A GRAPHIC MEMOIR

DEAR DAD

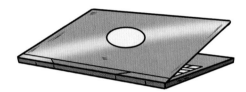

All rights reserved. Published by Graphix, an imprint of Scholastic Inc., *Publishers since 1920*.
SCHOLASTIC, GRAPHIX, and associated logos are trademarks and/or registered trademarks of Scholastic Inc.

The publisher does not have any control over and does not assume any responsibility for author or third-party websites or their content.

ISBN 978-1-5461-2837-3 (hardcover)
ISBN 978-1-338-89320-5 (paperback)

10 9 8 7 6 5 4 3 2 1   24 25 26 27 28

Printed in China   62

First edition September 2024

Stock art © Shutterstock.com

Edited by Michael Petranek
Lettering by Jesse Post
Book design by Veronica Mang
Art Direction by Salena Mahina

A GRAPHIC MEMOIR

DEAR DAD

Growing Up with a Parent in Prison—
and How We Stayed Connected

JAY JAY PATTON

WITH **KIARA VALDEZ** & **MARKIA JENAI**

An Imprint of
SCHOLASTIC

KAEPERNICK
PUBLISHING

For all the amazing mothers out there, but especially to my beautiful mom. Your sacrifices and unconditional love are the reasons I'm who I am and who I will continue to become. Your undeniable strength but equal amount of vulnerability is forever an inspiration to me. Thank you for always giving me your everything even when you have nothing. I love you forever and ever.

— Jay'Aina Patton

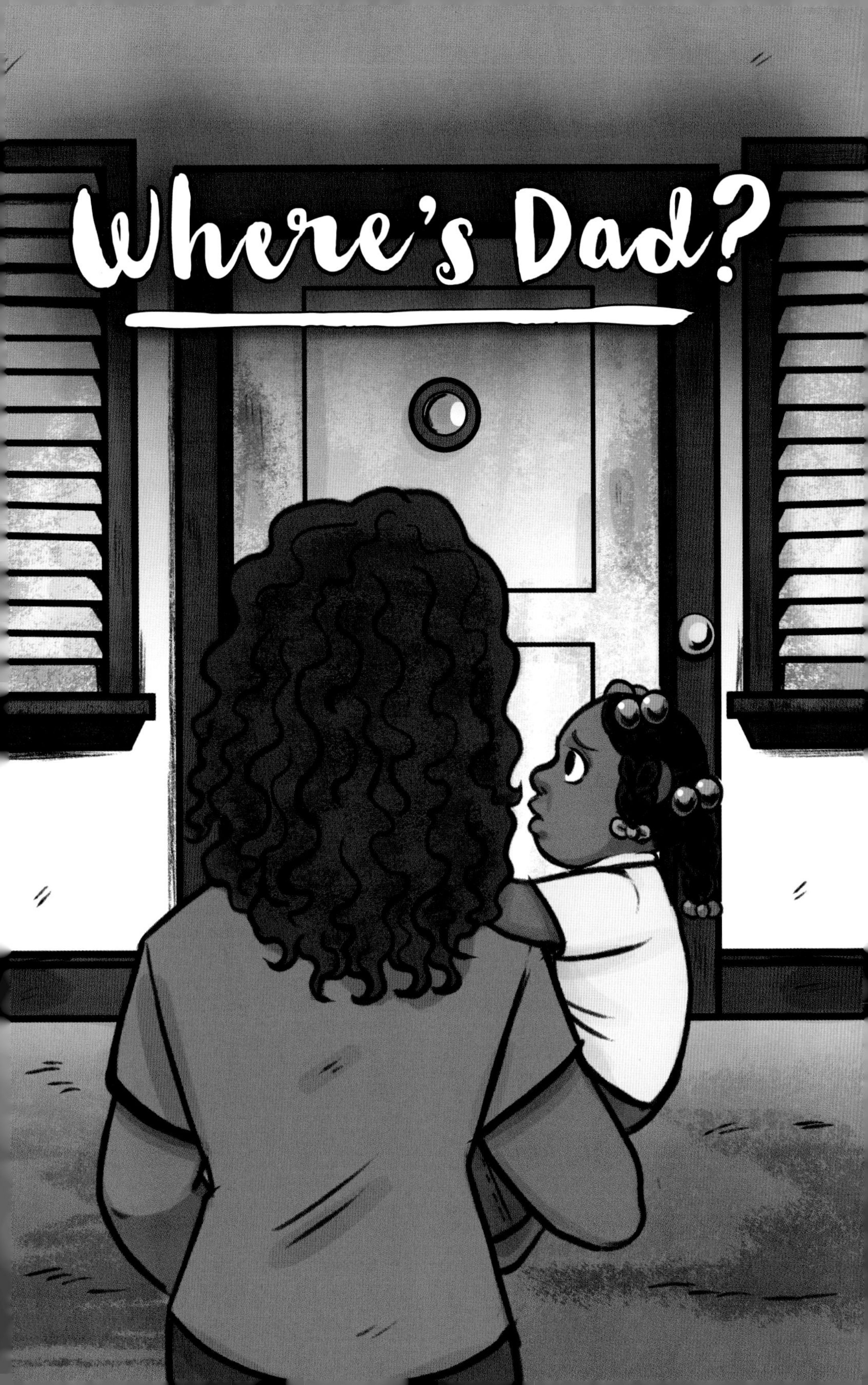
Where's Dad?

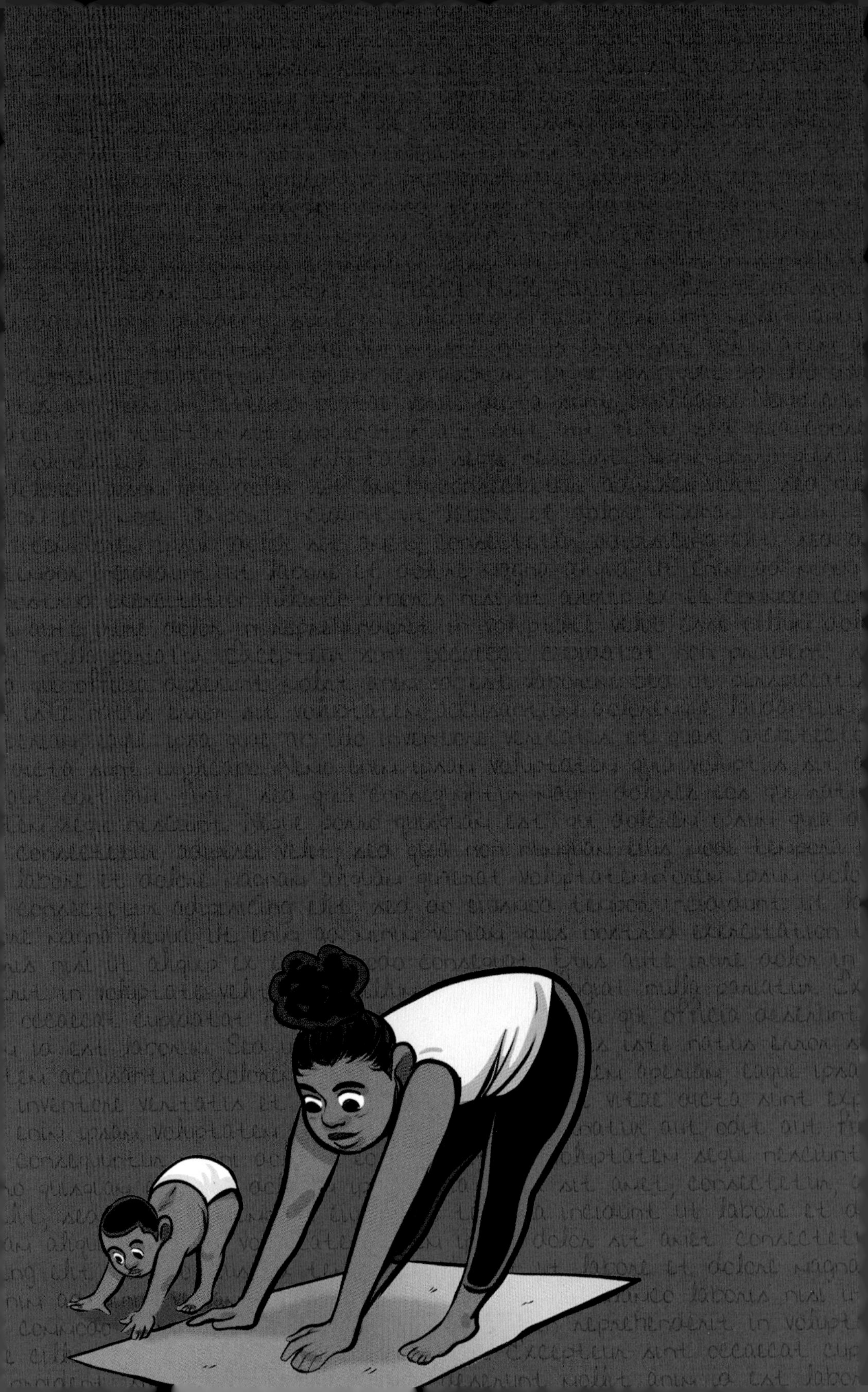

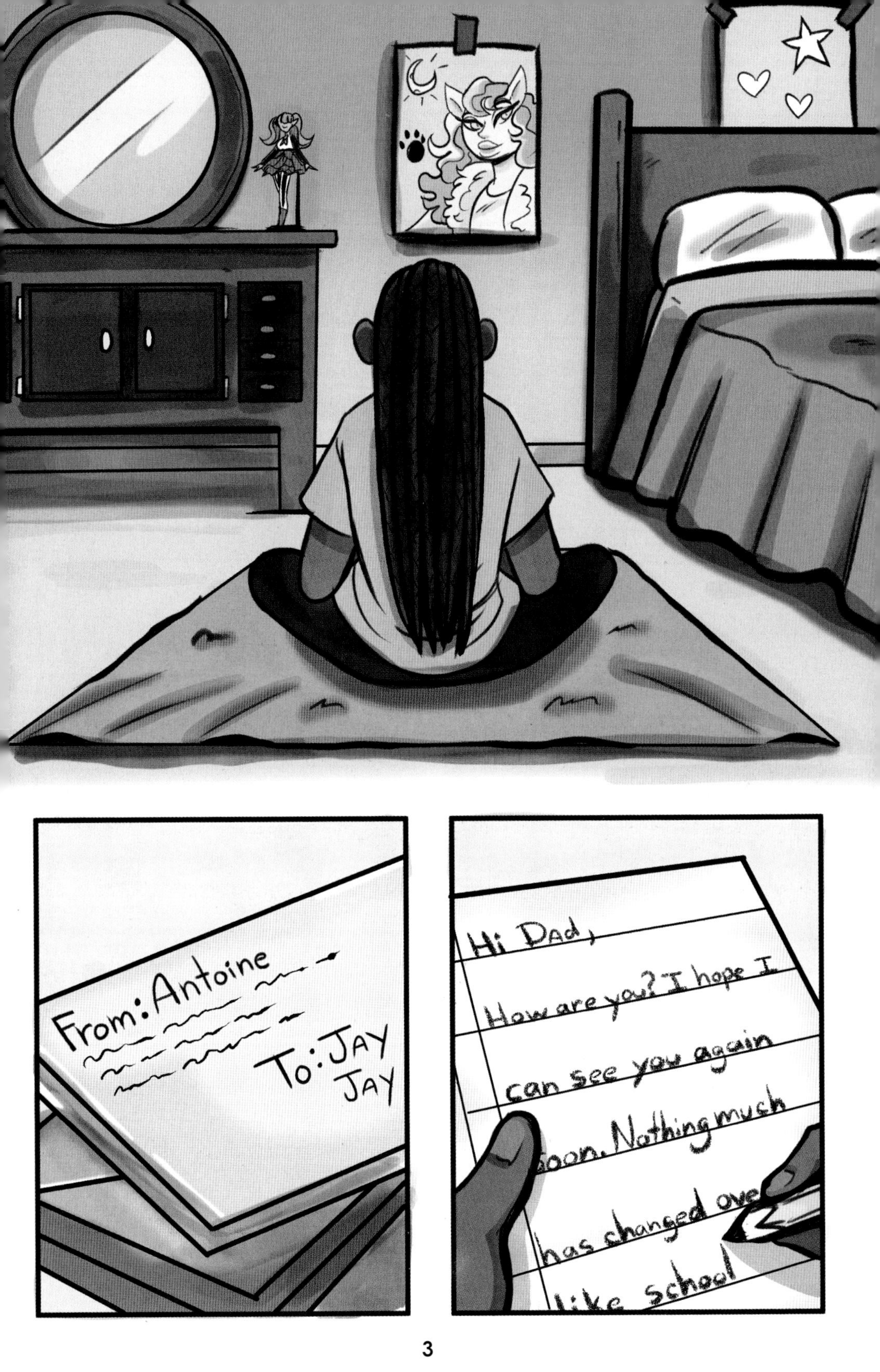
From: Antoine
To: JAY JAY
Hi Dad,
How are you? I hope I
can see you again
soon. Nothing much
has changed ove
like school

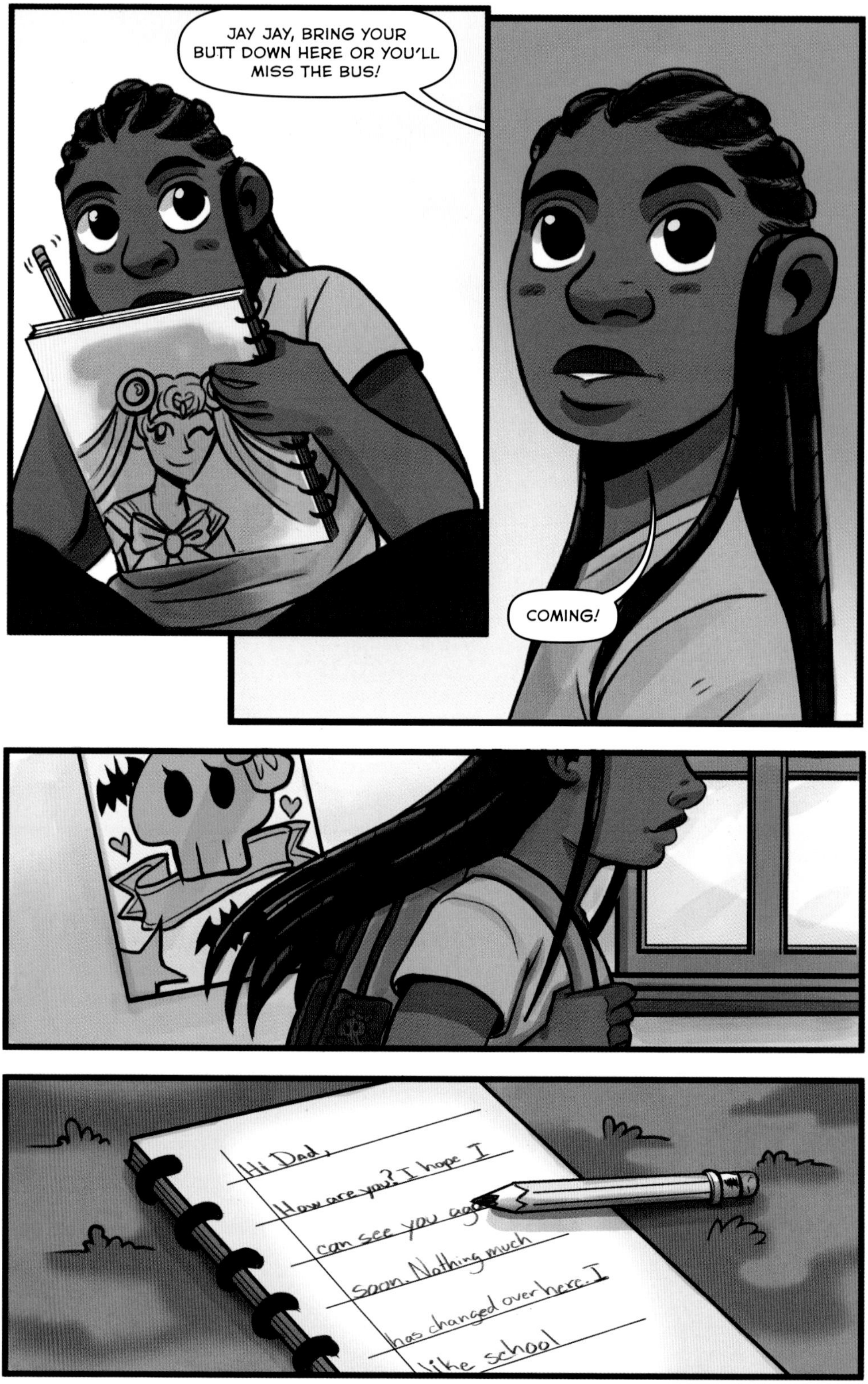
JAY JAY, BRING YOUR BUTT DOWN HERE OR YOU'LL MISS THE BUS!
COMING!
Hi Dad,
How are you? I hope I
can see you ag
soon. Nothing much
has changed over here. I
like school

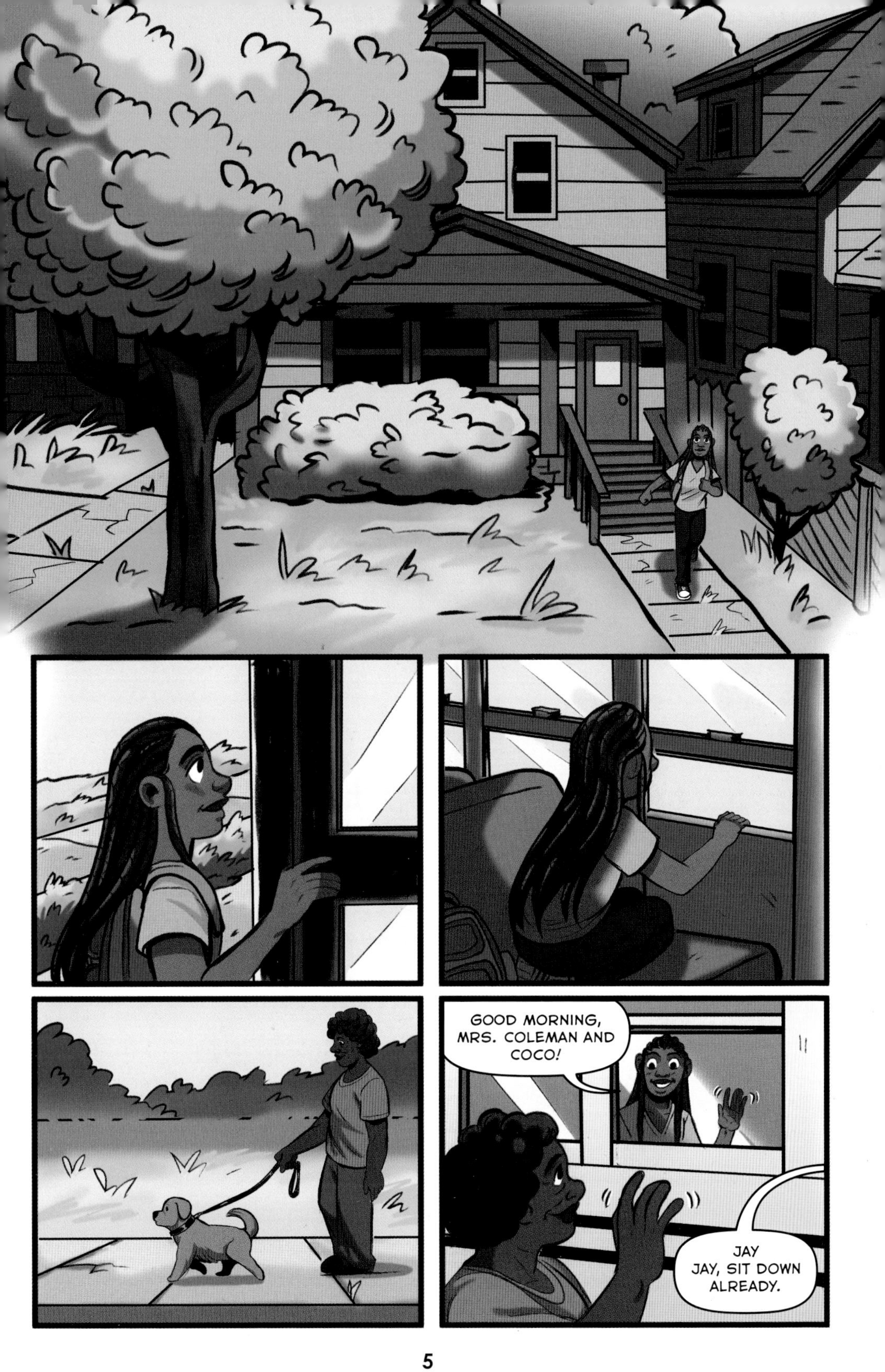
GOOD MORNING, MRS. COLEMAN AND COCO!
JAY JAY, SIT DOWN ALREADY.

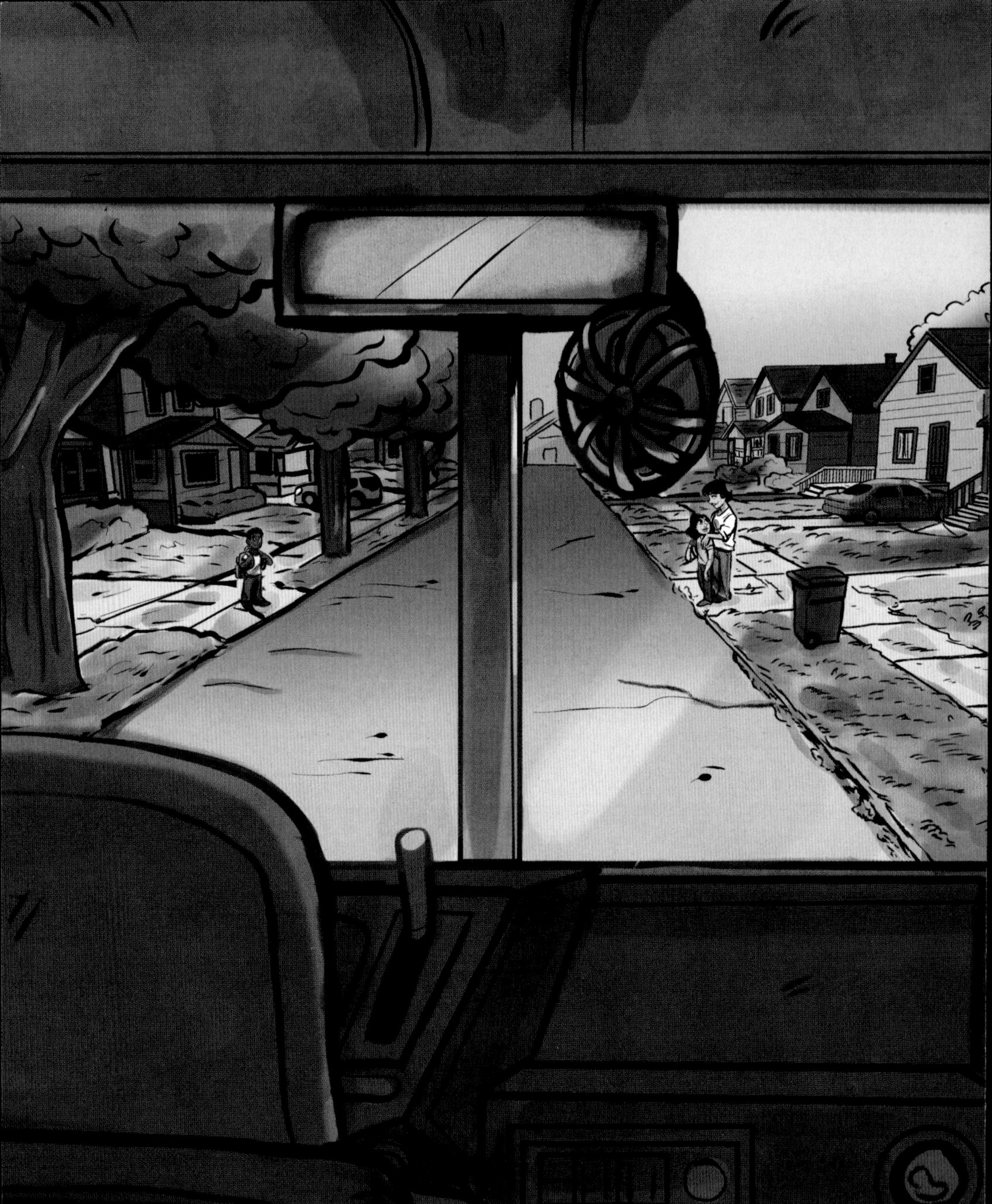

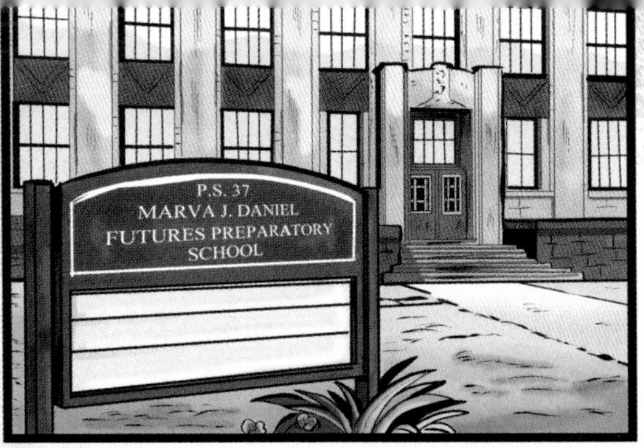
P.S. 37
MARVA J. DANIEL
FUTURES PREPARATORY
SCHOOL

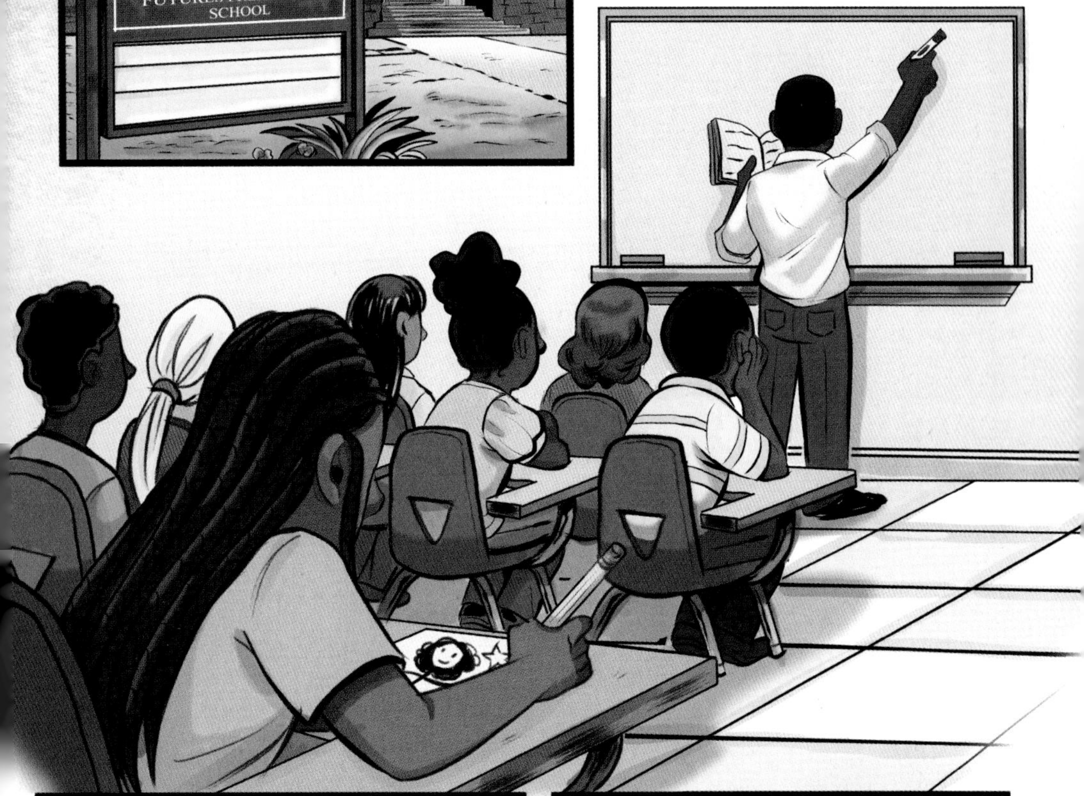

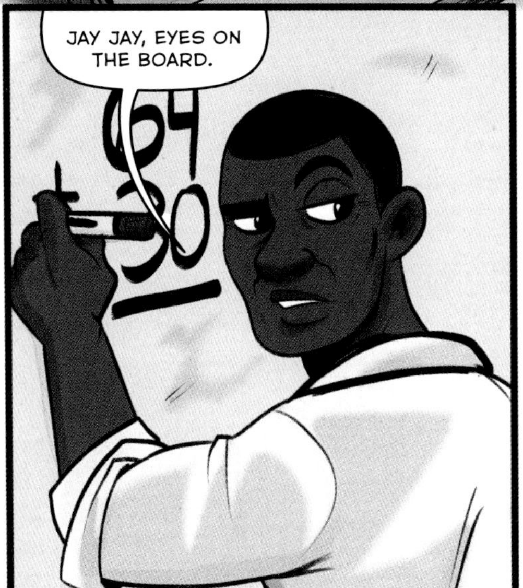
JAY JAY, EYES ON THE BOARD.
64
+30

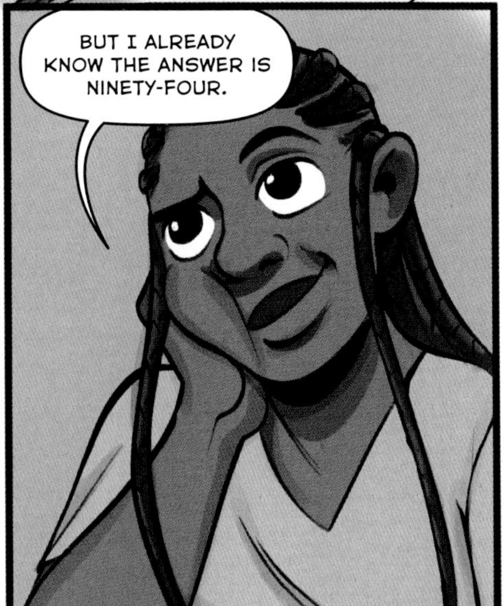
BUT I ALREADY KNOW THE ANSWER IS NINETY-FOUR.

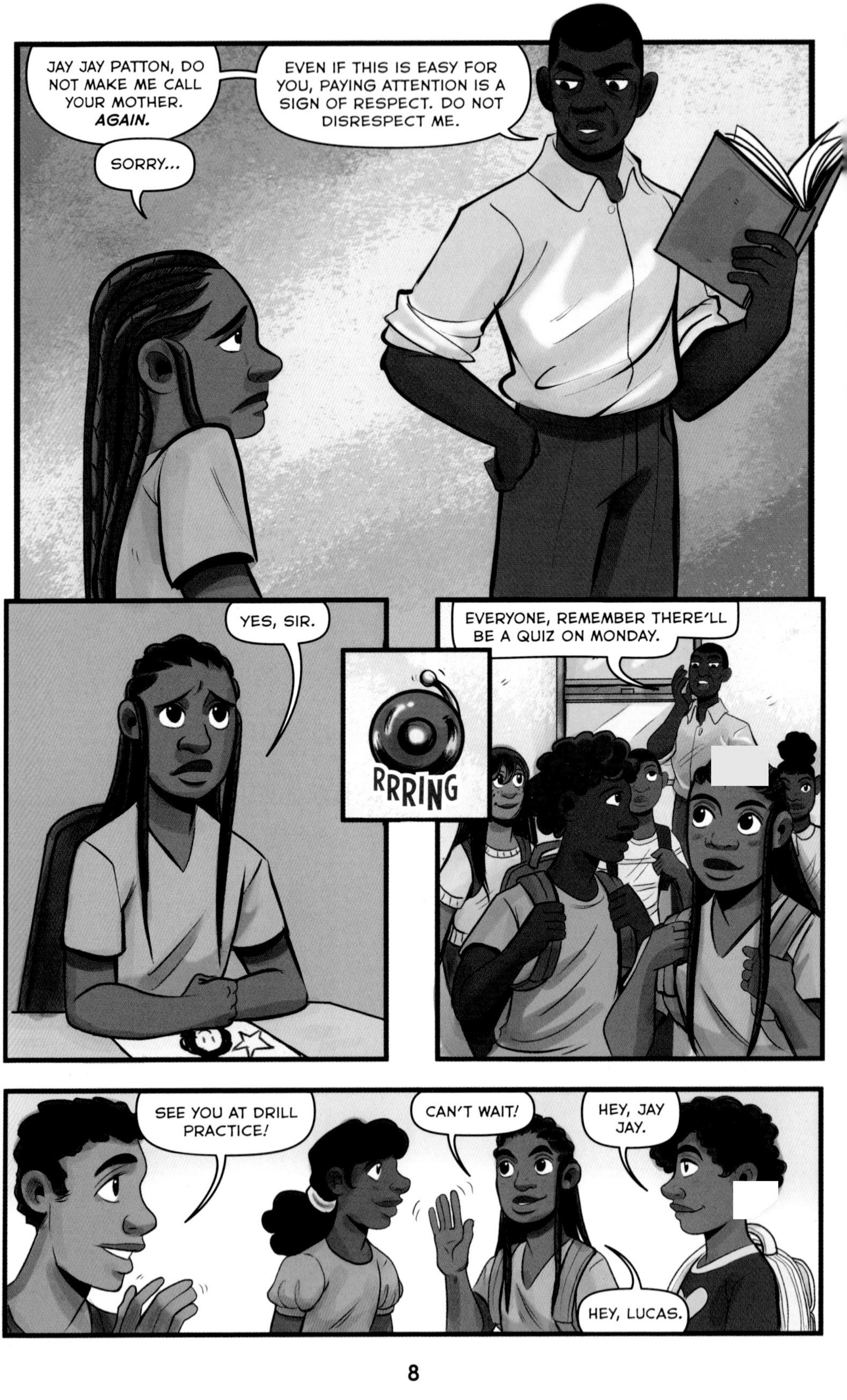
JAY JAY PATTON, DO NOT MAKE ME CALL YOUR MOTHER. ***AGAIN.***
EVEN IF THIS IS EASY FOR YOU, PAYING ATTENTION IS A SIGN OF RESPECT. DO NOT DISRESPECT ME.
SORRY...
YES, SIR.
RRRING
EVERYONE, REMEMBER THERE'LL BE A QUIZ ON MONDAY.
SEE YOU AT DRILL PRACTICE!
CAN'T WAIT!
HEY, JAY JAY.
HEY, LUCAS.

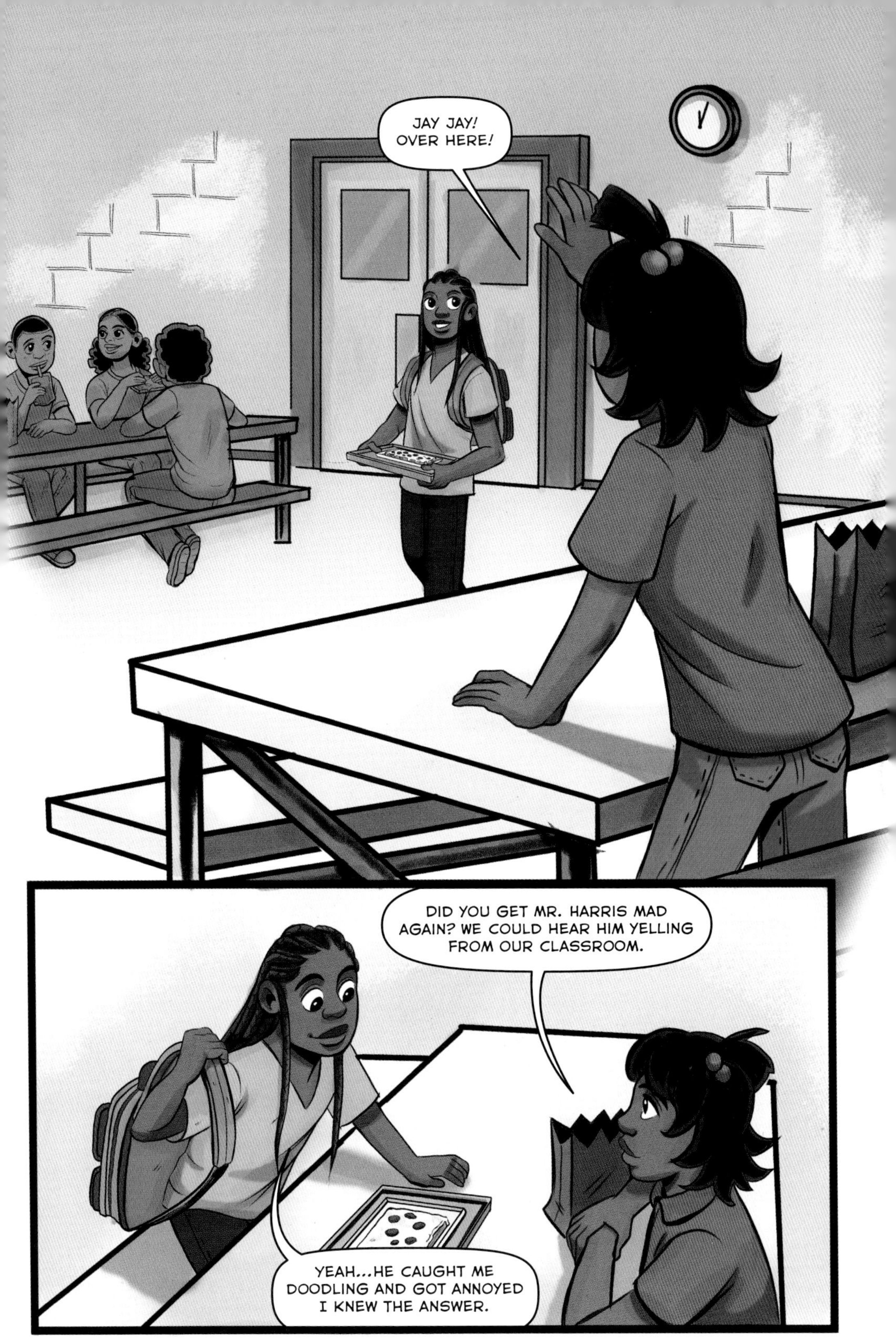
JAY JAY! OVER HERE!
DID YOU GET MR. HARRIS MAD AGAIN? WE COULD HEAR HIM YELLING FROM OUR CLASSROOM.
YEAH...HE CAUGHT ME DOODLING AND GOT ANNOYED I KNEW THE ANSWER.

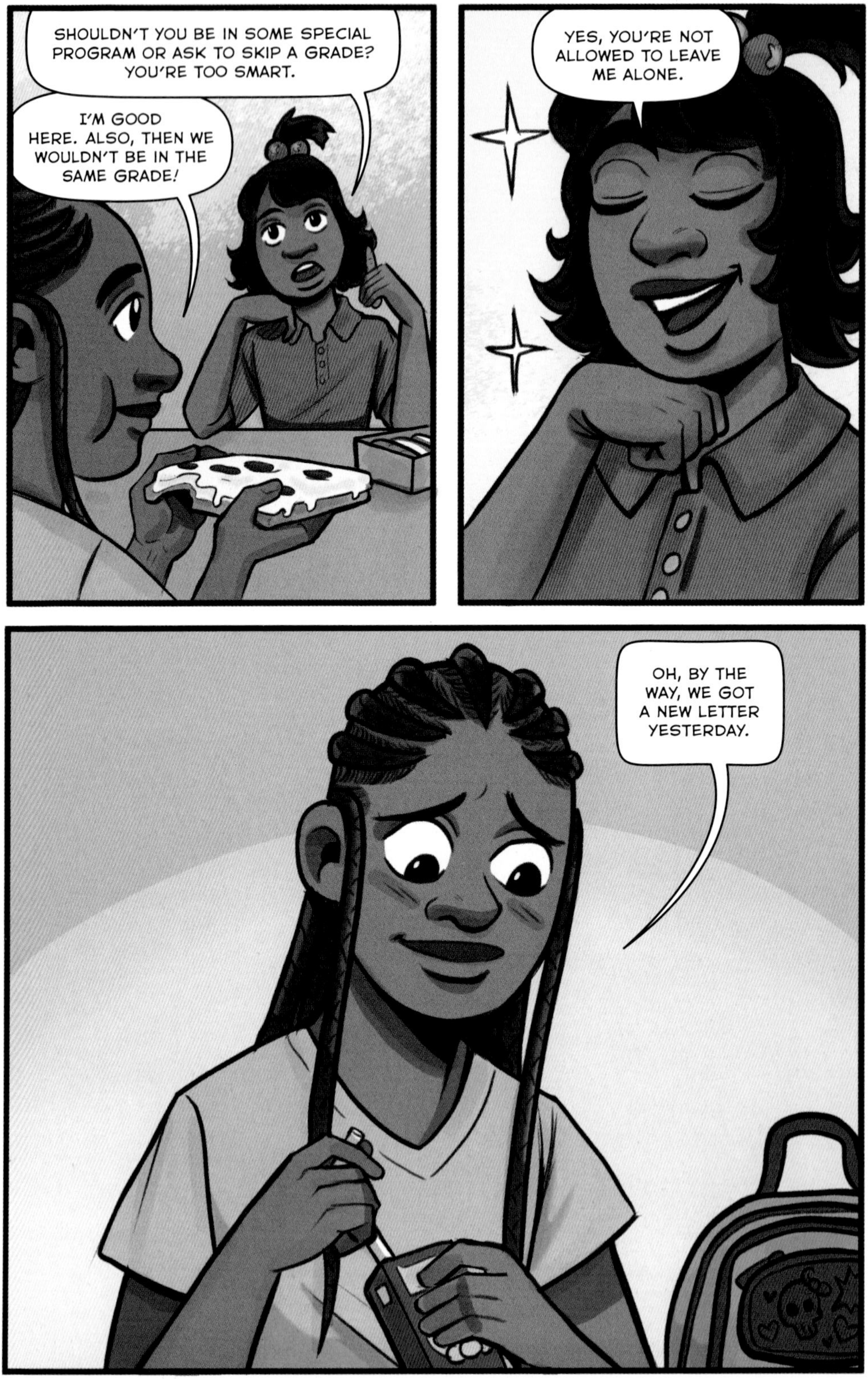
SHOULDN'T YOU BE IN SOME SPECIAL PROGRAM OR ASK TO SKIP A GRADE? YOU'RE TOO SMART.
I'M GOOD HERE. ALSO, THEN WE WOULDN'T BE IN THE SAME GRADE!
YES, YOU'RE NOT ALLOWED TO LEAVE ME ALONE.
OH, BY THE WAY, WE GOT A NEW LETTER YESTERDAY.

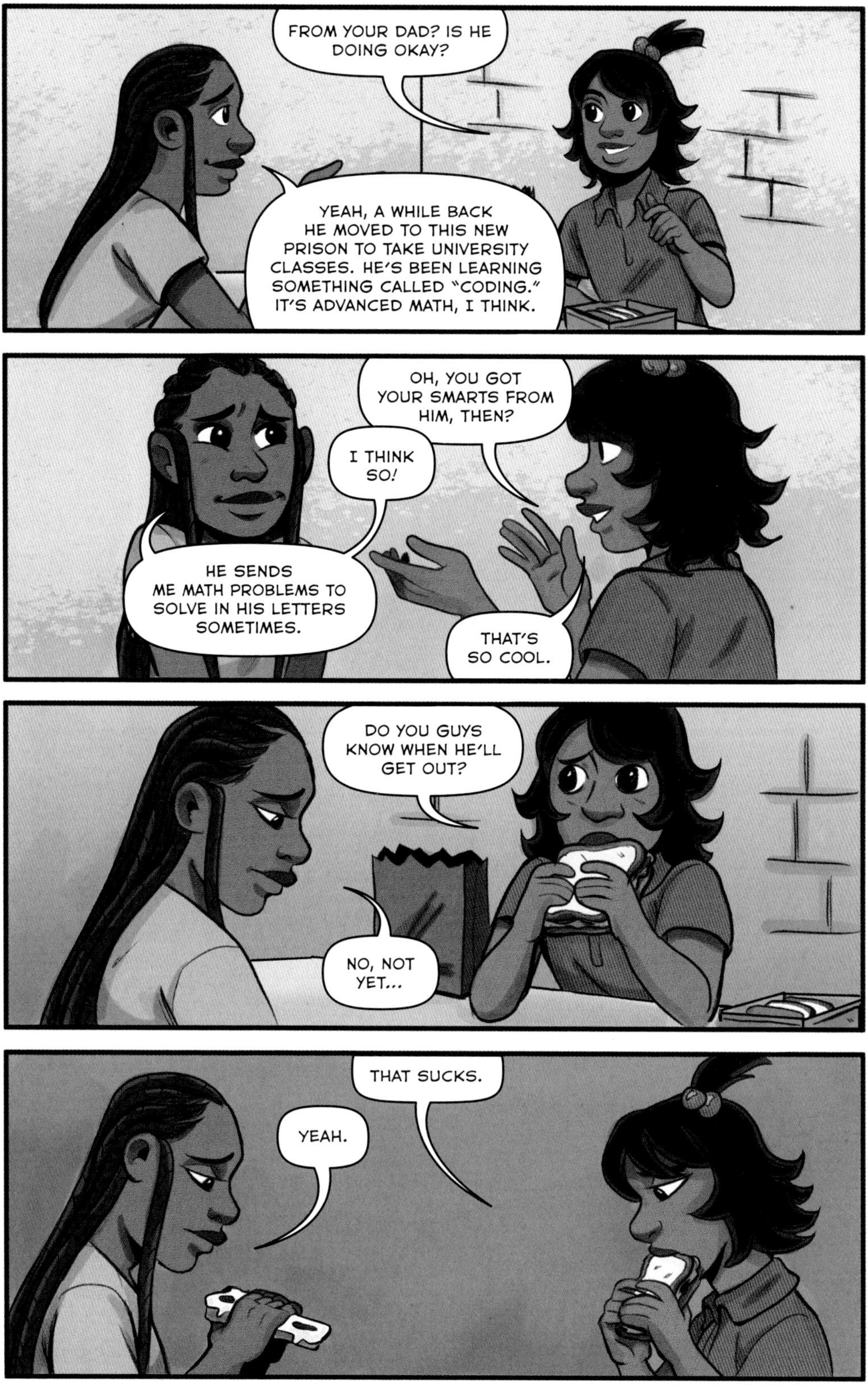
FROM YOUR DAD? IS HE DOING OKAY?
YEAH, A WHILE BACK HE MOVED TO THIS NEW PRISON TO TAKE UNIVERSITY CLASSES. HE'S BEEN LEARNING SOMETHING CALLED "CODING." IT'S ADVANCED MATH, I THINK.
OH, YOU GOT YOUR SMARTS FROM HIM, THEN?
I THINK SO!
HE SENDS ME MATH PROBLEMS TO SOLVE IN HIS LETTERS SOMETIMES.
THAT'S SO COOL.
DO YOU GUYS KNOW WHEN HE'LL GET OUT?
NO, NOT YET...
THAT SUCKS.
YEAH.

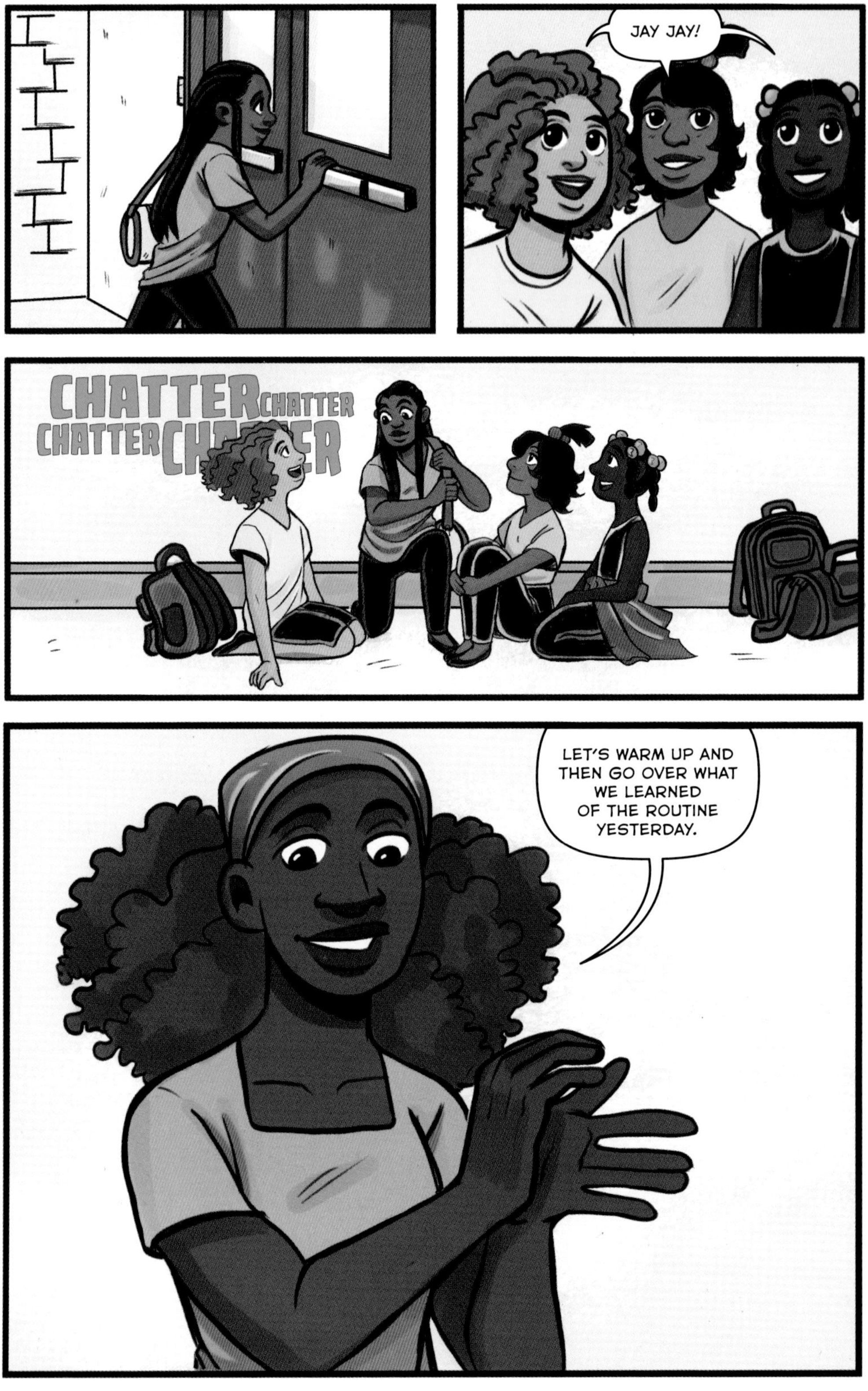
JAY JAY!
CHATTER CHATTER
CHATTER CHATTER
LET'S WARM UP AND THEN GO OVER WHAT WE LEARNED OF THE ROUTINE YESTERDAY.

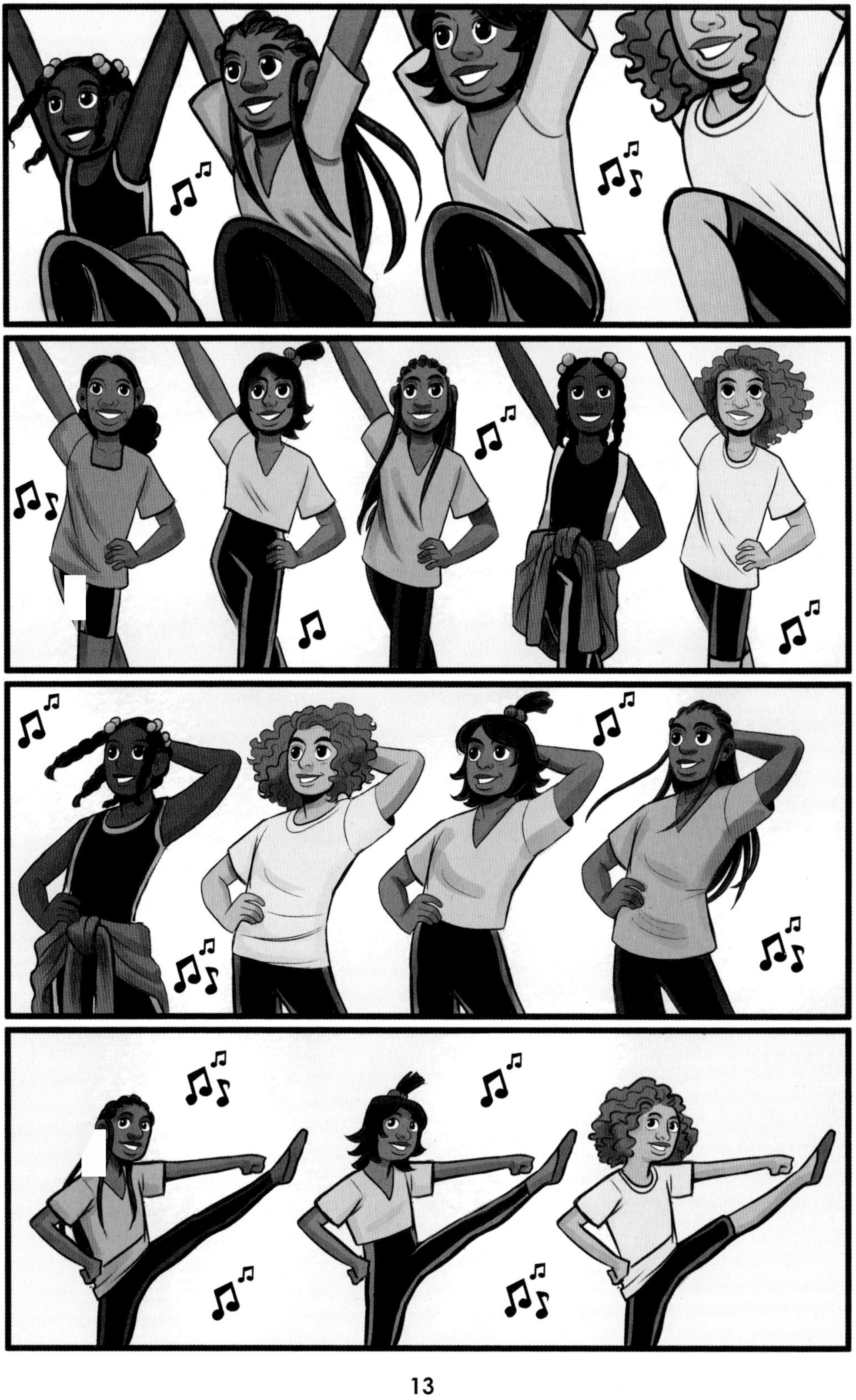

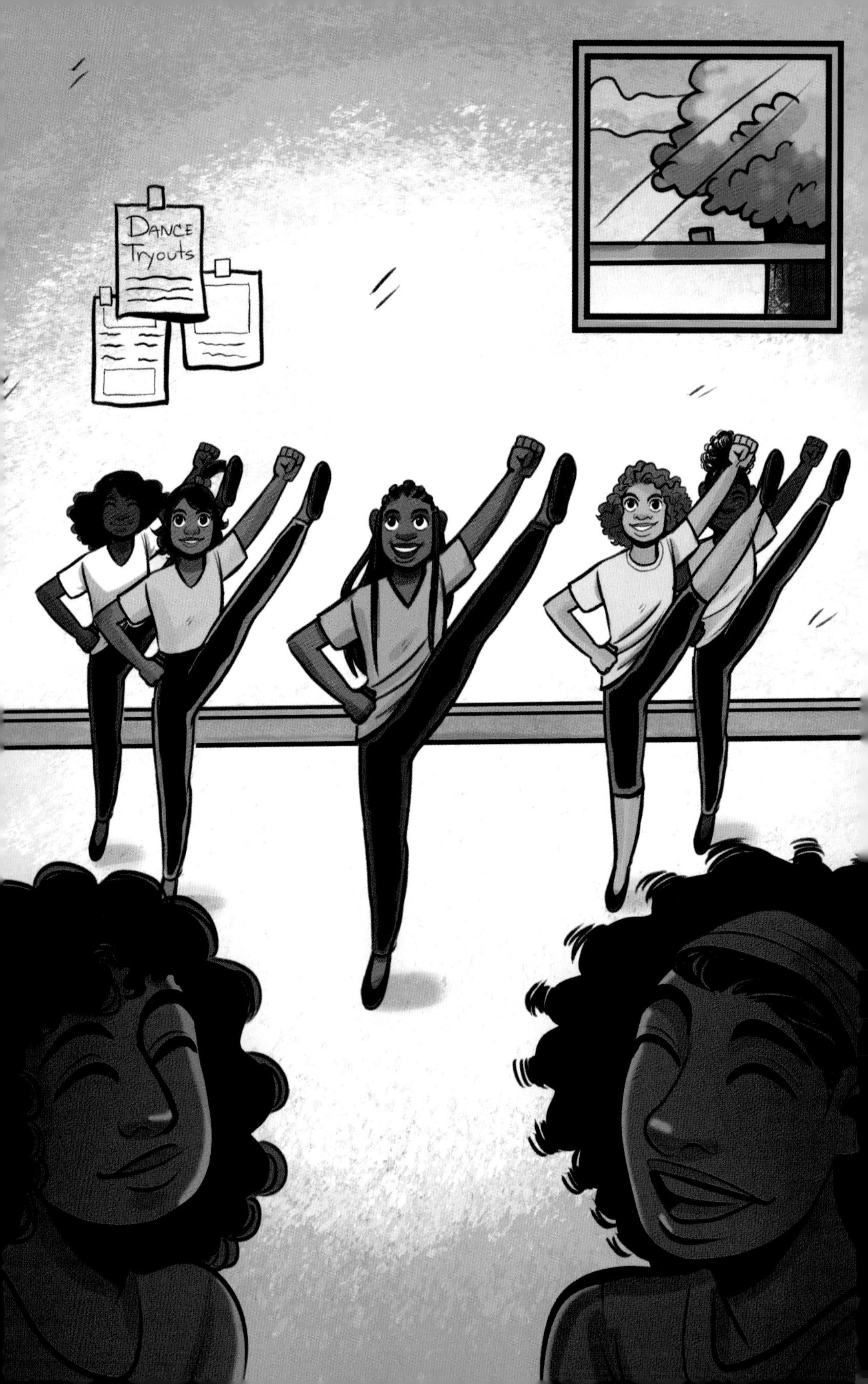
Dance Tryouts

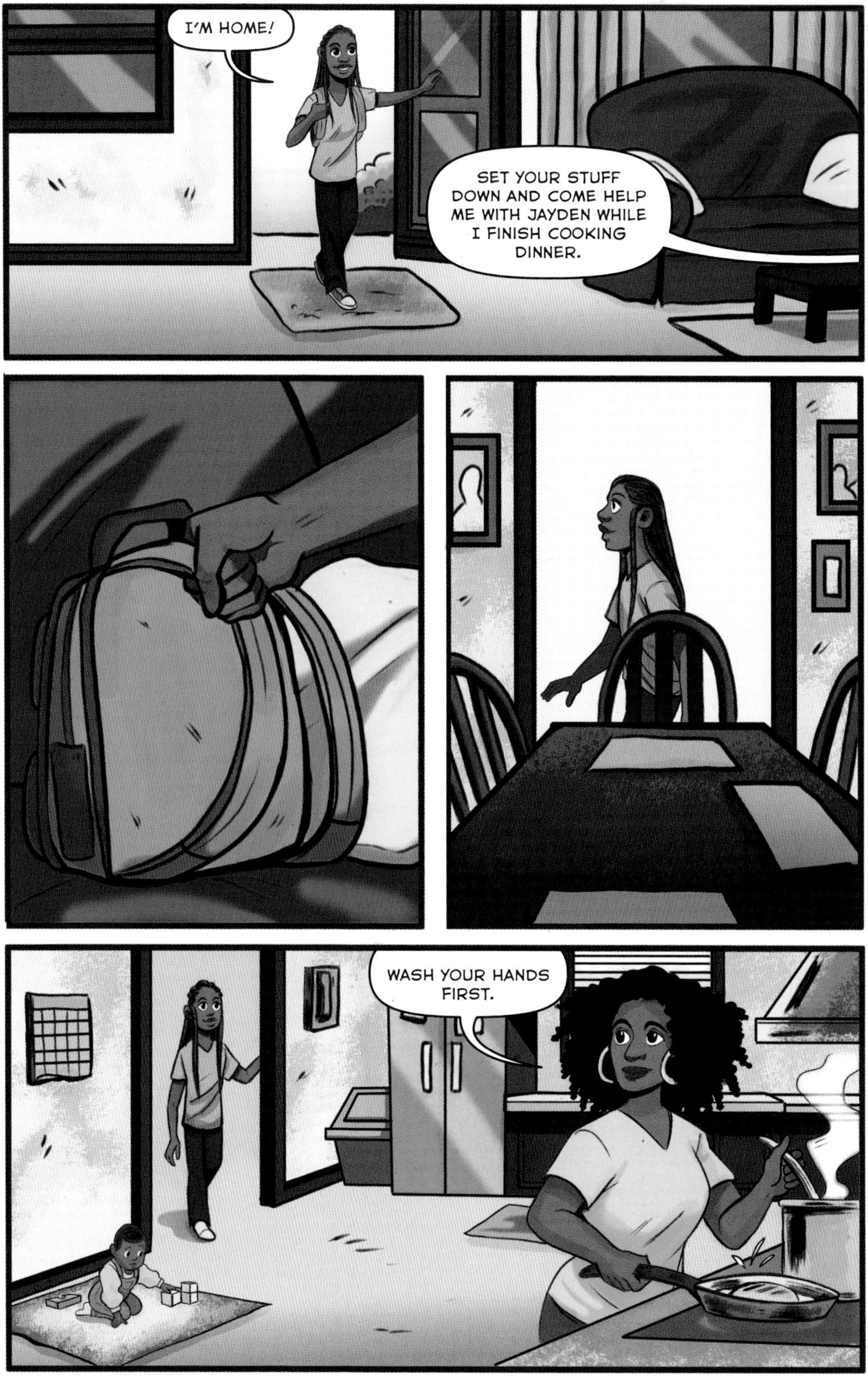
I'M HOME!
SET YOUR STUFF DOWN AND COME HELP ME WITH JAYDEN WHILE I FINISH COOKING DINNER.
WASH YOUR HANDS FIRST.

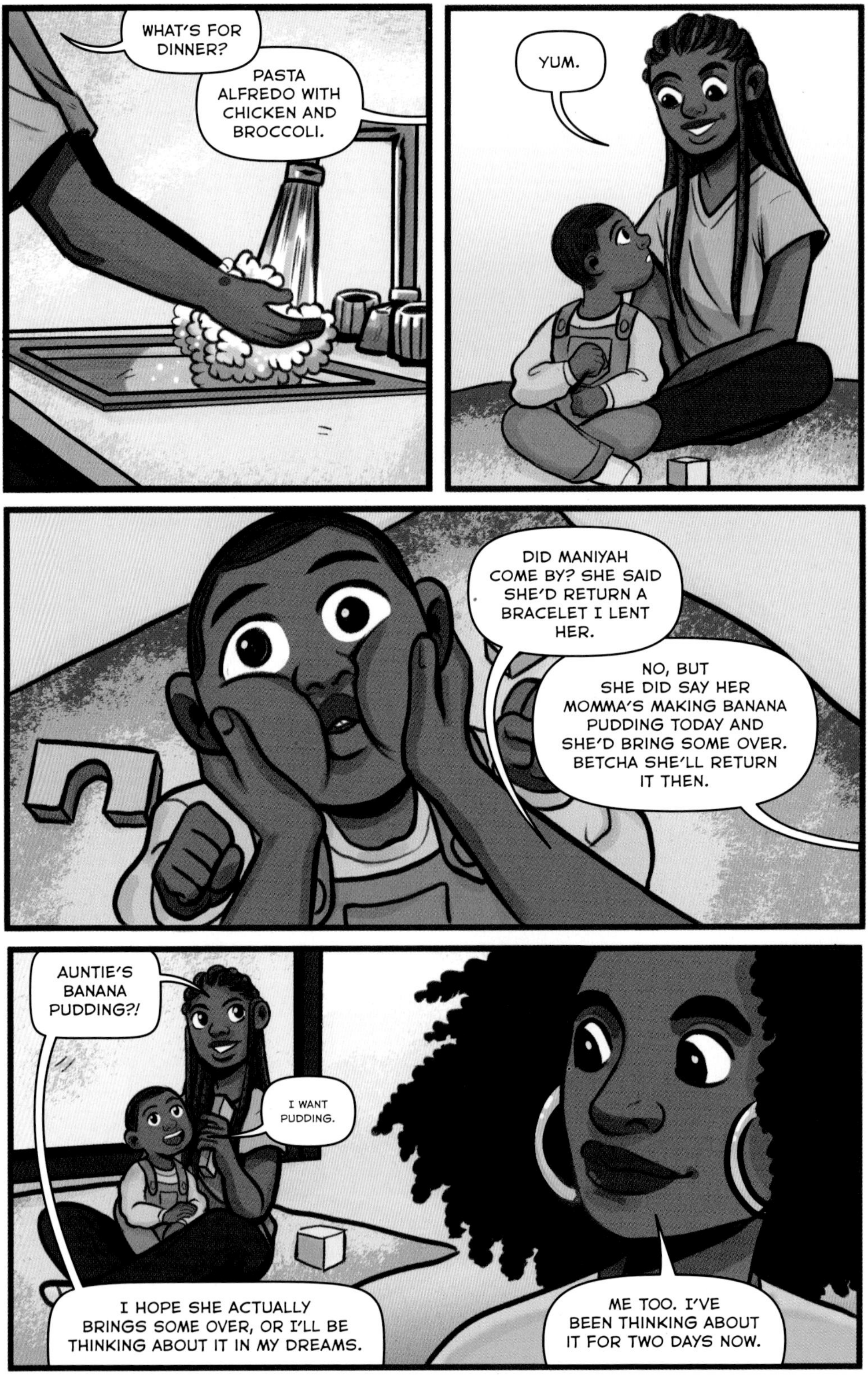
WHAT'S FOR DINNER?
PASTA ALFREDO WITH CHICKEN AND BROCCOLI.
YUM.
DID MANIYAH COME BY? SHE SAID SHE'D RETURN A BRACELET I LENT HER.
NO, BUT SHE DID SAY HER MOMMA'S MAKING BANANA PUDDING TODAY AND SHE'D BRING SOME OVER. BETCHA SHE'LL RETURN IT THEN.
AUNTIE'S BANANA PUDDING?!
I WANT PUDDING.
I HOPE SHE ACTUALLY BRINGS SOME OVER, OR I'LL BE THINKING ABOUT IT IN MY DREAMS.
ME TOO. I'VE BEEN THINKING ABOUT IT FOR TWO DAYS NOW.

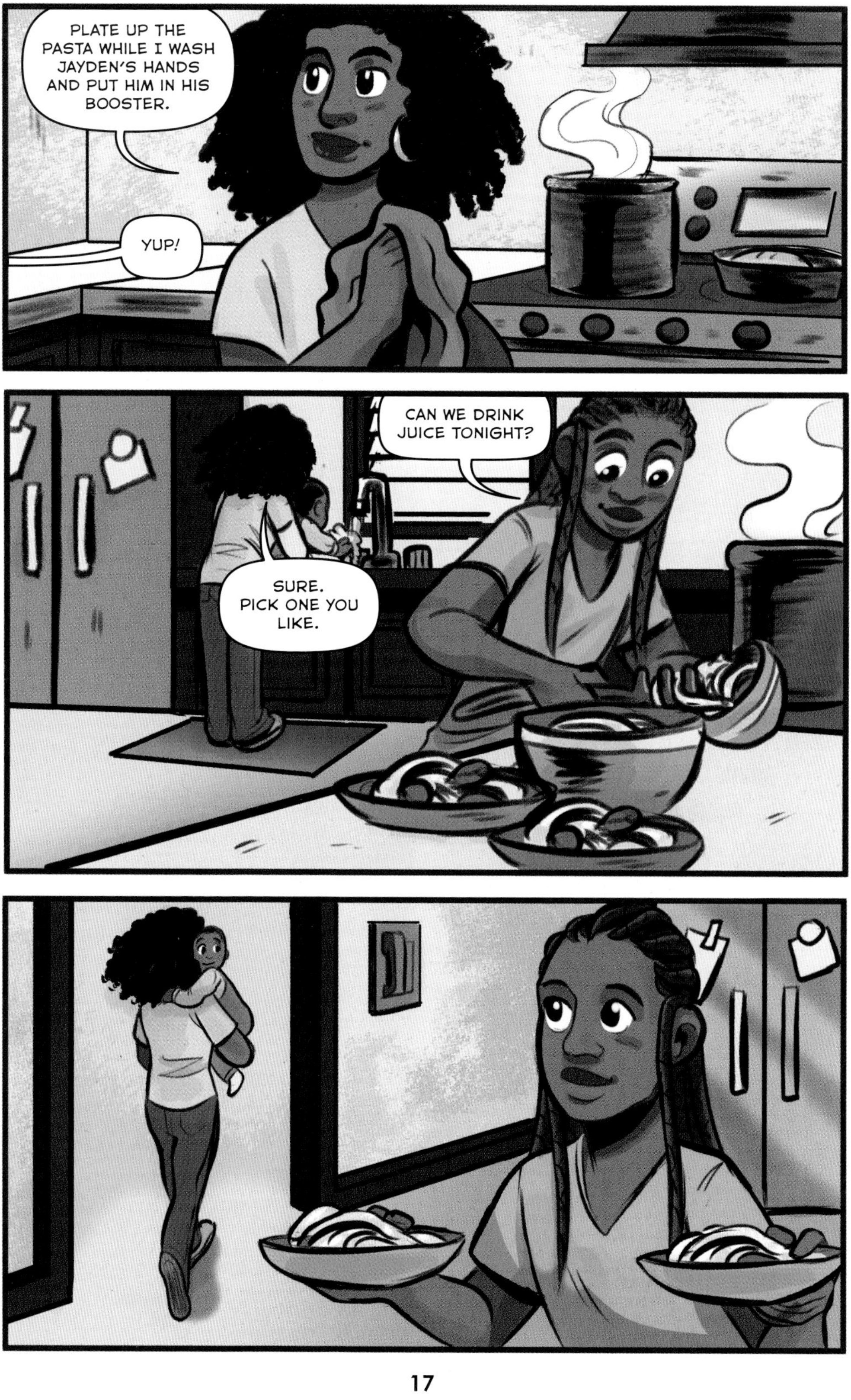
PLATE UP THE PASTA WHILE I WASH JAYDEN'S HANDS AND PUT HIM IN HIS BOOSTER.
YUP!
CAN WE DRINK JUICE TONIGHT?
SURE. PICK ONE YOU LIKE.

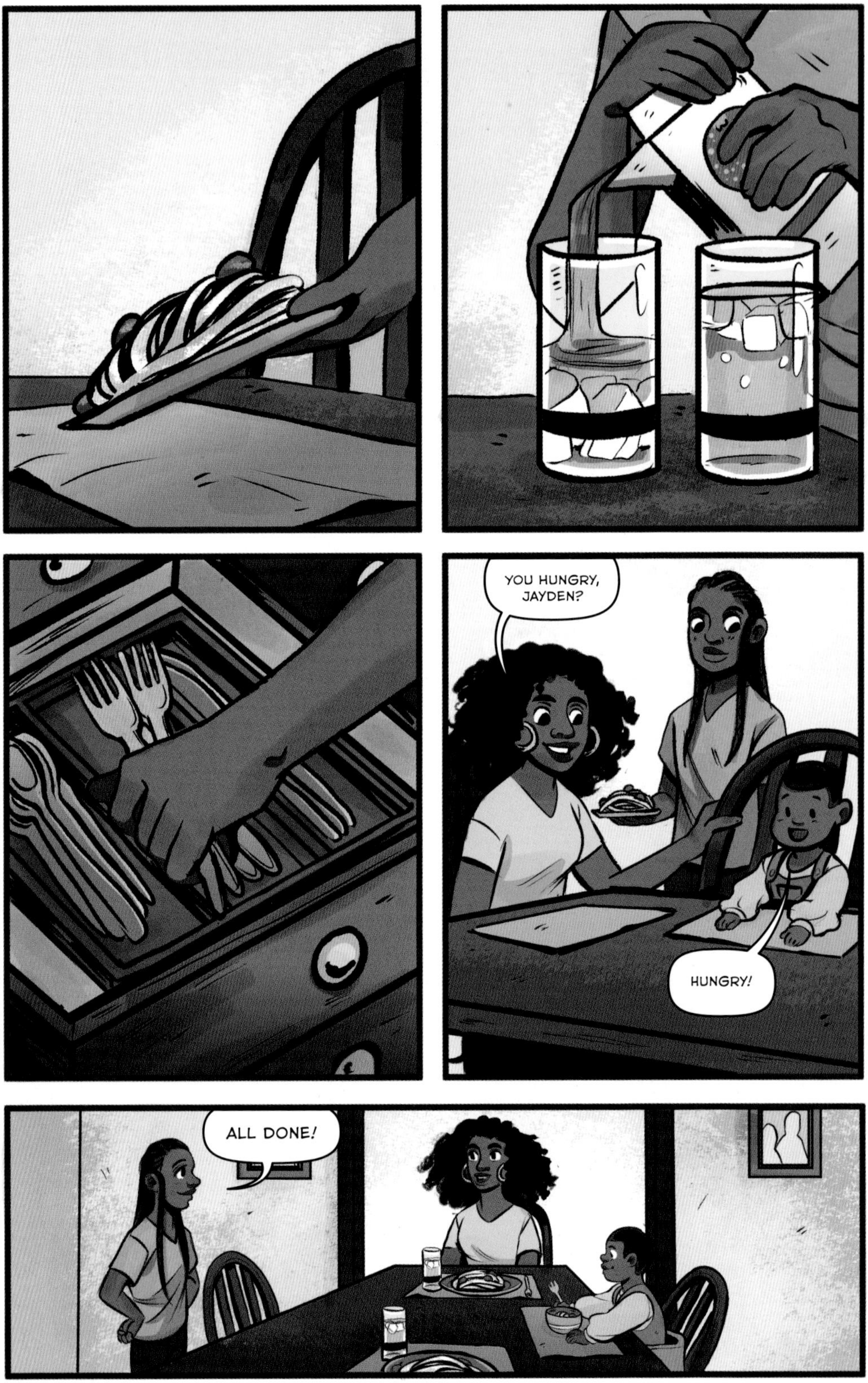
YOU HUNGRY, JAYDEN?
HUNGRY!
ALL DONE!

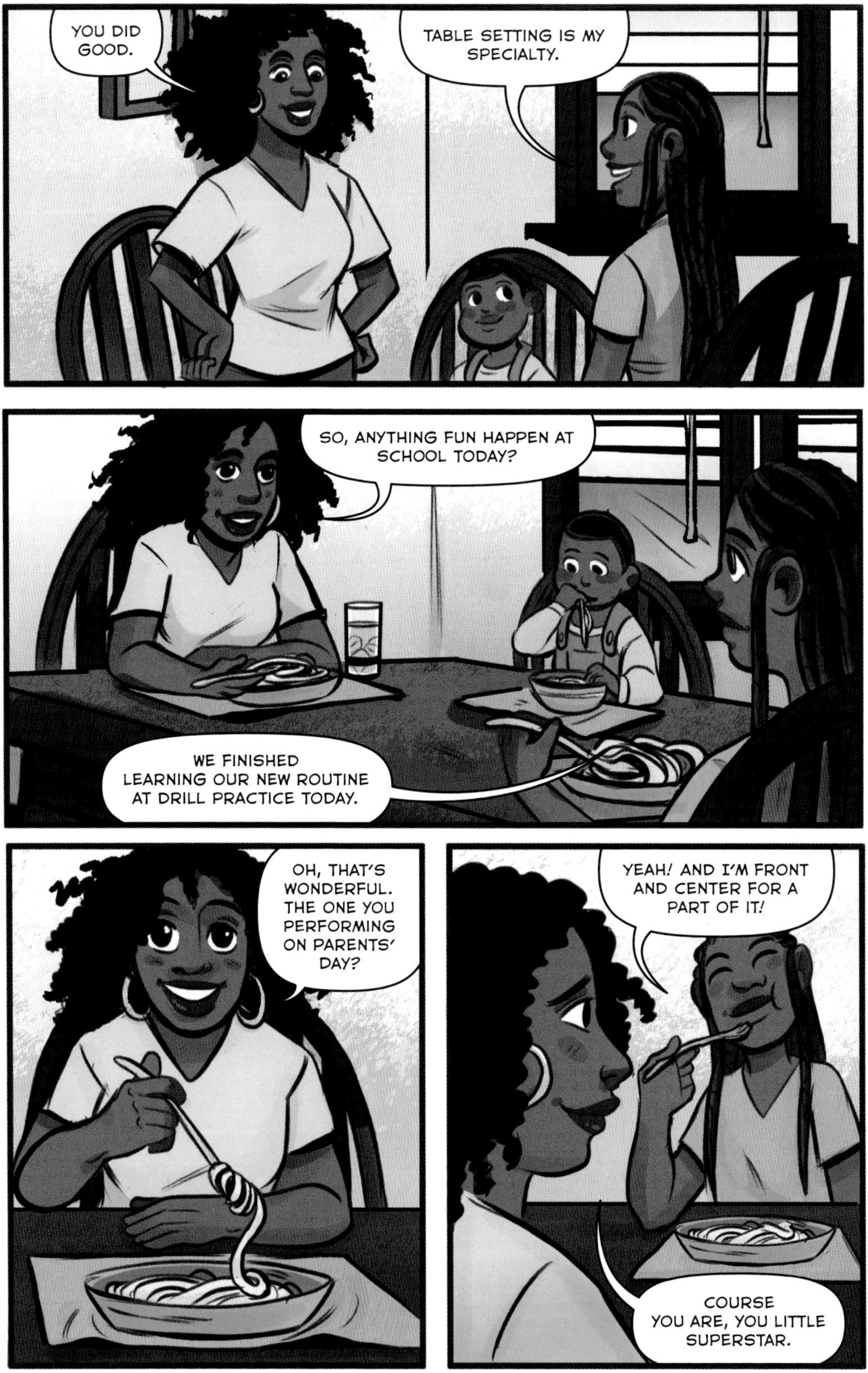
YOU DID GOOD.
TABLE SETTING IS MY SPECIALTY.
SO, ANYTHING FUN HAPPEN AT SCHOOL TODAY?
WE FINISHED LEARNING OUR NEW ROUTINE AT DRILL PRACTICE TODAY.
OH, THAT'S WONDERFUL. THE ONE YOU PERFORMING ON PARENTS' DAY?
YEAH! AND I'M FRONT AND CENTER FOR A PART OF IT!
COURSE YOU ARE, YOU LITTLE SUPERSTAR.

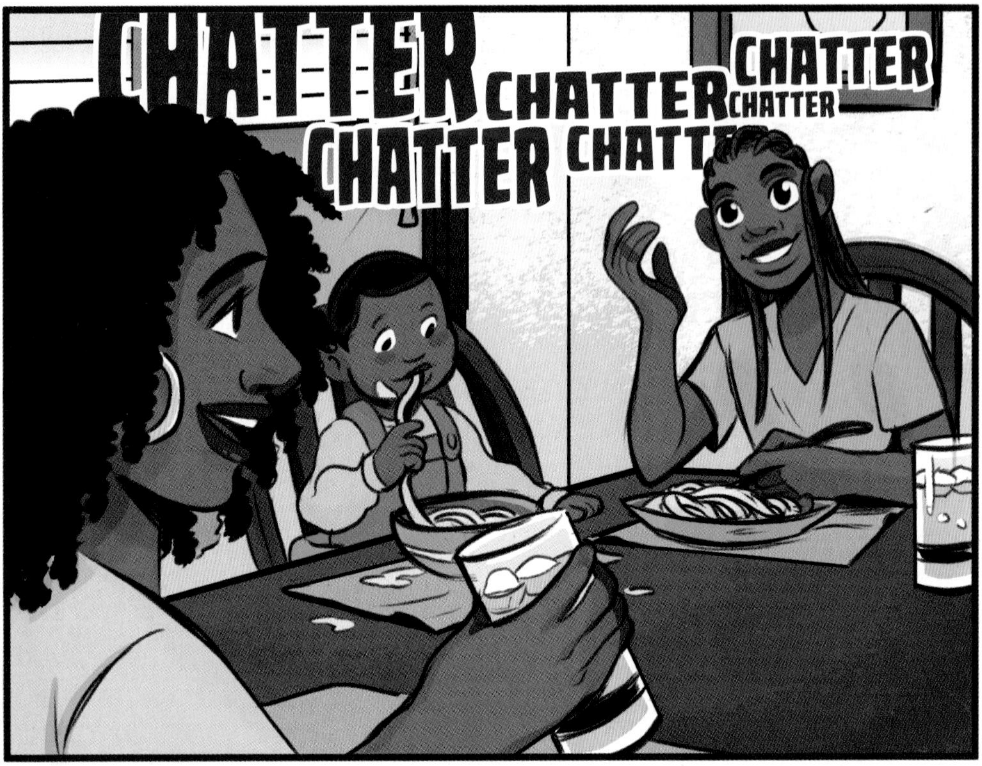
CHATTER
CHATTER
CHATTER
CHATTER
CHATTER
CHATT

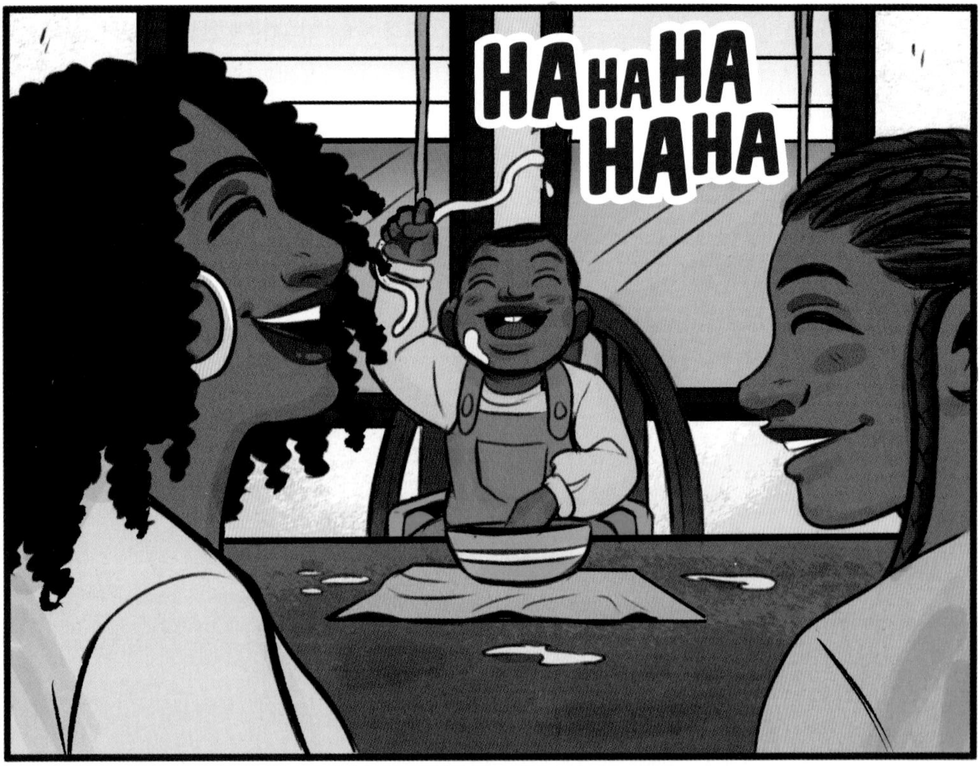
HAHAHA
HAHA

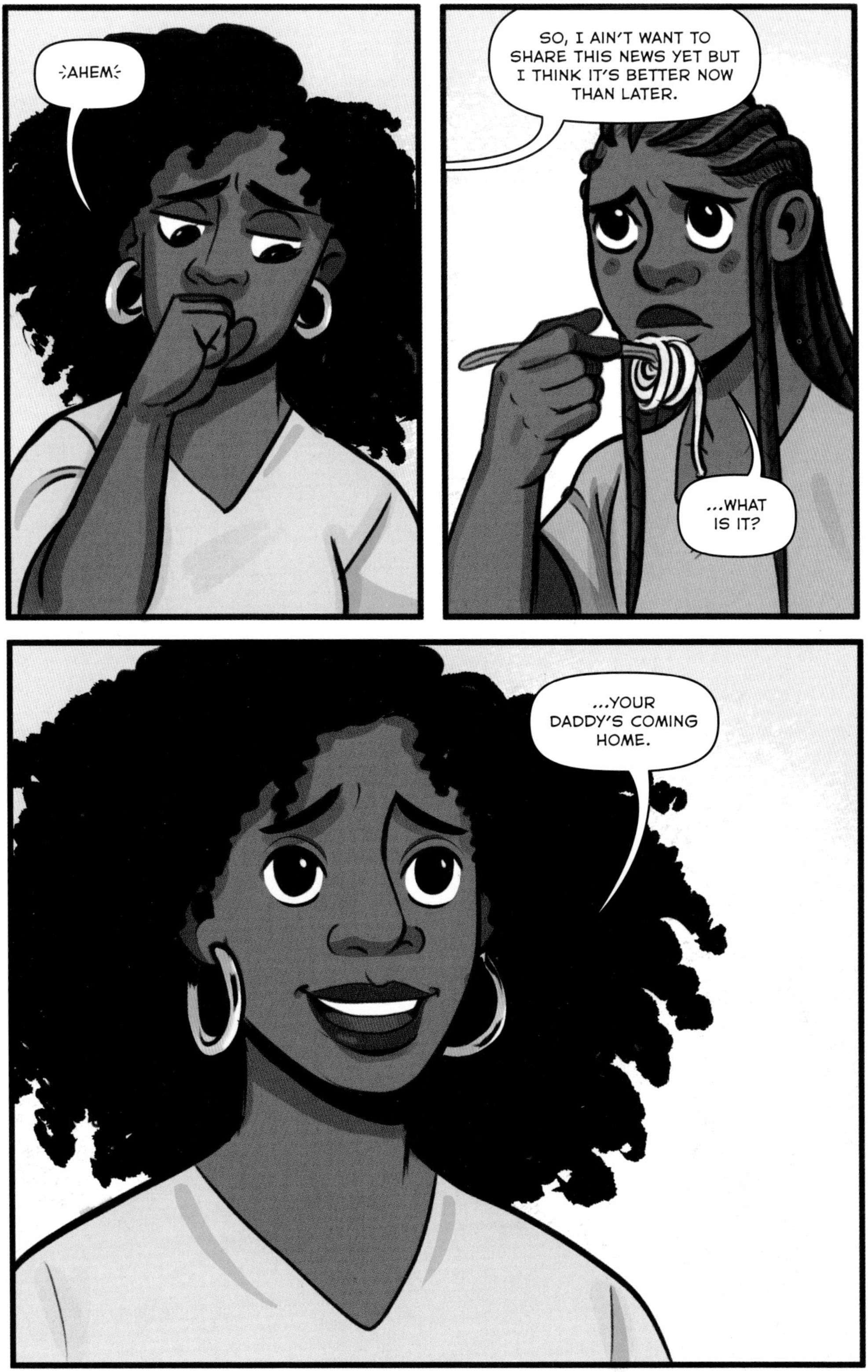

AHEM
SO, I AIN'T WANT TO SHARE THIS NEWS YET BUT I THINK IT'S BETTER NOW THAN LATER.
...WHAT IS IT?
...YOUR DADDY'S COMING HOME.

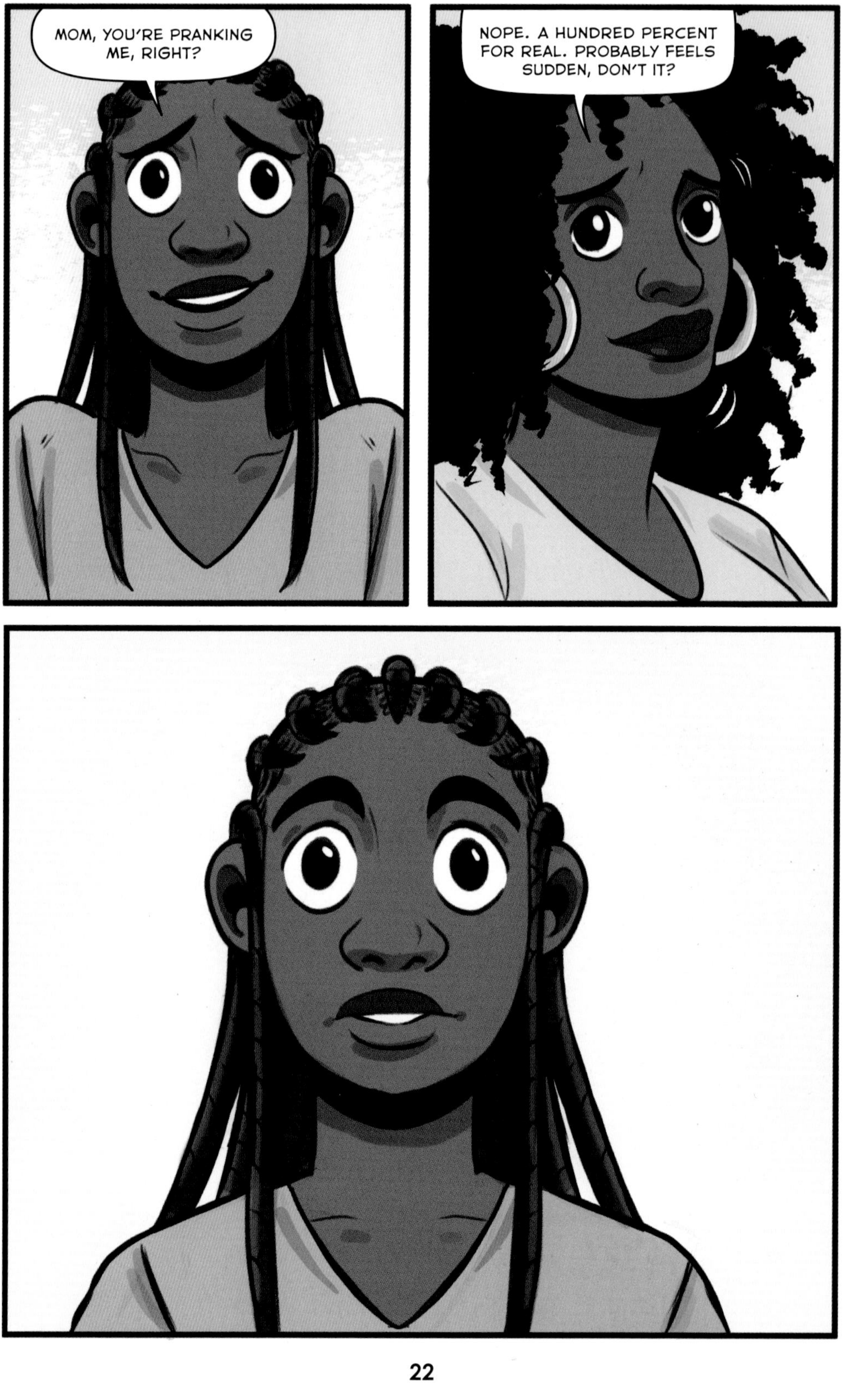
MOM, YOU'RE PRANKING ME, RIGHT?
NOPE. A HUNDRED PERCENT FOR REAL. PROBABLY FEELS SUDDEN, DON'T IT?

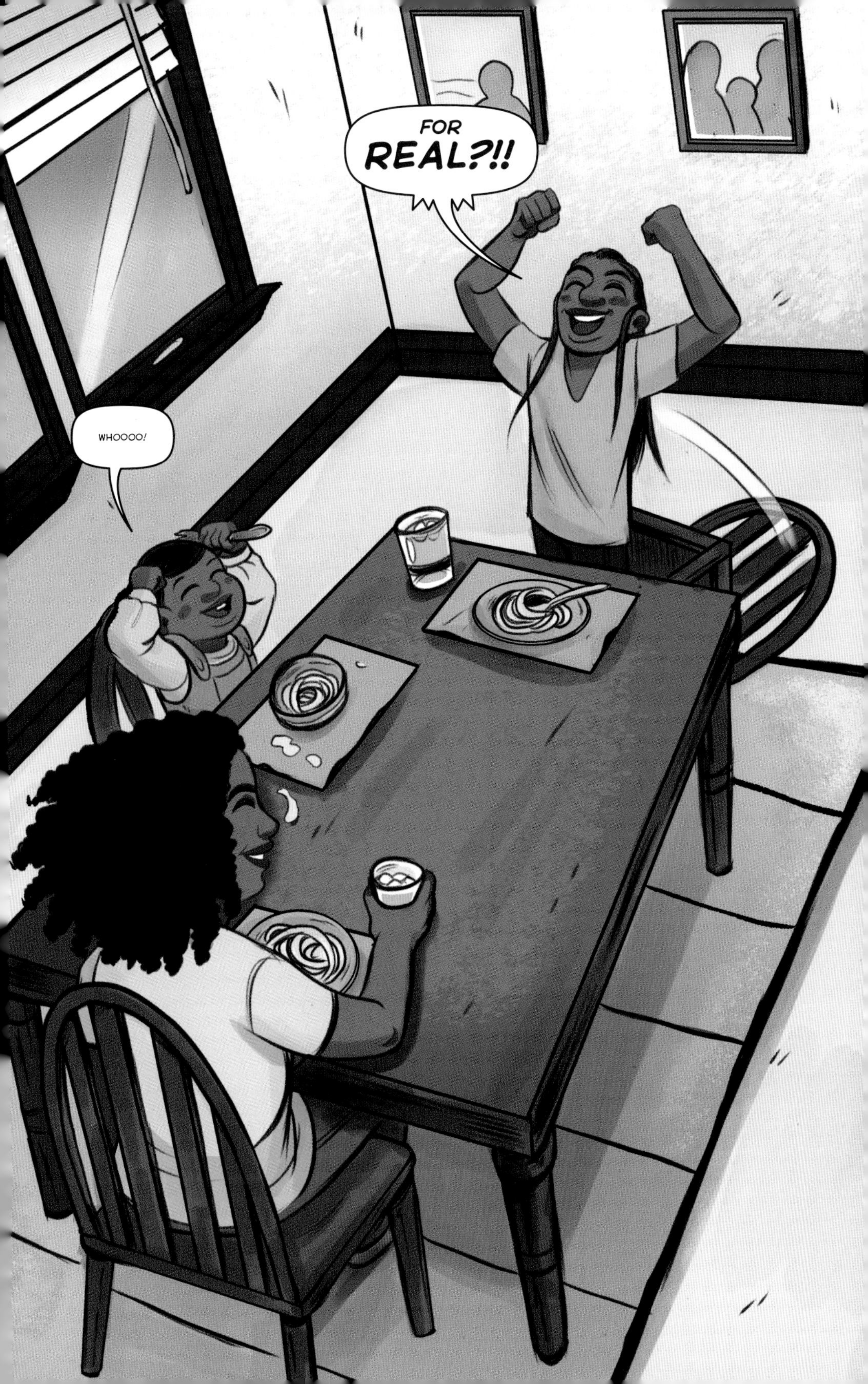
FOR REAL?!!
WHOOOO!

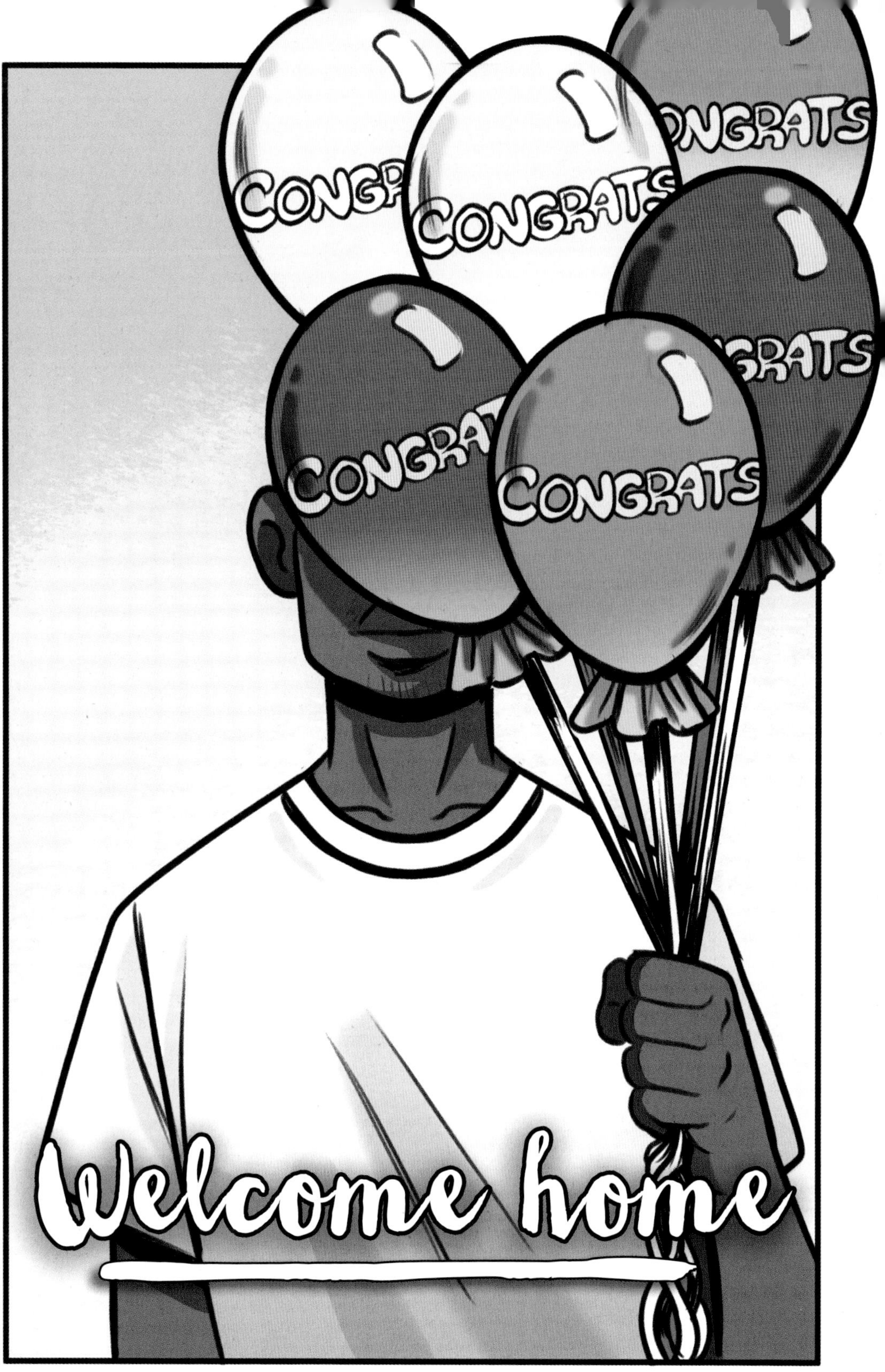
CONGRATS
CONGRATS
Welcome home

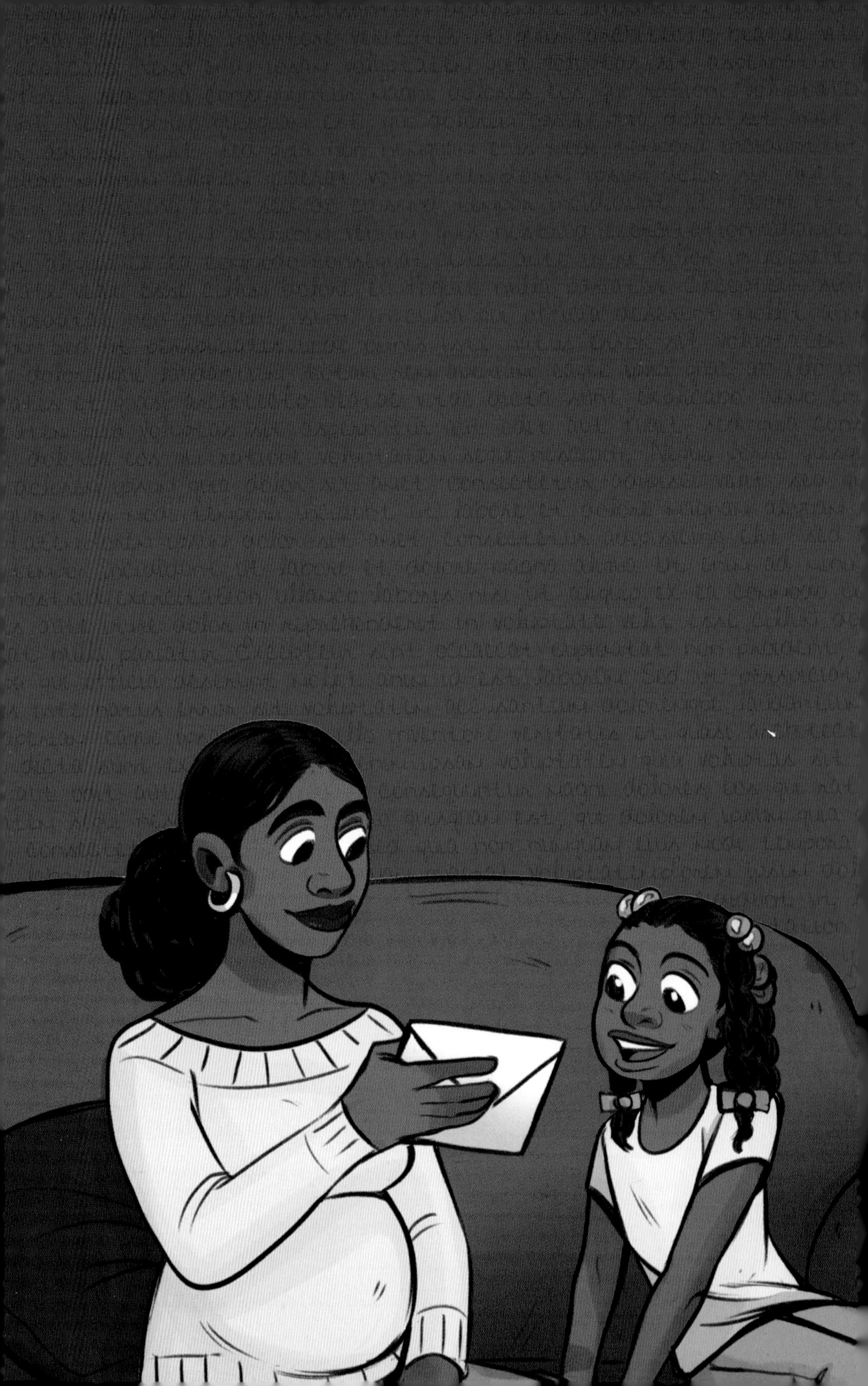

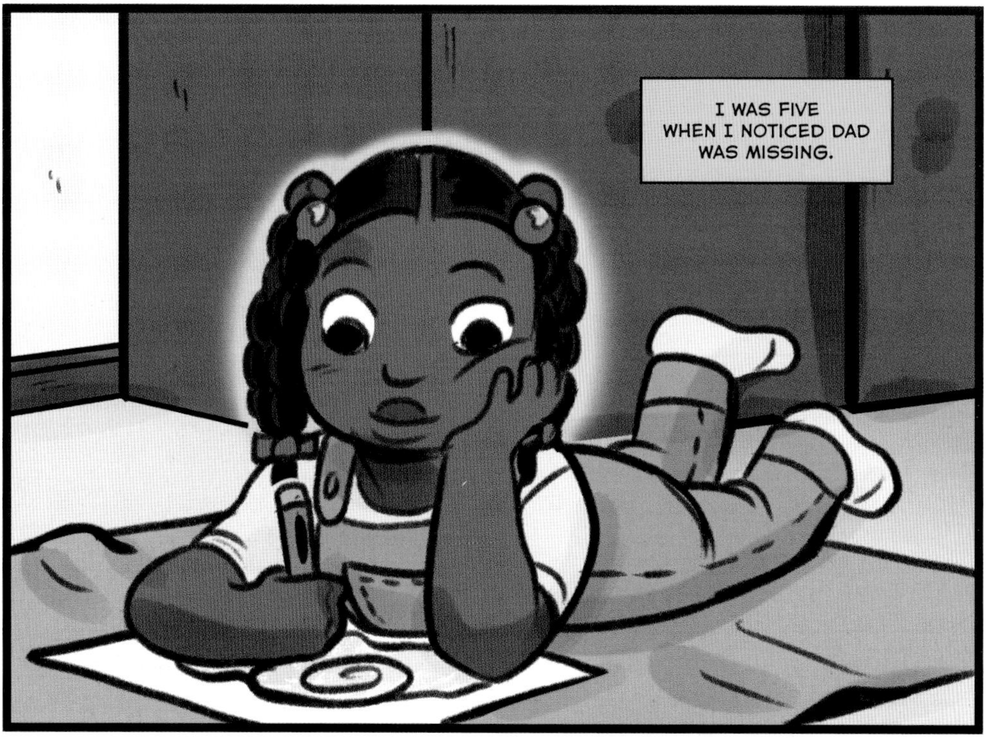
I WAS FIVE WHEN I NOTICED DAD WAS MISSING.

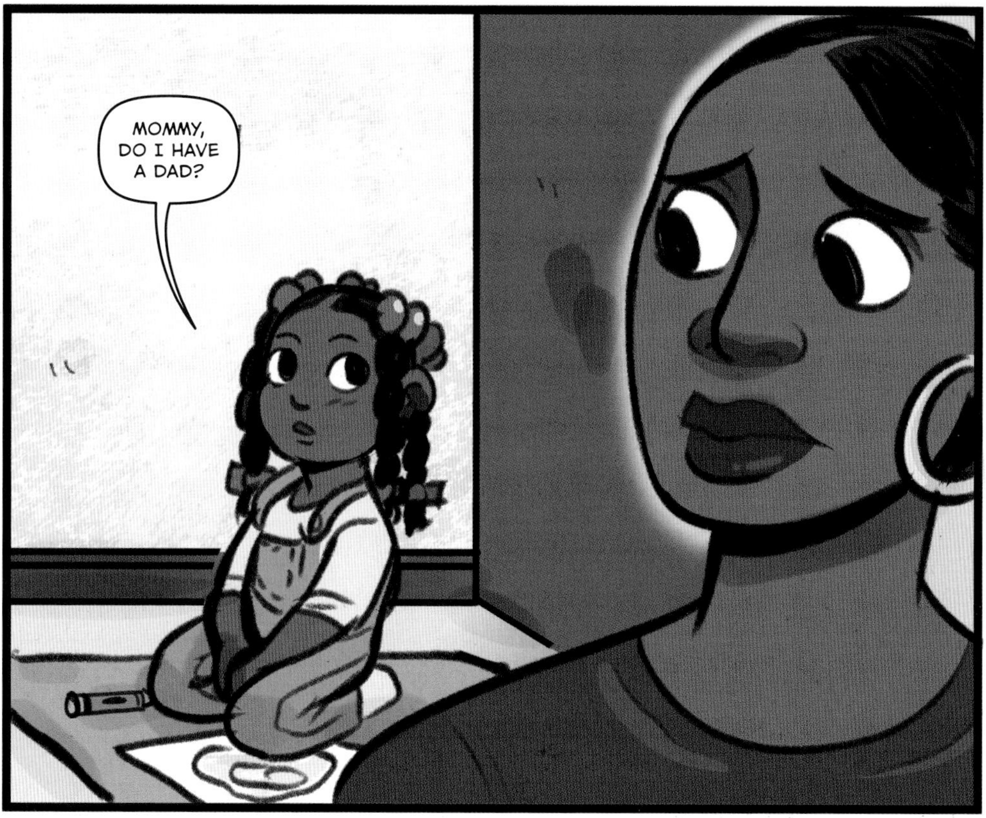
MOMMY, DO I HAVE A DAD?

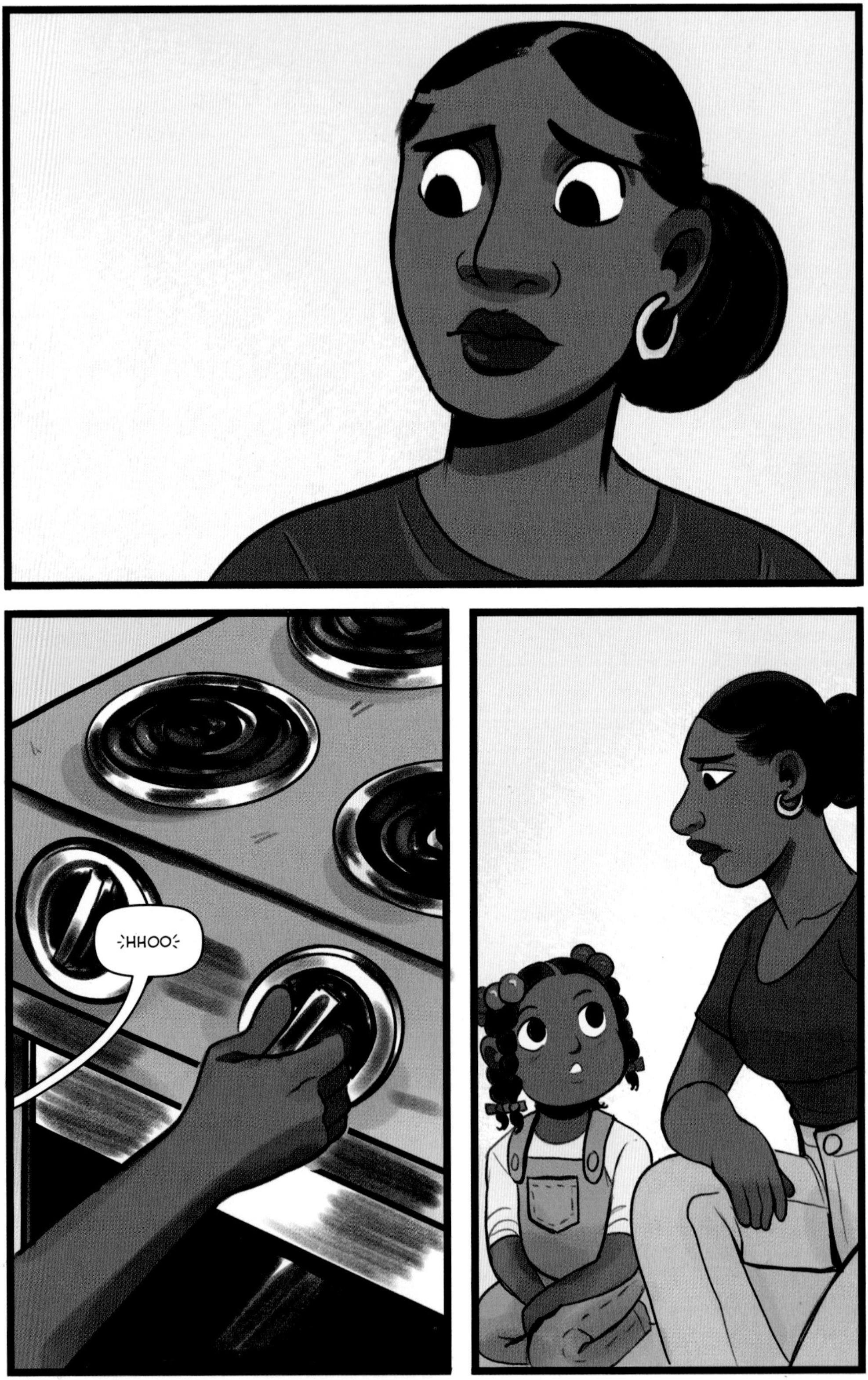
HHOO

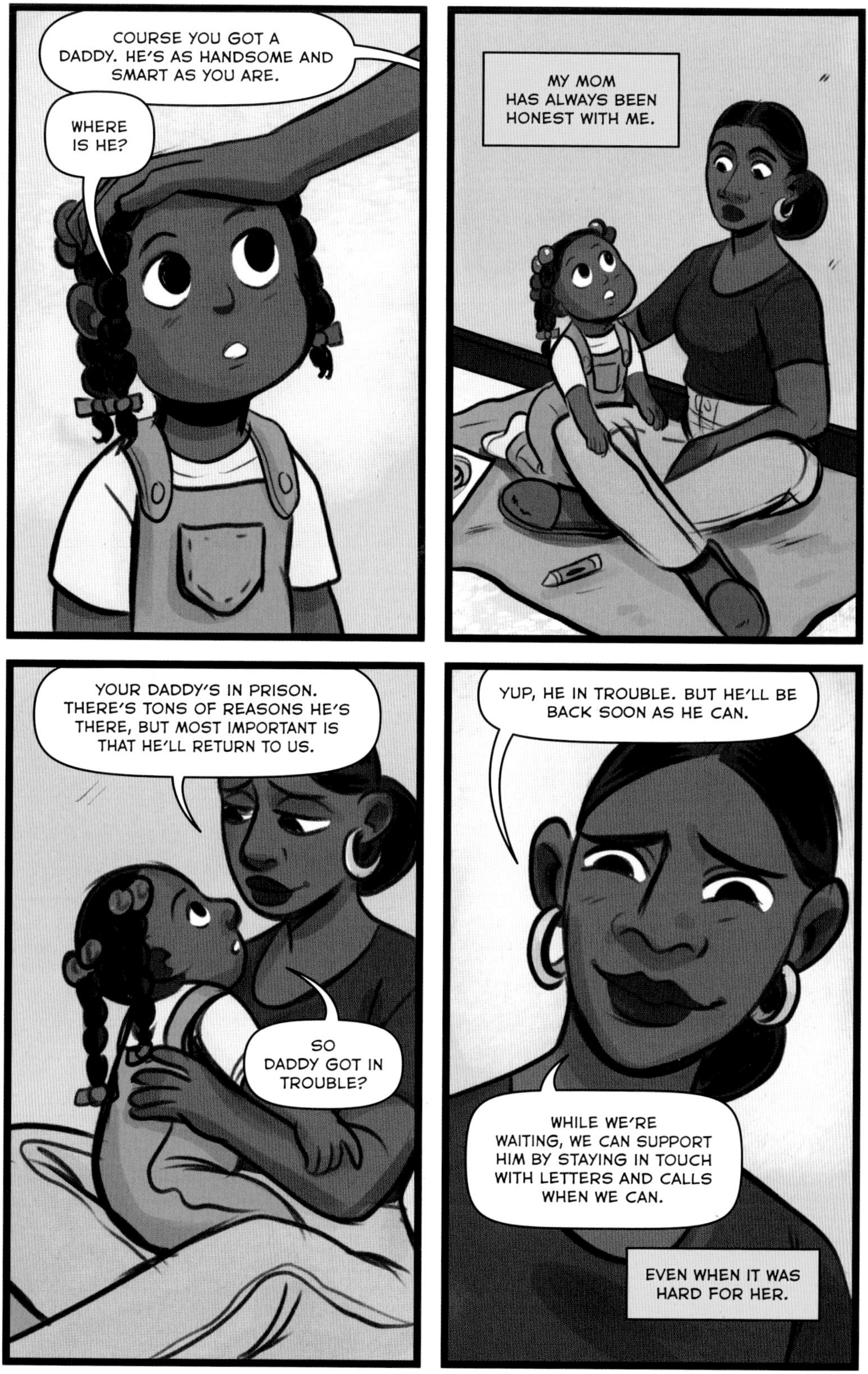
COURSE YOU GOT A DADDY. HE'S AS HANDSOME AND SMART AS YOU ARE.
WHERE IS HE?
MY MOM HAS ALWAYS BEEN HONEST WITH ME.
YOUR DADDY'S IN PRISON. THERE'S TONS OF REASONS HE'S THERE, BUT MOST IMPORTANT IS THAT HE'LL RETURN TO US.
SO DADDY GOT IN TROUBLE?
YUP, HE IN TROUBLE. BUT HE'LL BE BACK SOON AS HE CAN.
WHILE WE'RE WAITING, WE CAN SUPPORT HIM BY STAYING IN TOUCH WITH LETTERS AND CALLS WHEN WE CAN.
EVEN WHEN IT WAS HARD FOR HER.

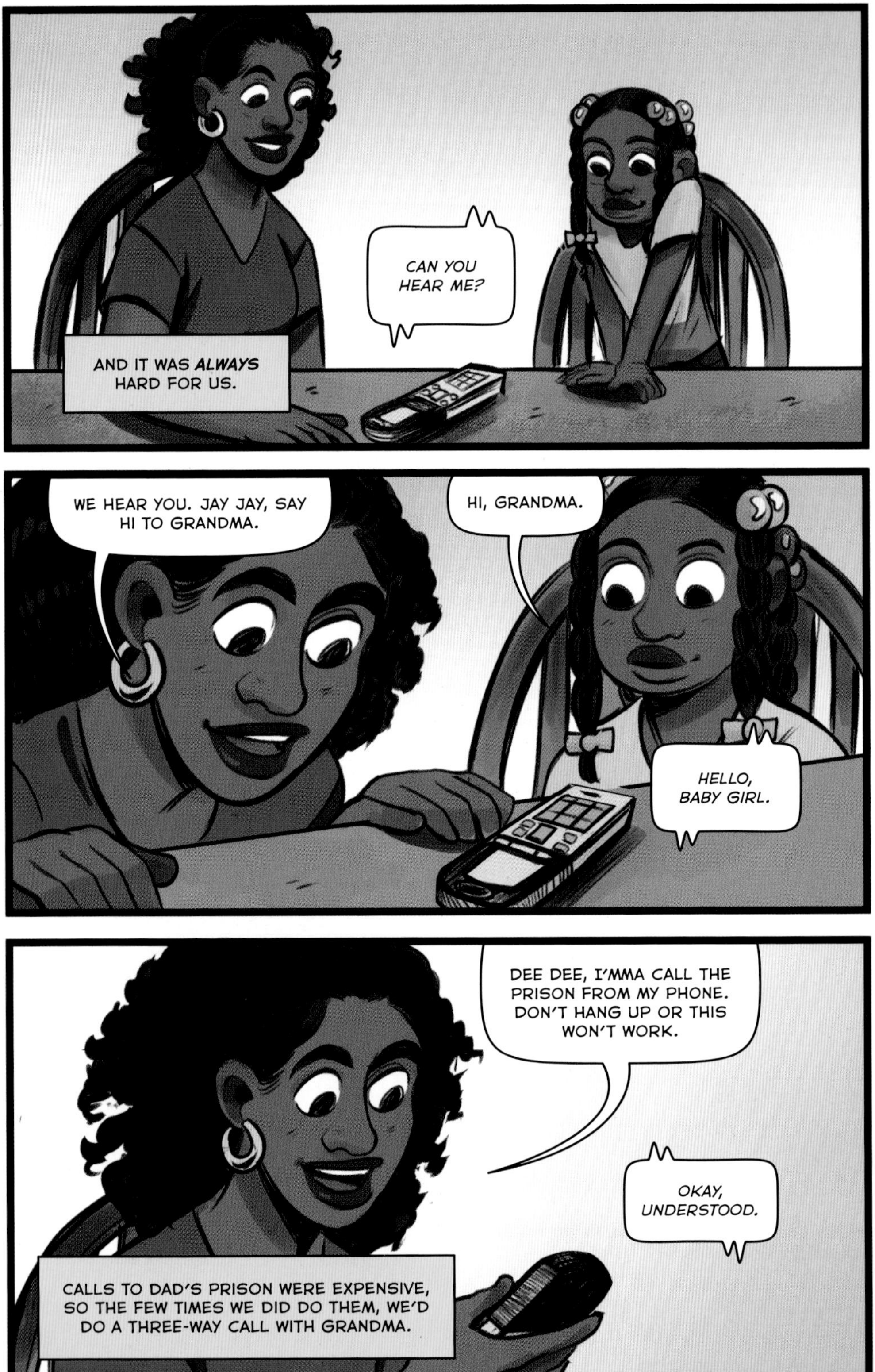
CAN YOU HEAR ME?
AND IT WAS *ALWAYS* HARD FOR US.
WE HEAR YOU. JAY JAY, SAY HI TO GRANDMA.
HI, GRANDMA.
HELLO, BABY GIRL.
DEE DEE, I'MMA CALL THE PRISON FROM MY PHONE. DON'T HANG UP OR THIS WON'T WORK.
OKAY, UNDERSTOOD.
CALLS TO DAD'S PRISON WERE EXPENSIVE, SO THE FEW TIMES WE DID DO THEM, WE'D DO A THREE-WAY CALL WITH GRANDMA.

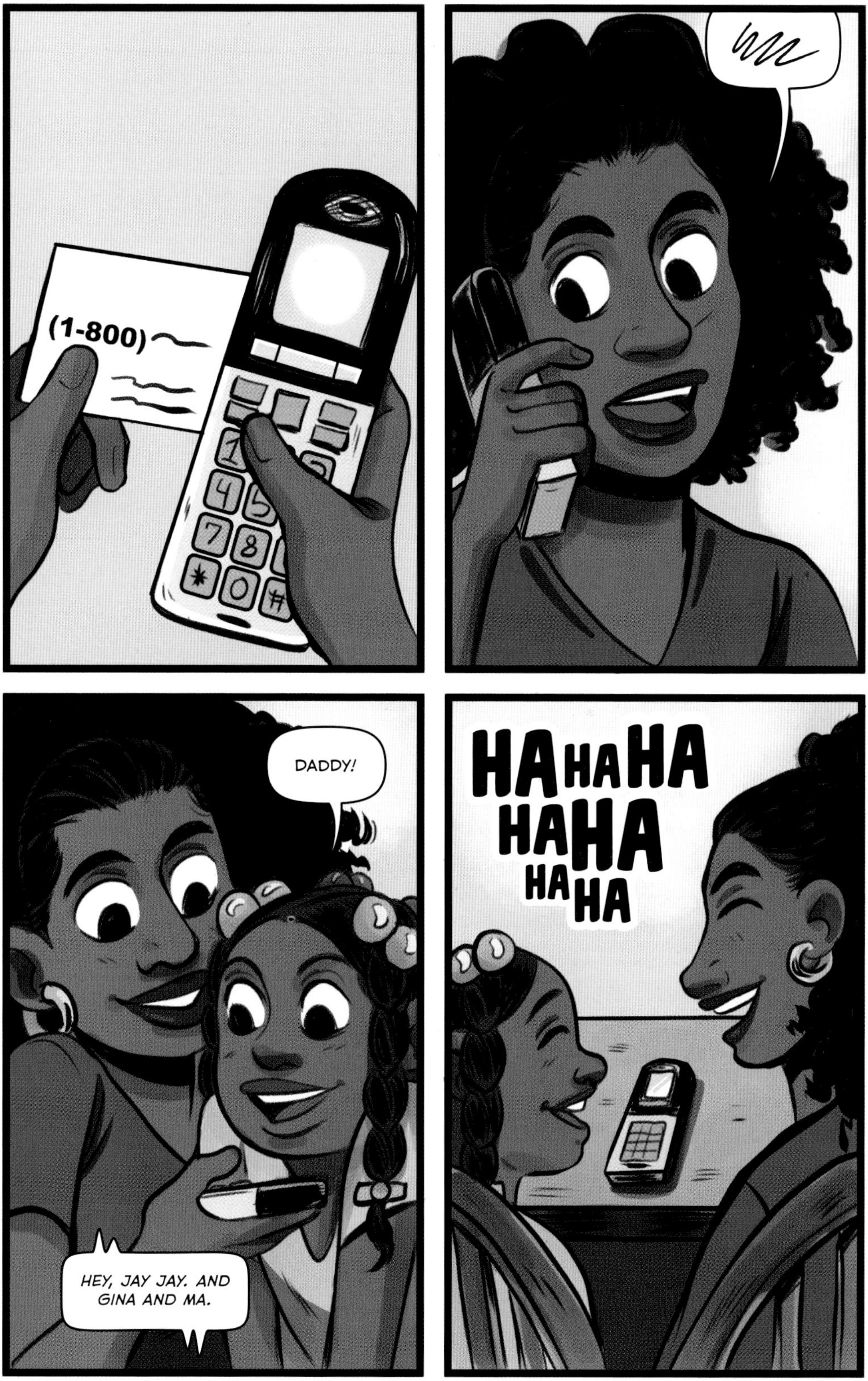
(1-800)
DADDY!
HEY, JAY JAY. AND GINA AND MA.
HAHAHAHA
HAHAHA
HAHA

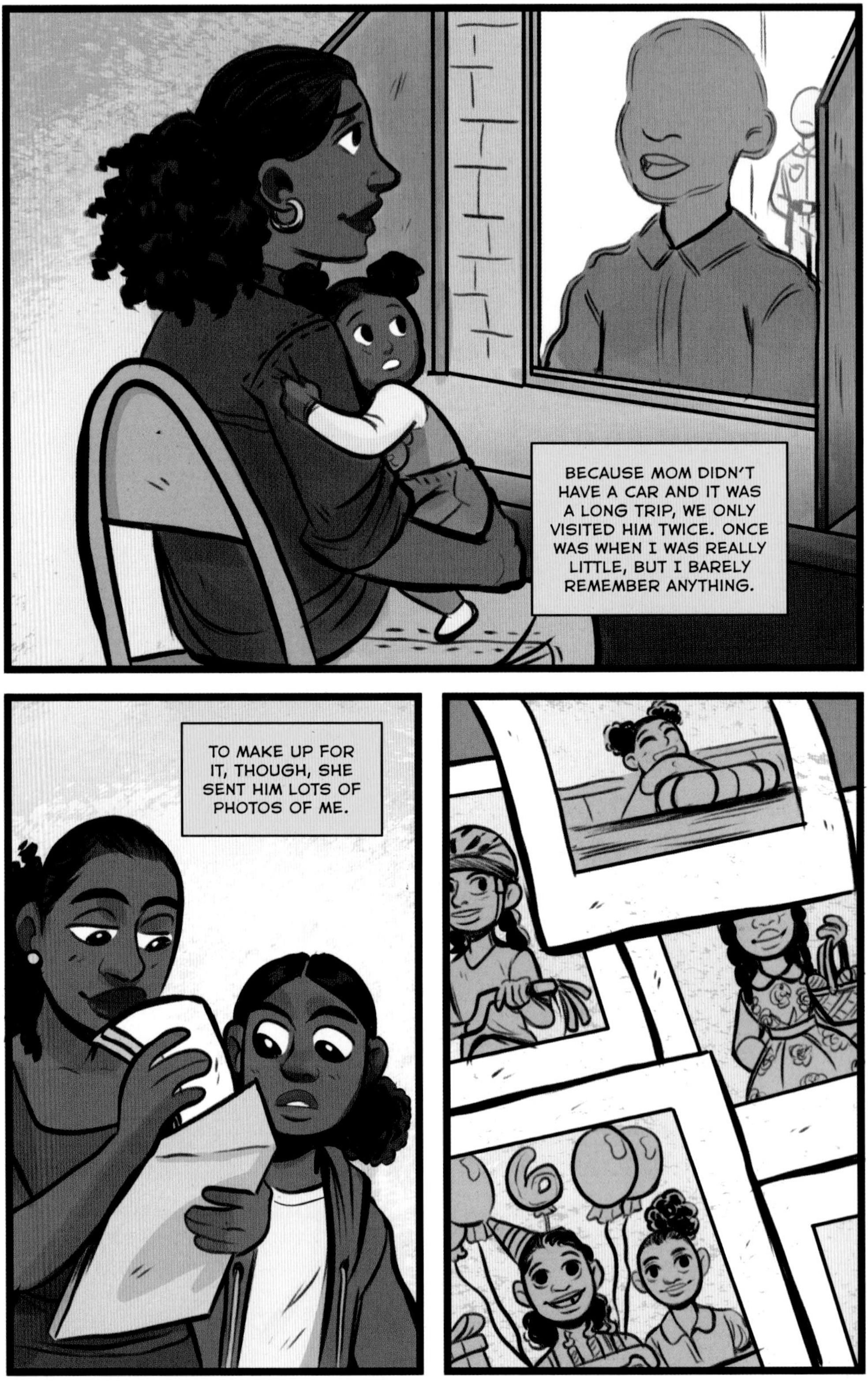
BECAUSE MOM DIDN'T HAVE A CAR AND IT WAS A LONG TRIP, WE ONLY VISITED HIM TWICE. ONCE WAS WHEN I WAS REALLY LITTLE, BUT I BARELY REMEMBER ANYTHING.
TO MAKE UP FOR IT, THOUGH, SHE SENT HIM LOTS OF PHOTOS OF ME.

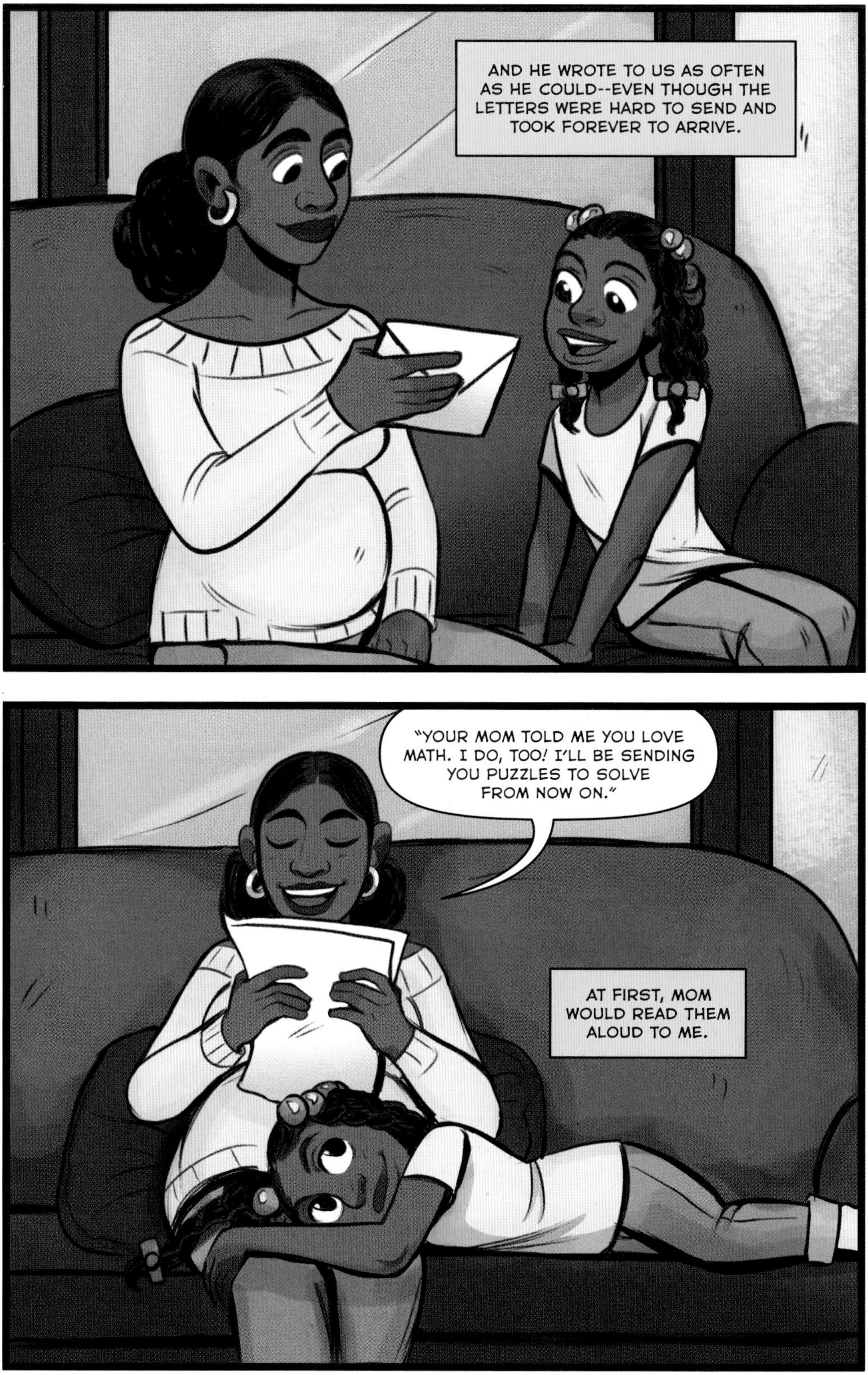
AND HE WROTE TO US AS OFTEN AS HE COULD--EVEN THOUGH THE LETTERS WERE HARD TO SEND AND TOOK FOREVER TO ARRIVE.
"YOUR MOM TOLD ME YOU LOVE MATH. I DO, TOO! I'LL BE SENDING YOU PUZZLES TO SOLVE FROM NOW ON."
AT FIRST, MOM WOULD READ THEM ALOUD TO ME.

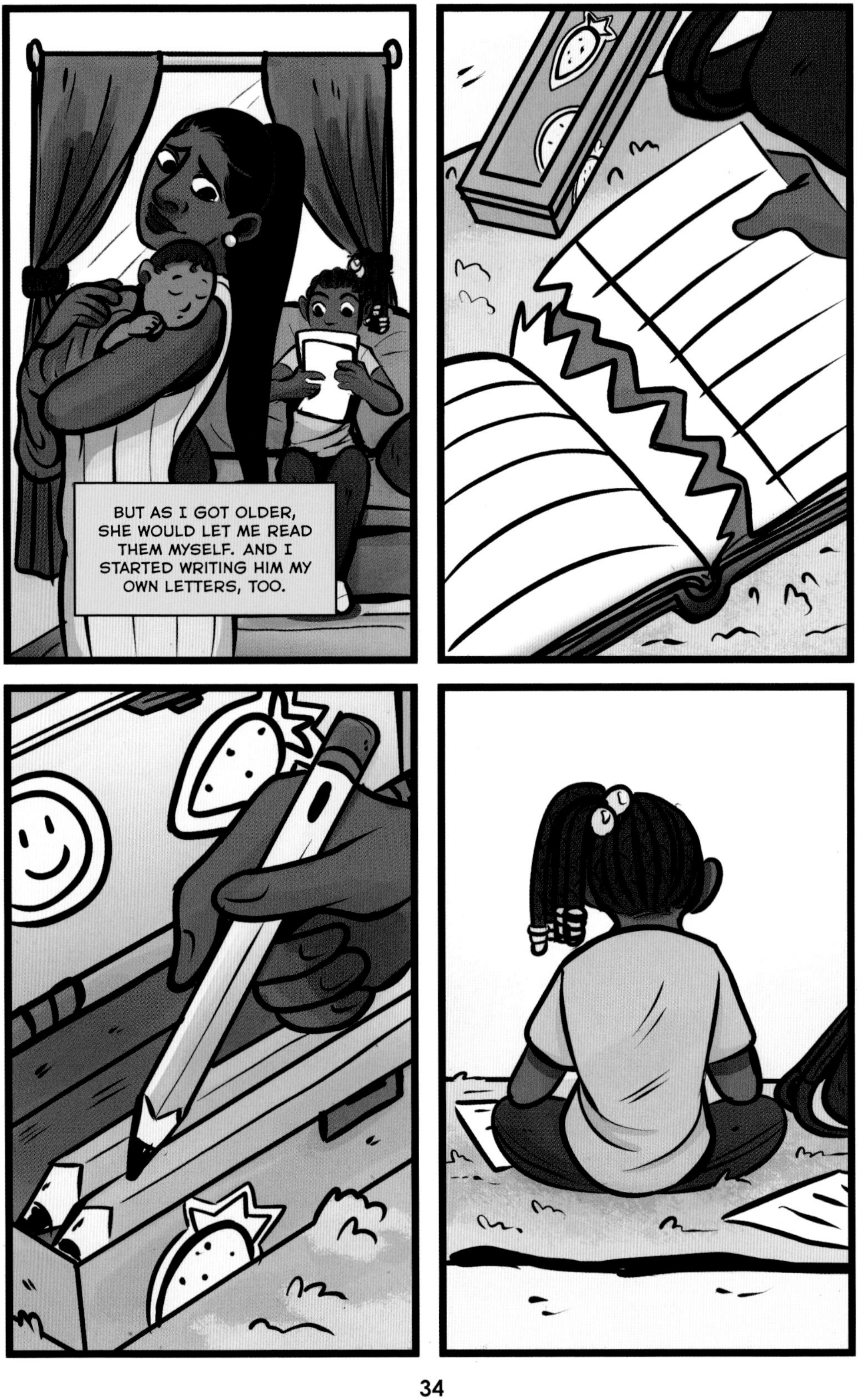
BUT AS I GOT OLDER, SHE WOULD LET ME READ THEM MYSELF. AND I STARTED WRITING HIM MY OWN LETTERS, TOO.

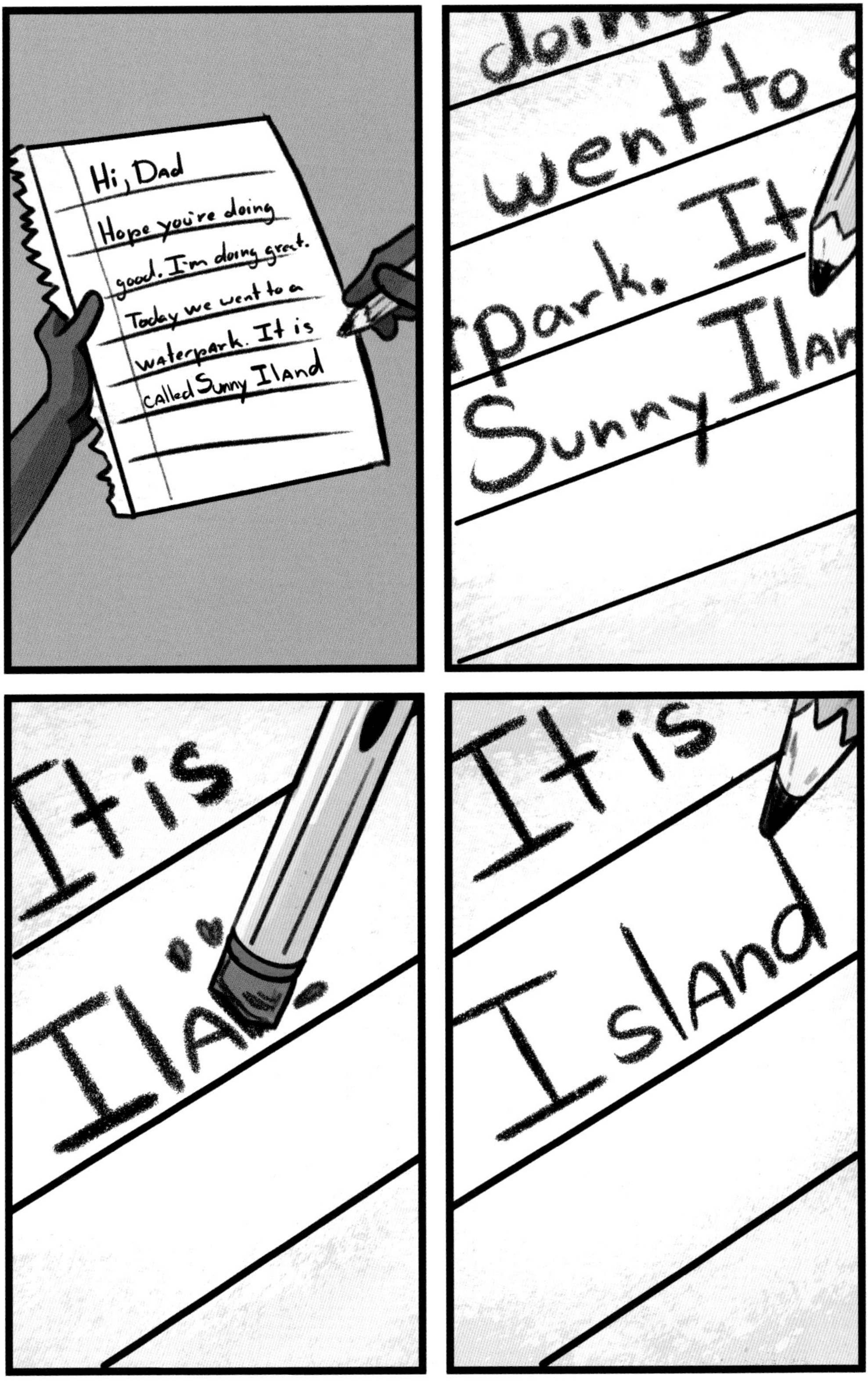
Hi, Dad
Hope you're doing good. I'm doing great. Today we went to a waterpark. It is called Sunny Iland
doing
went to
park. It
Sunny Ilan
It is
It is
Island

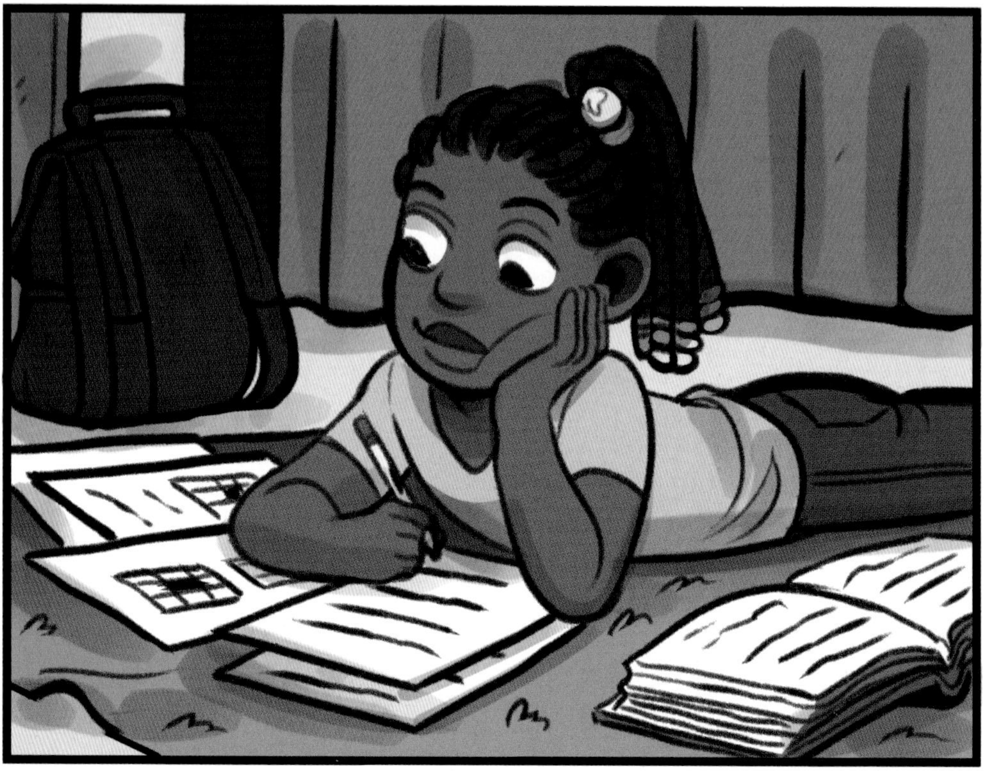

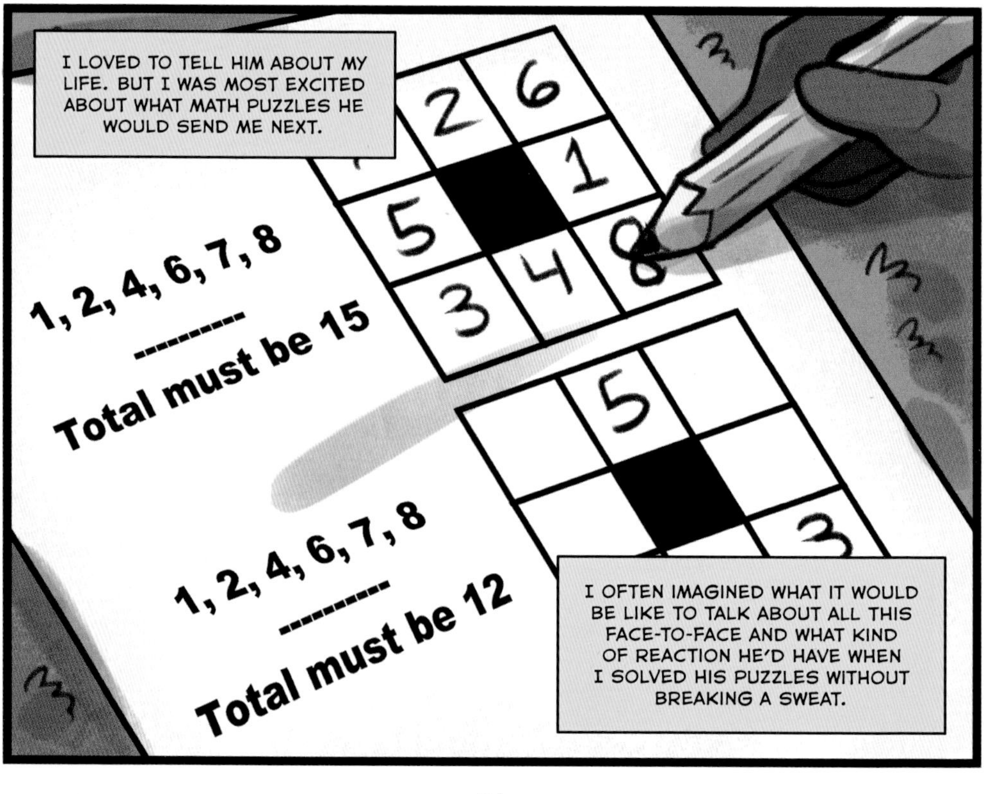
I LOVED TO TELL HIM ABOUT MY LIFE. BUT I WAS MOST EXCITED ABOUT WHAT MATH PUZZLES HE WOULD SEND ME NEXT.
2
6
1
5
8
3
4
8
1, 2, 4, 6, 7, 8
Total must be 15
5
3
1, 2, 4, 6, 7, 8
Total must be 12
I OFTEN IMAGINED WHAT IT WOULD BE LIKE TO TALK ABOUT ALL THIS FACE-TO-FACE AND WHAT KIND OF REACTION HE'D HAVE WHEN I SOLVED HIS PUZZLES WITHOUT BREAKING A SWEAT.

15

12

$$\text{🍎} + \text{🍎} + \text{🍎} + \text{🍎} = \underline{28}$$

$$\text{🍎} \times \text{🍐} = \underline{21}$$

$$\text{🍐} \times \text{🍄} - \text{🍎} = \underline{17}$$

$$\text{🍎} \times \text{🍄} + \text{🍐} - \text{🍄} = \underline{51}$$

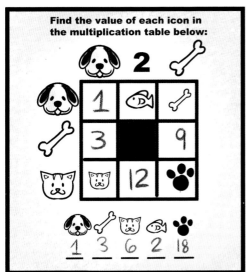

Find the value of each icon in the multiplication table below:

MY MOM ALWAYS SAID I WAS SMART, JUST LIKE HIM.

I WANTED TO SHOW HIM I WAS.

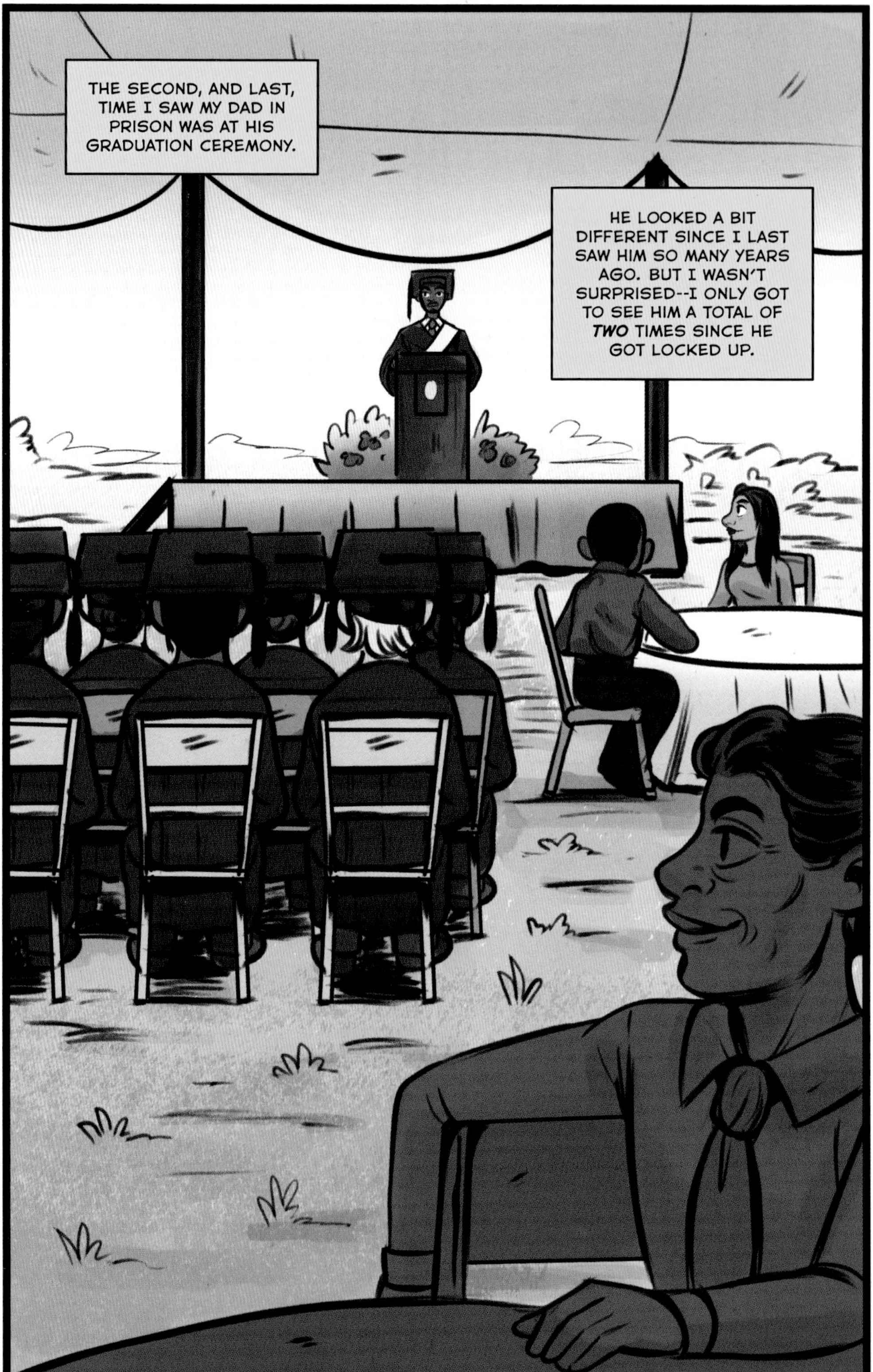
THE SECOND, AND LAST, TIME I SAW MY DAD IN PRISON WAS AT HIS GRADUATION CEREMONY.
HE LOOKED A BIT DIFFERENT SINCE I LAST SAW HIM SO MANY YEARS AGO. BUT I WASN'T SURPRISED--I ONLY GOT TO SEE HIM A TOTAL OF *TWO* TIMES SINCE HE GOT LOCKED UP.

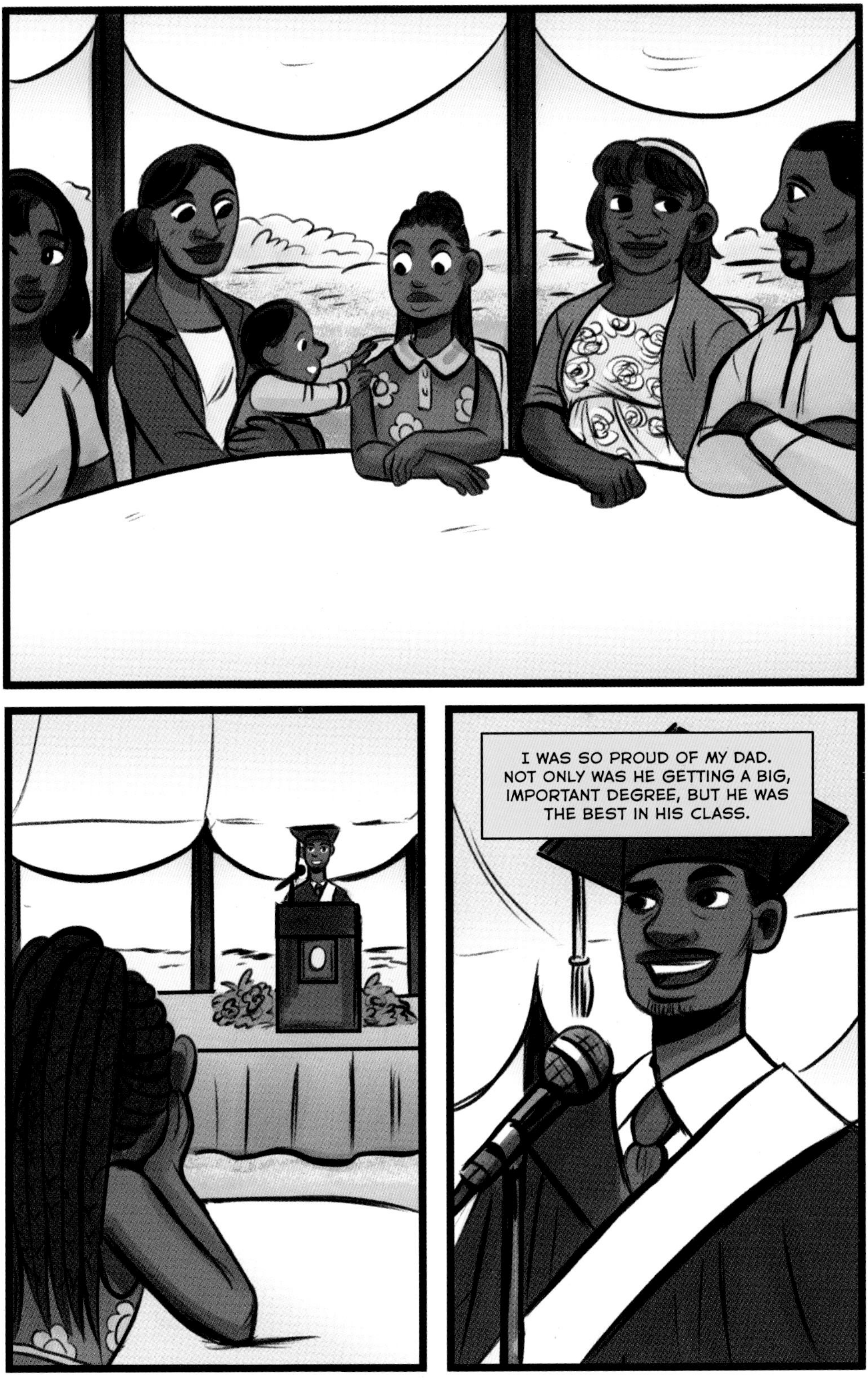
I WAS SO PROUD OF MY DAD. NOT ONLY WAS HE GETTING A BIG, IMPORTANT DEGREE, BUT HE WAS THE BEST IN HIS CLASS.

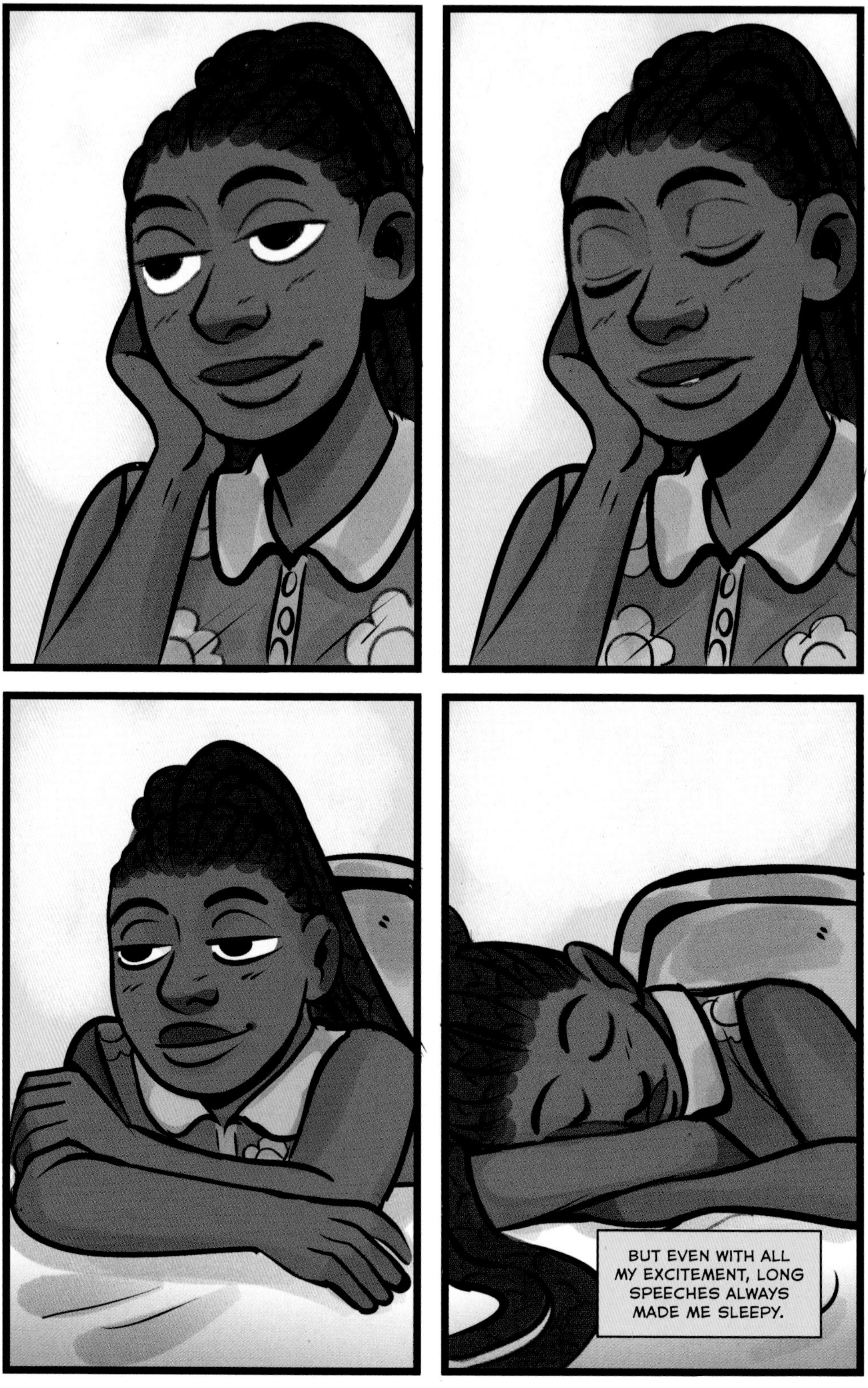
BUT EVEN WITH ALL MY EXCITEMENT, LONG SPEECHES ALWAYS MADE ME SLEEPY.

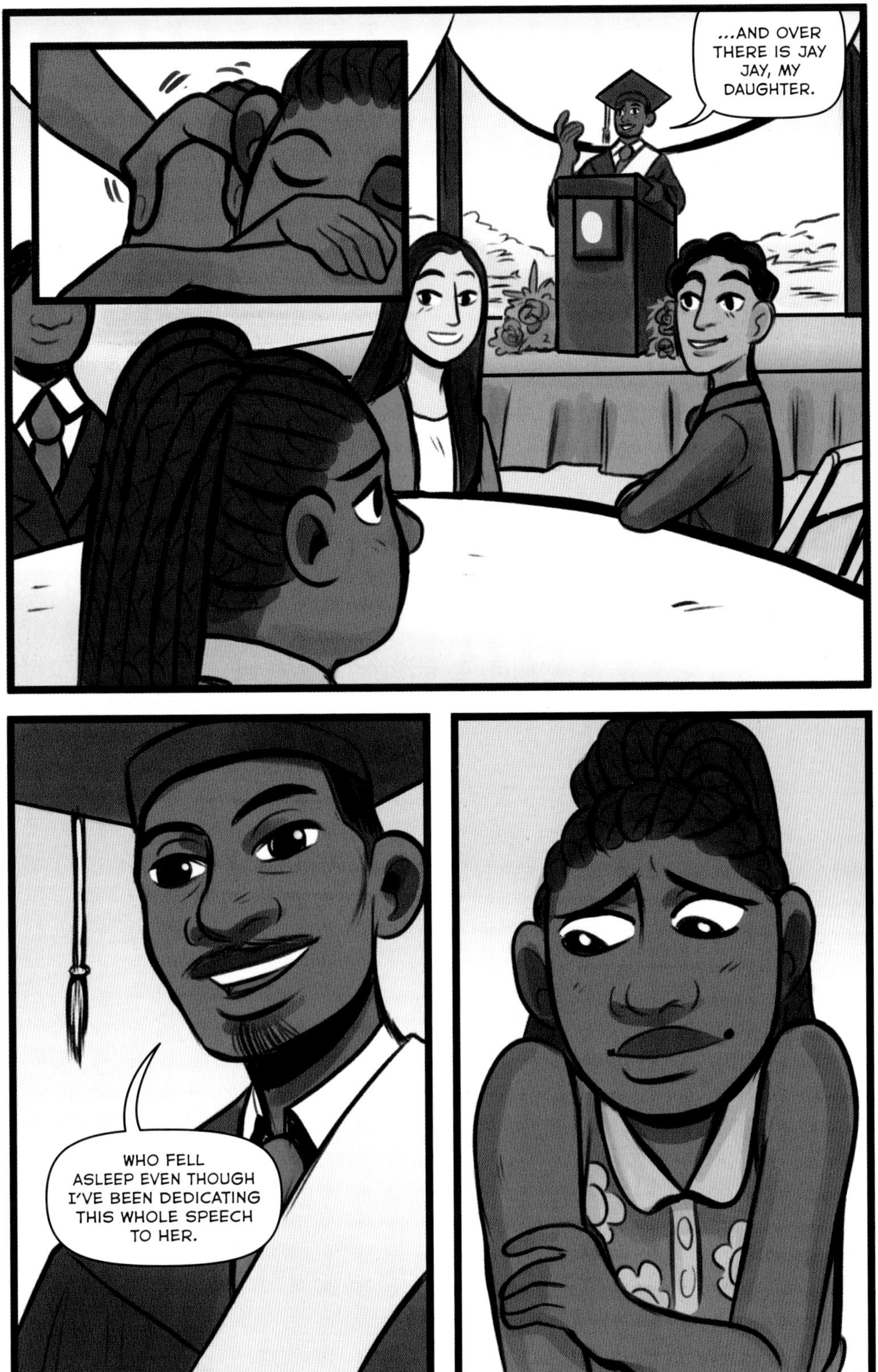
...AND OVER THERE IS JAY JAY, MY DAUGHTER.
WHO FELL ASLEEP EVEN THOUGH I'VE BEEN DEDICATING THIS WHOLE SPEECH TO HER.

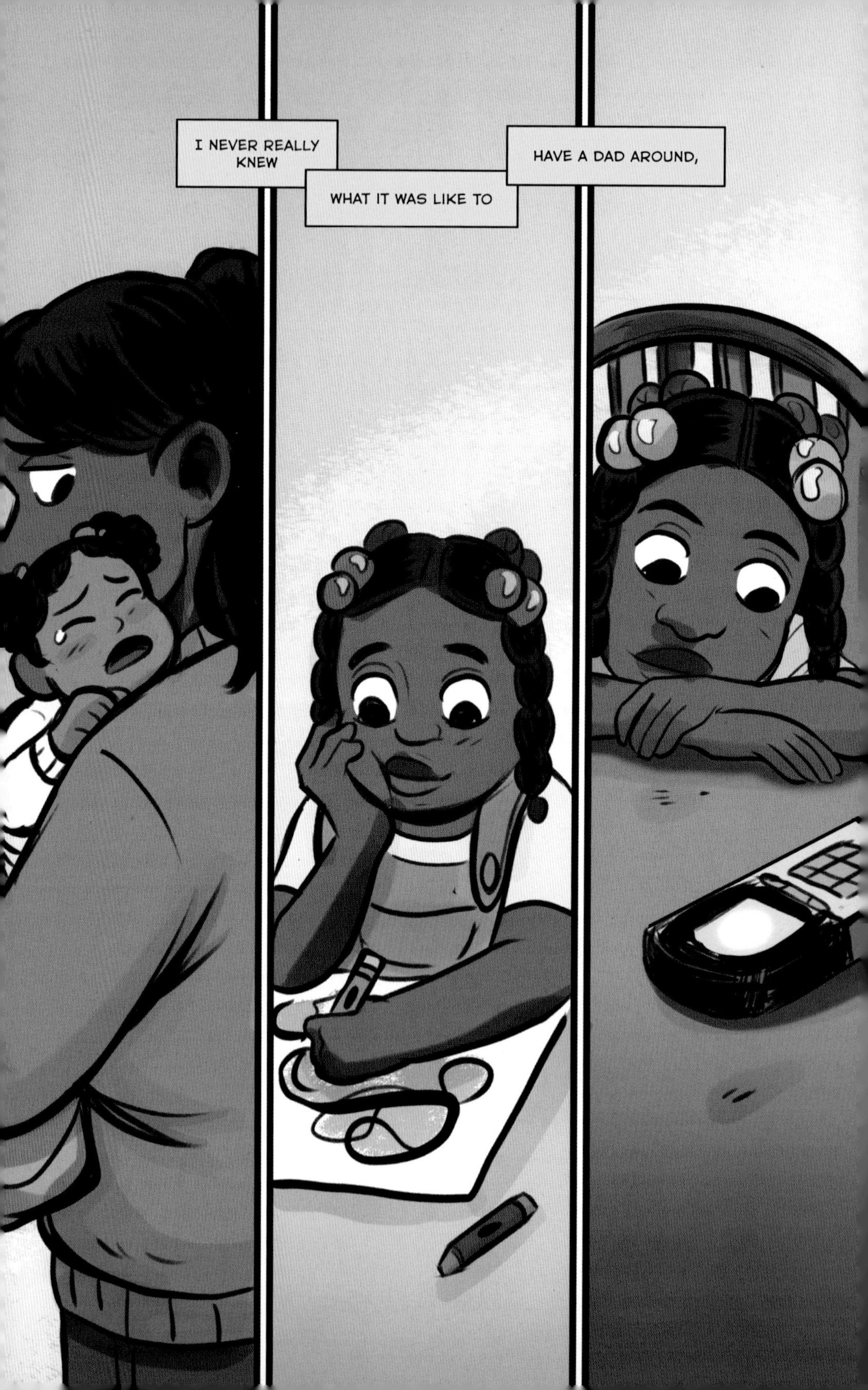
I NEVER REALLY KNEW
WHAT IT WAS LIKE TO
HAVE A DAD AROUND,

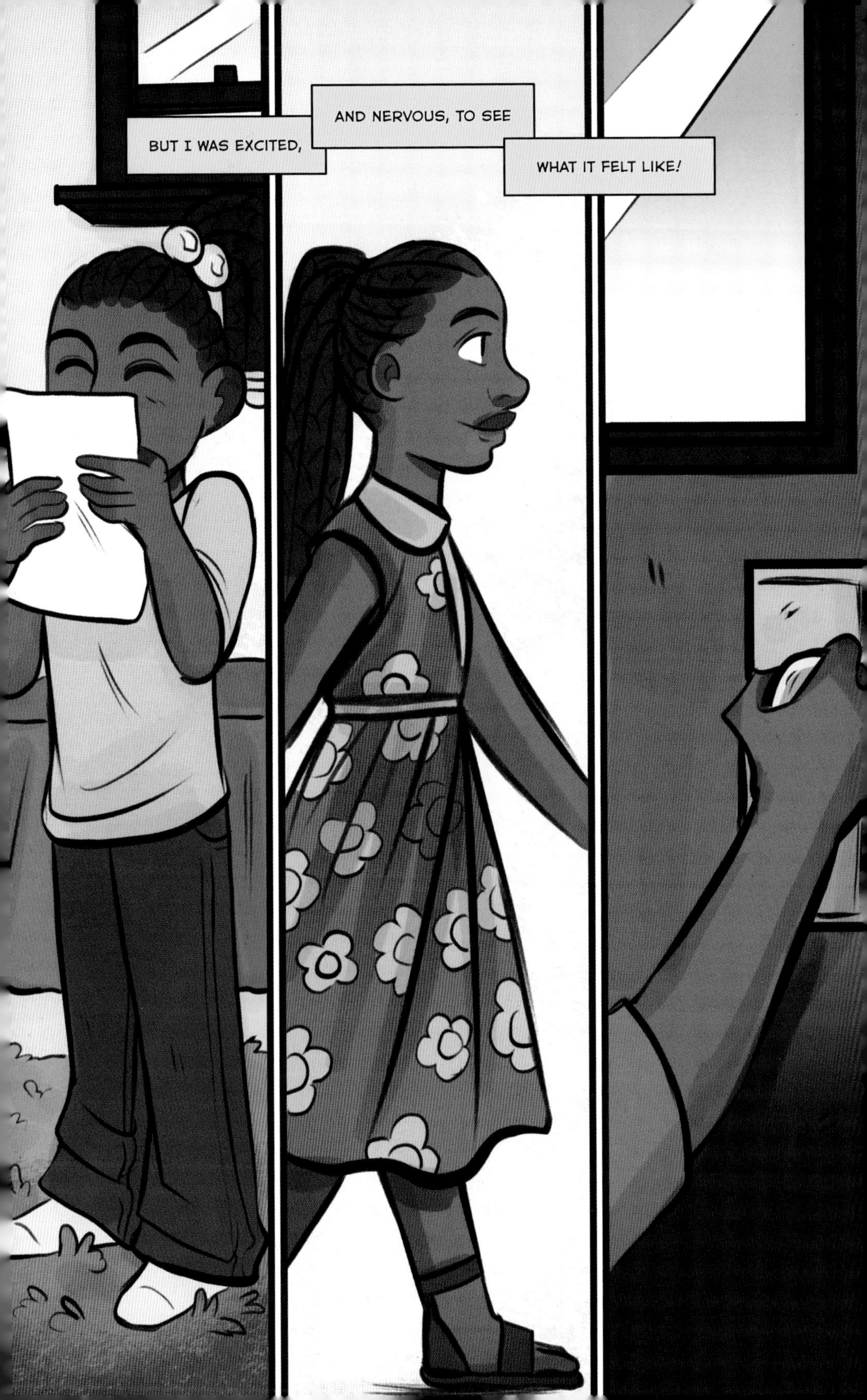
BUT I WAS EXCITED,
AND NERVOUS, TO SEE
WHAT IT FELT LIKE!

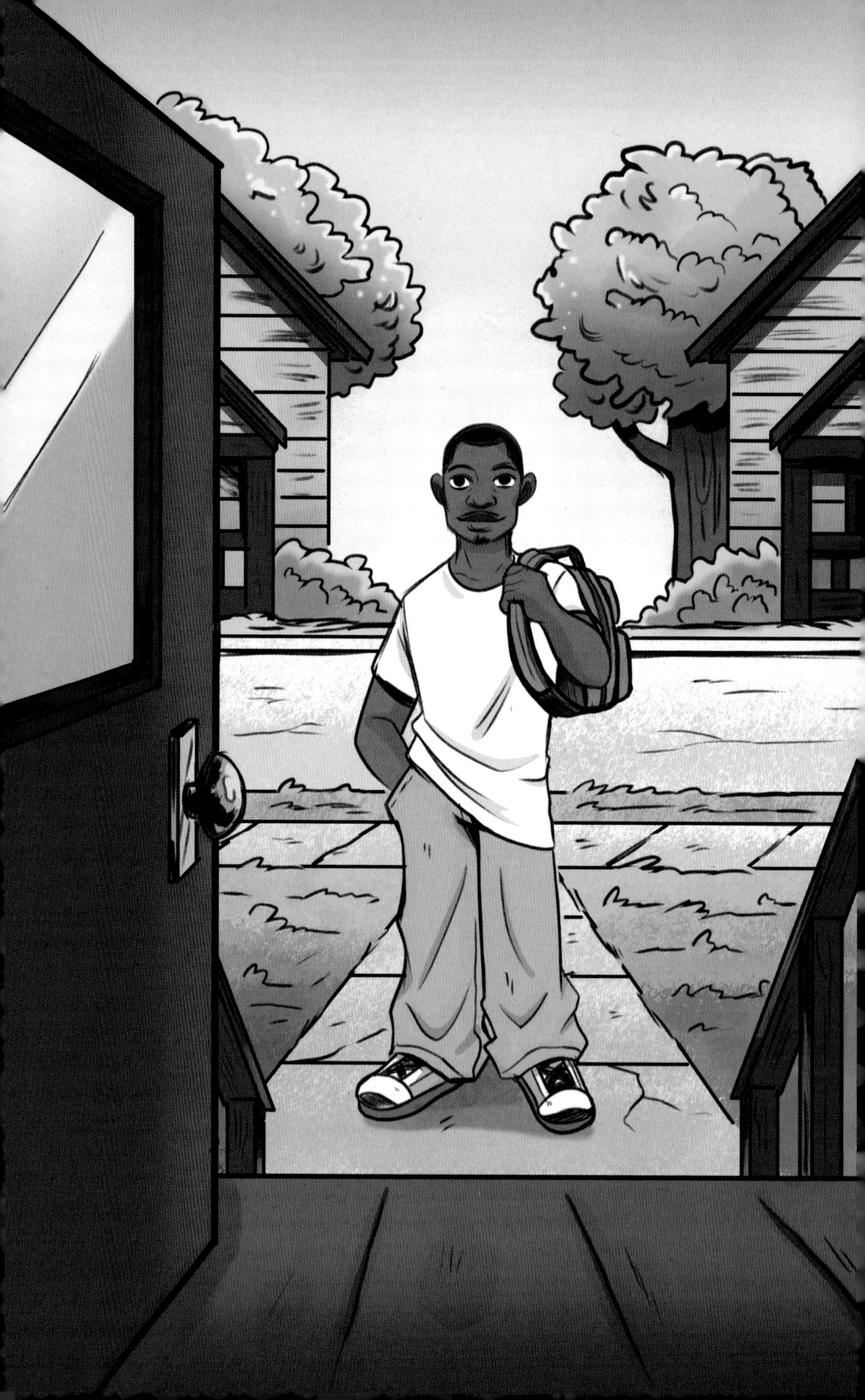

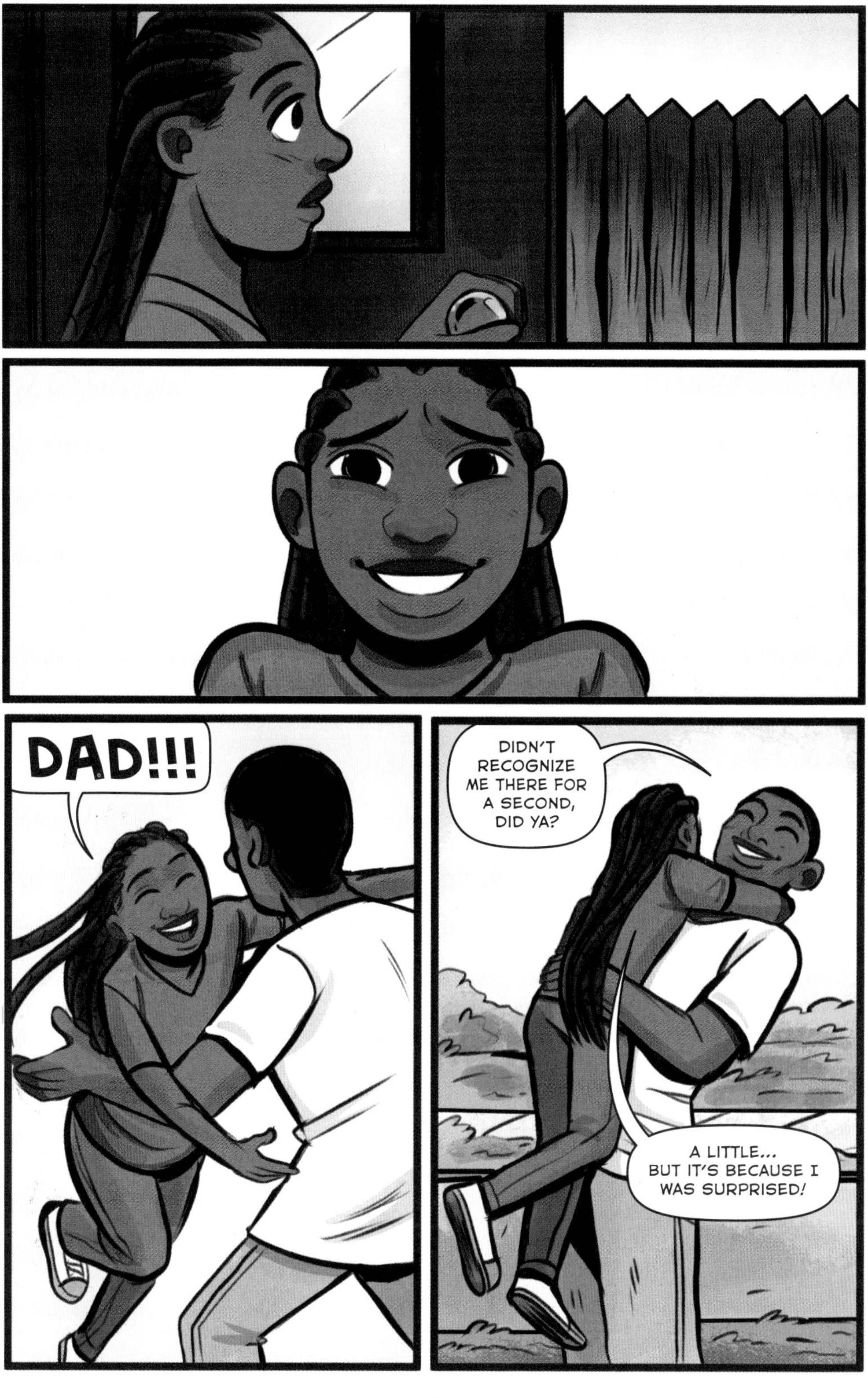
DAD!!!
DIDN'T RECOGNIZE ME THERE FOR A SECOND, DID YA?
A LITTLE... BUT IT'S BECAUSE I WAS SURPRISED!

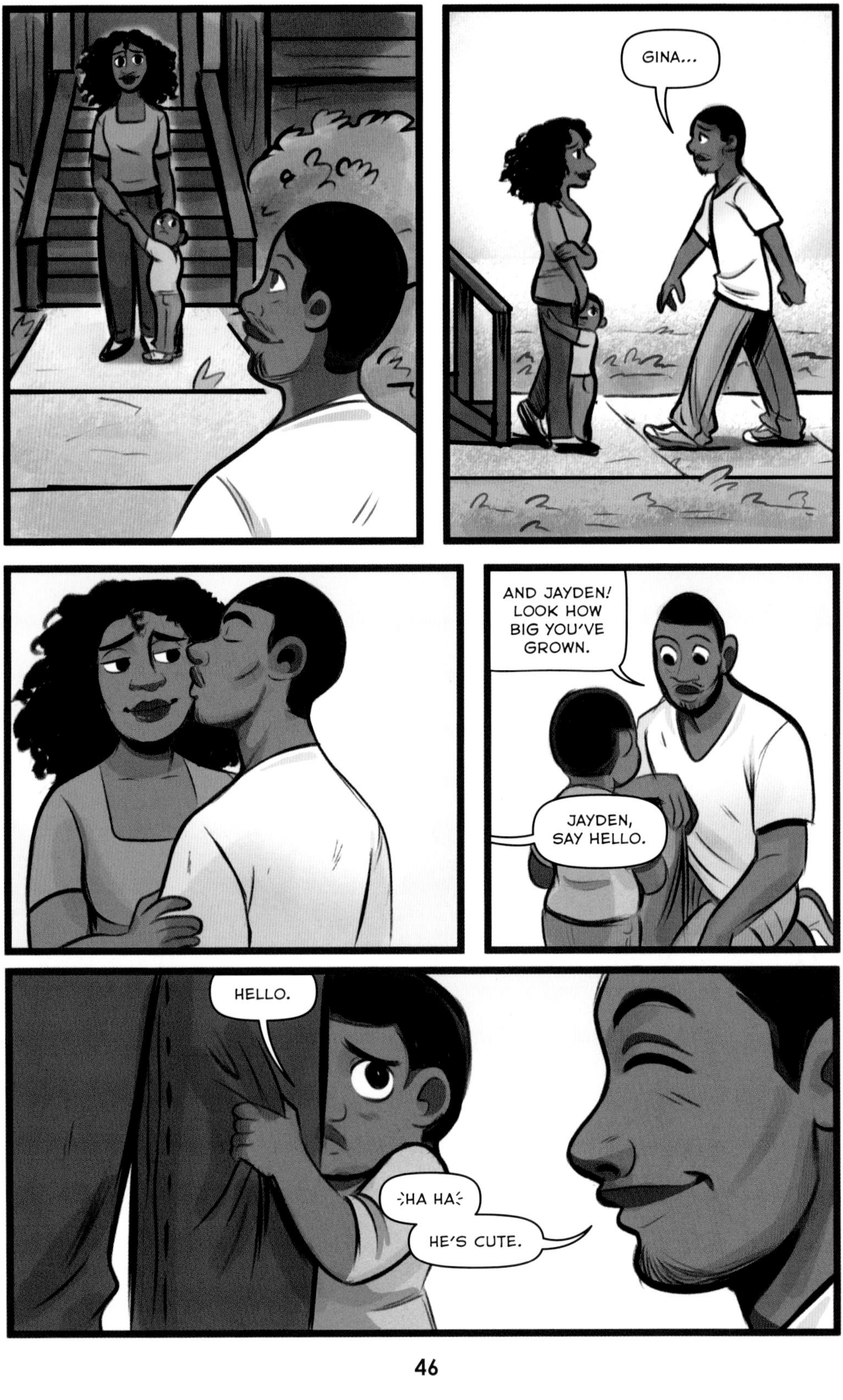
GINA...
AND JAYDEN! LOOK HOW BIG YOU'VE GROWN.
JAYDEN, SAY HELLO.
HELLO.
HA HA
HE'S CUTE.

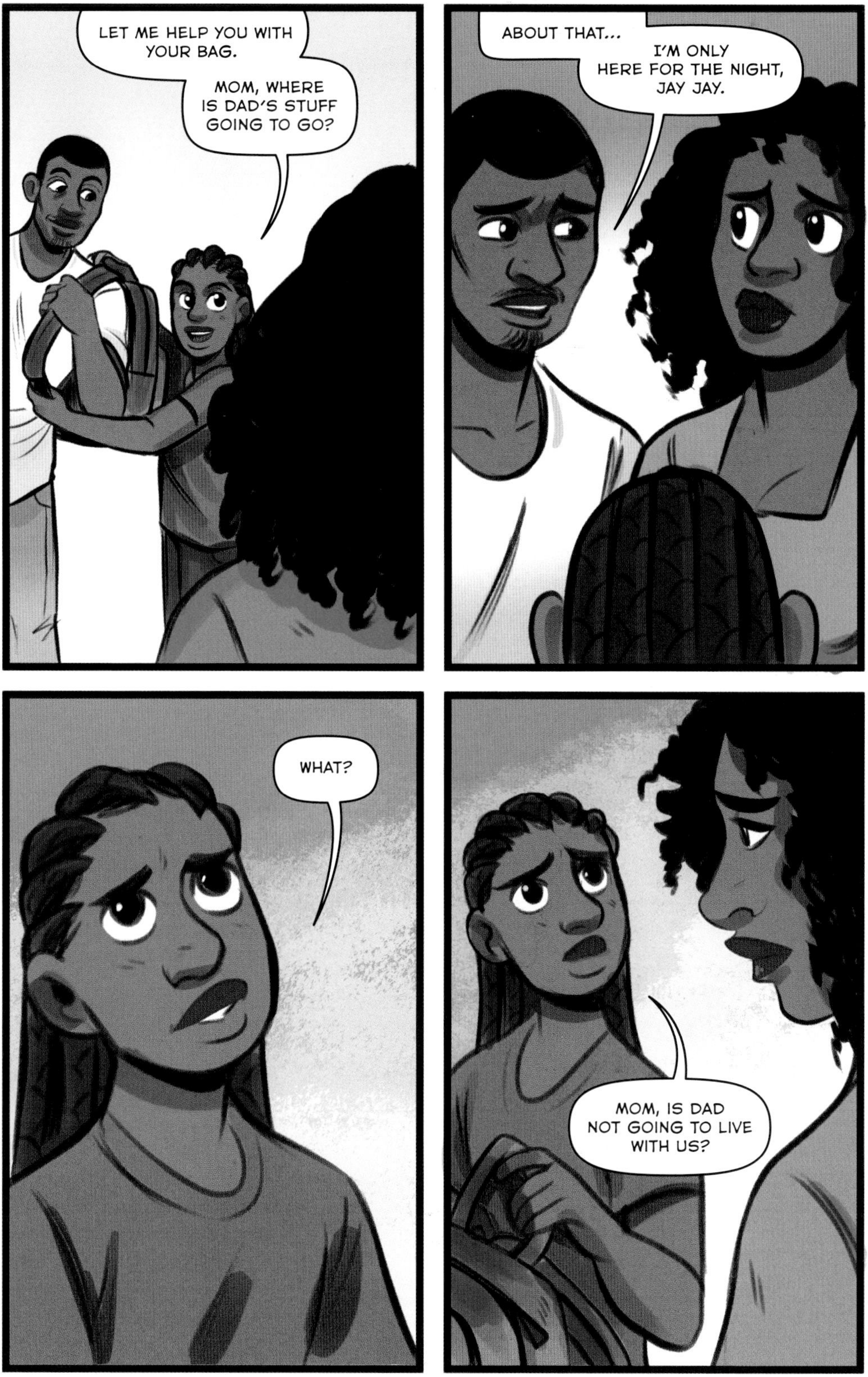
LET ME HELP YOU WITH YOUR BAG.
MOM, WHERE IS DAD'S STUFF GOING TO GO?
ABOUT THAT...
I'M ONLY HERE FOR THE NIGHT, JAY JAY.
WHAT?
MOM, IS DAD NOT GOING TO LIVE WITH US?

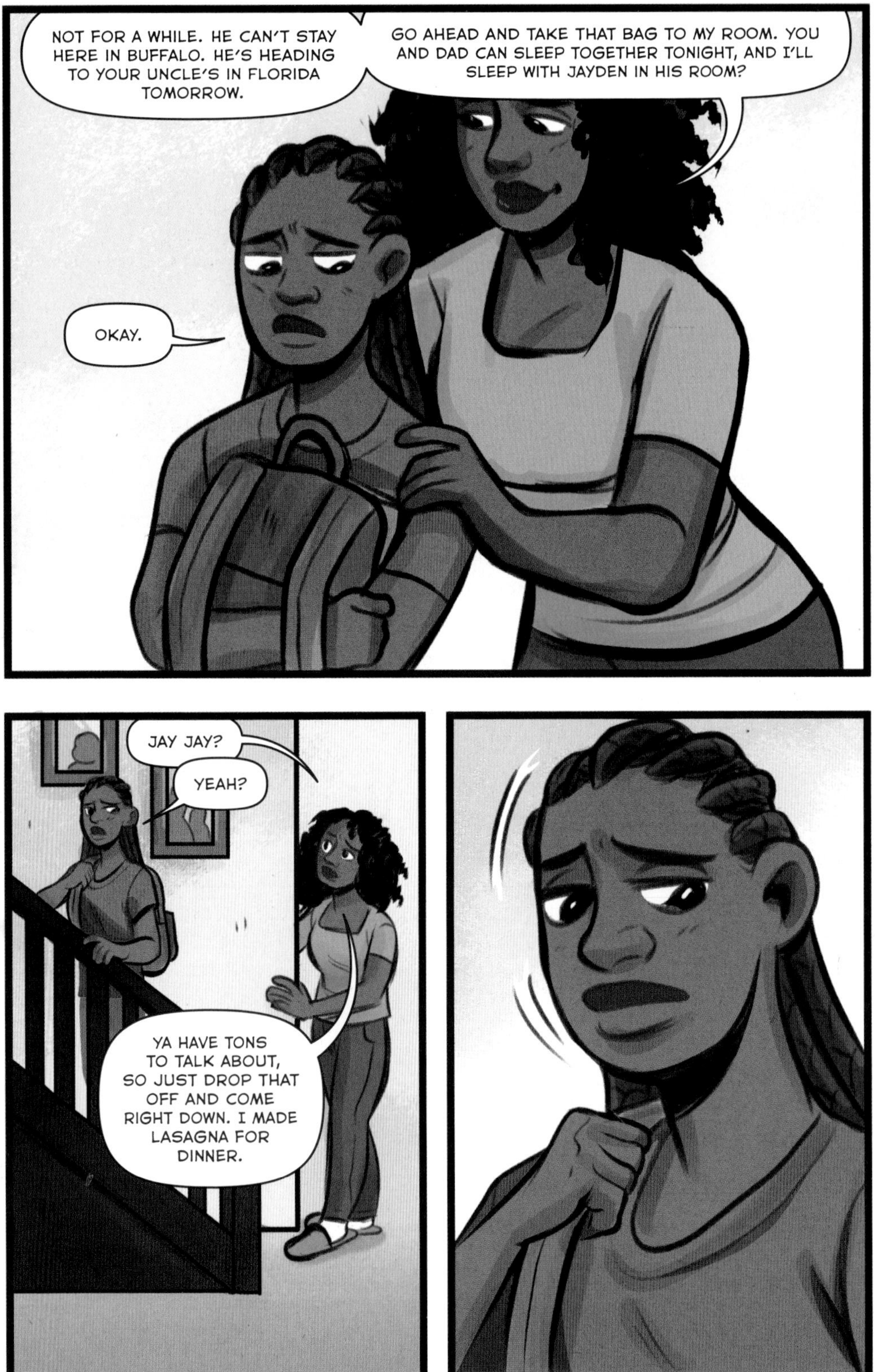
NOT FOR A WHILE. HE CAN'T STAY HERE IN BUFFALO. HE'S HEADING TO YOUR UNCLE'S IN FLORIDA TOMORROW.
GO AHEAD AND TAKE THAT BAG TO MY ROOM. YOU AND DAD CAN SLEEP TOGETHER TONIGHT, AND I'LL SLEEP WITH JAYDEN IN HIS ROOM?
OKAY.
JAY JAY?
YEAH?
YA HAVE TONS TO TALK ABOUT, SO JUST DROP THAT OFF AND COME RIGHT DOWN. I MADE LASAGNA FOR DINNER.

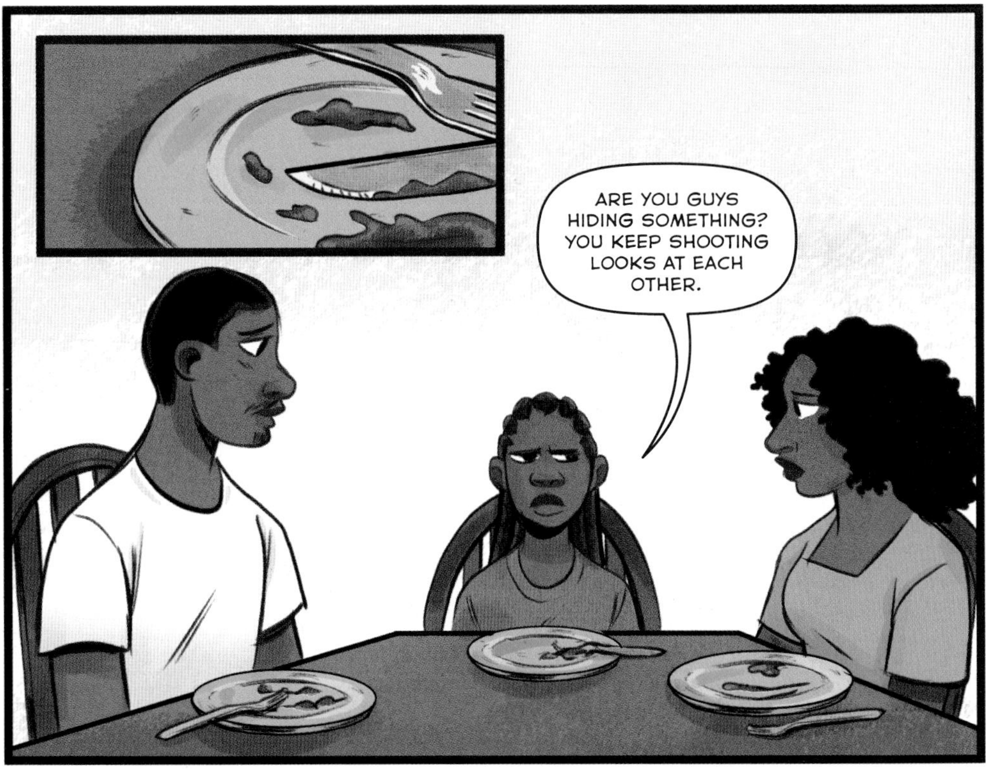
ARE YOU GUYS HIDING SOMETHING? YOU KEEP SHOOTING LOOKS AT EACH OTHER.

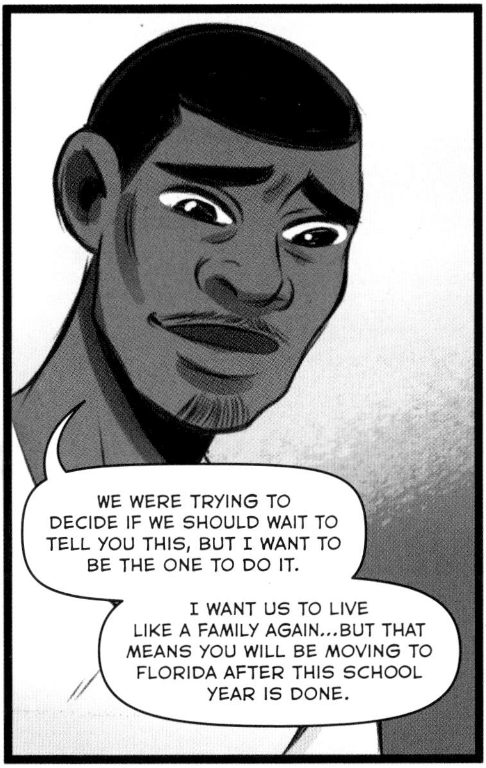
WE WERE TRYING TO DECIDE IF WE SHOULD WAIT TO TELL YOU THIS, BUT I WANT TO BE THE ONE TO DO IT.
I WANT US TO LIVE LIKE A FAMILY AGAIN...BUT THAT MEANS YOU WILL BE MOVING TO FLORIDA AFTER THIS SCHOOL YEAR IS DONE.

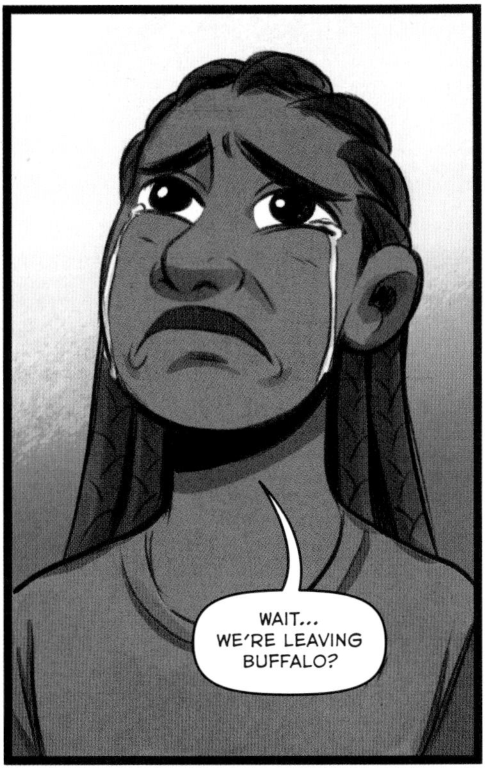
WAIT... WE'RE LEAVING BUFFALO?

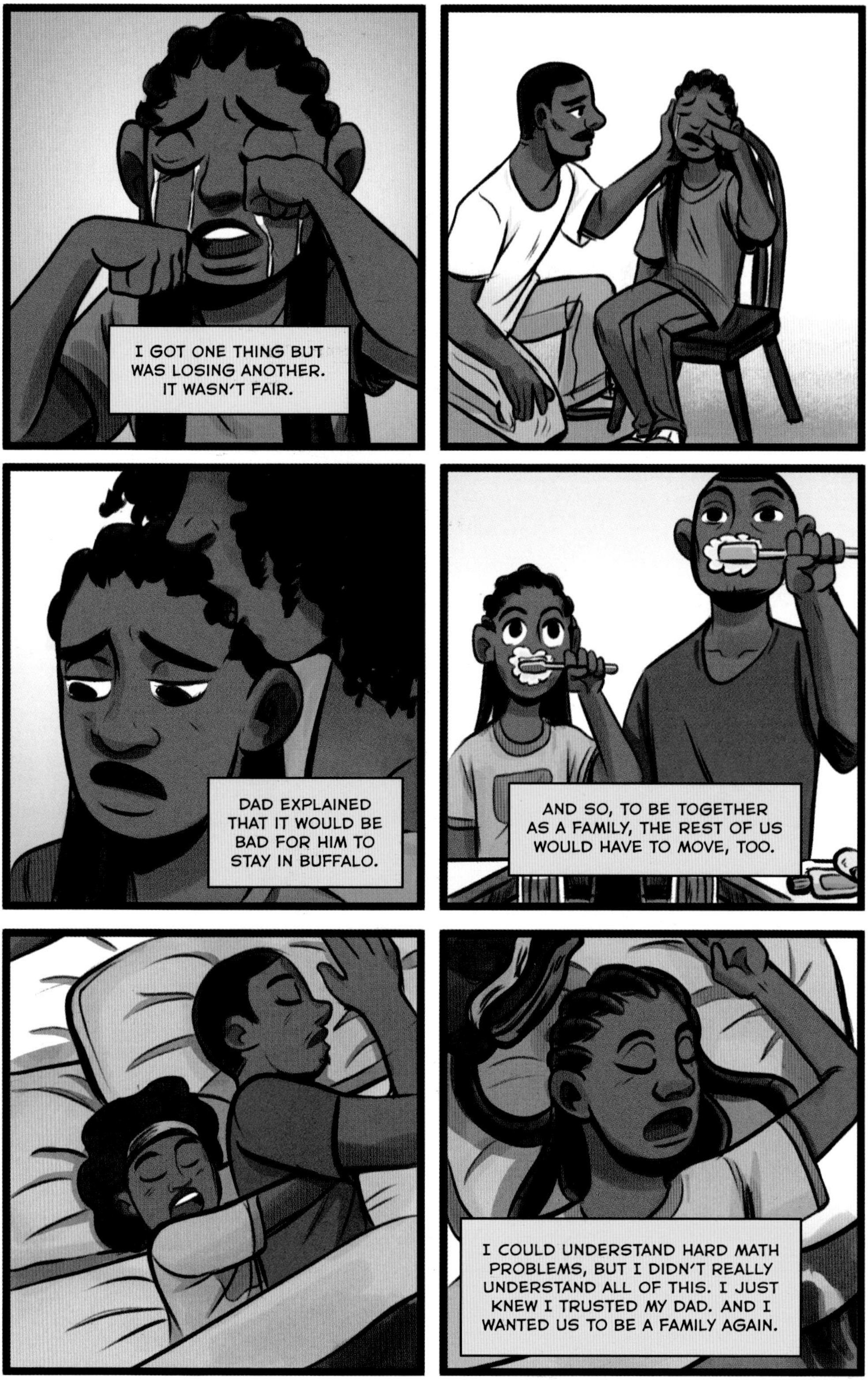
I GOT ONE THING BUT WAS LOSING ANOTHER. IT WASN'T FAIR.
DAD EXPLAINED THAT IT WOULD BE BAD FOR HIM TO STAY IN BUFFALO.
AND SO, TO BE TOGETHER AS A FAMILY, THE REST OF US WOULD HAVE TO MOVE, TOO.
I COULD UNDERSTAND HARD MATH PROBLEMS, BUT I DIDN'T REALLY UNDERSTAND ALL OF THIS. I JUST KNEW I TRUSTED MY DAD. AND I WANTED US TO BE A FAMILY AGAIN.

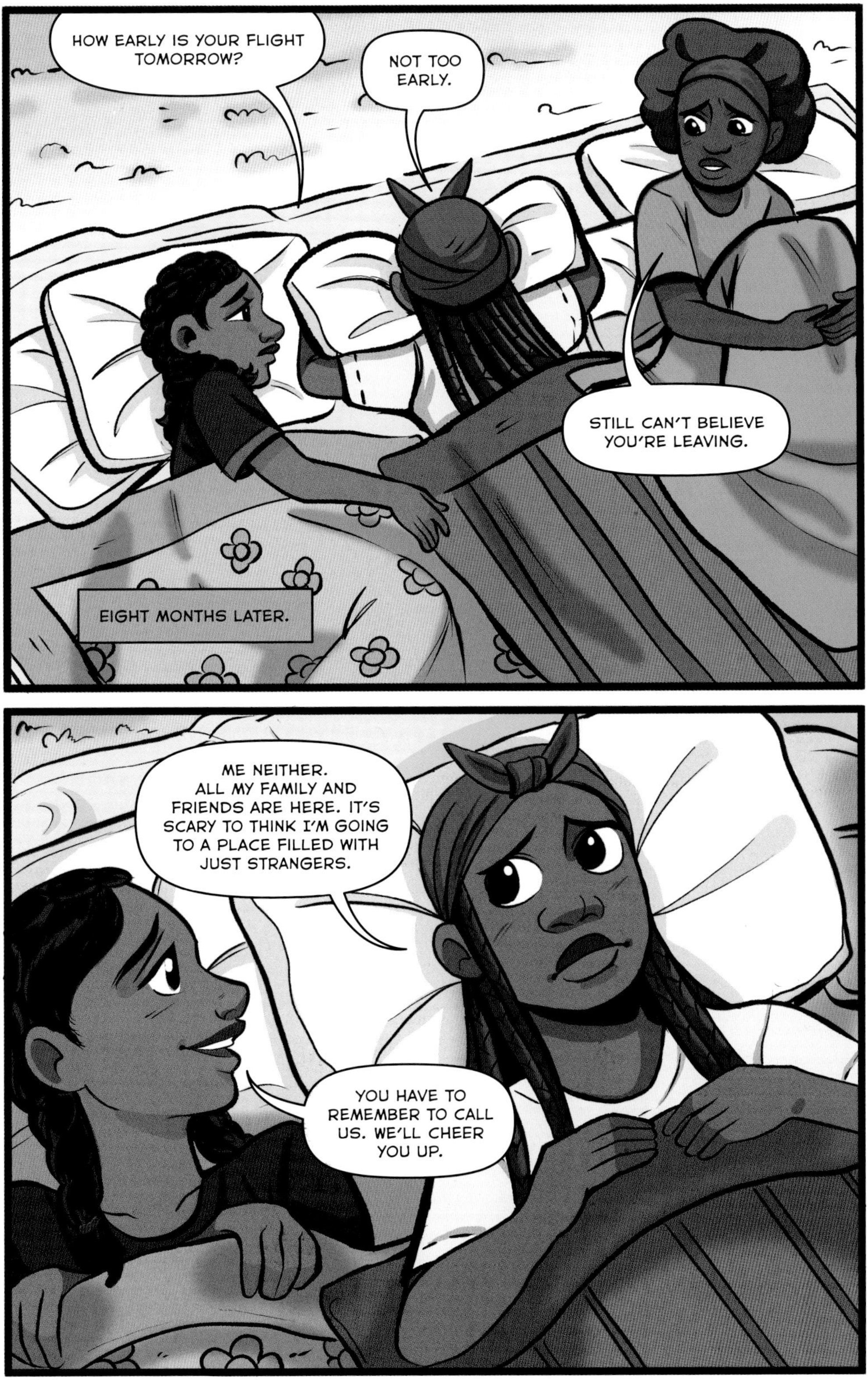
HOW EARLY IS YOUR FLIGHT TOMORROW?
NOT TOO EARLY.
STILL CAN'T BELIEVE YOU'RE LEAVING.
EIGHT MONTHS LATER.
ME NEITHER. ALL MY FAMILY AND FRIENDS ARE HERE. IT'S SCARY TO THINK I'M GOING TO A PLACE FILLED WITH JUST STRANGERS.
YOU HAVE TO REMEMBER TO CALL US. WE'LL CHEER YOU UP.

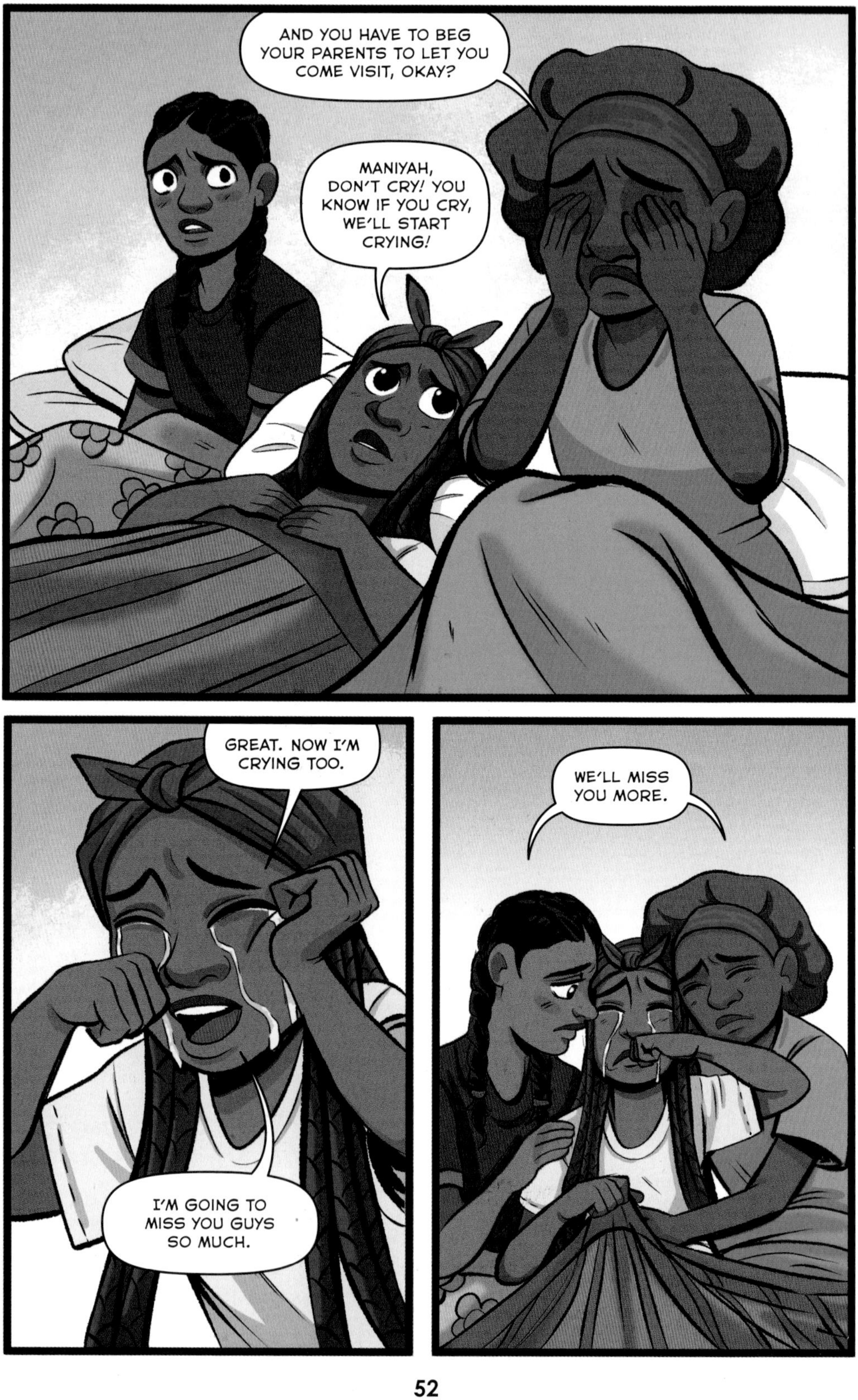
AND YOU HAVE TO BEG YOUR PARENTS TO LET YOU COME VISIT, OKAY?
MANIYAH, DON'T CRY! YOU KNOW IF YOU CRY, WE'LL START CRYING!
GREAT. NOW I'M CRYING TOO.
I'M GOING TO MISS YOU GUYS SO MUCH.
WE'LL MISS YOU MORE.

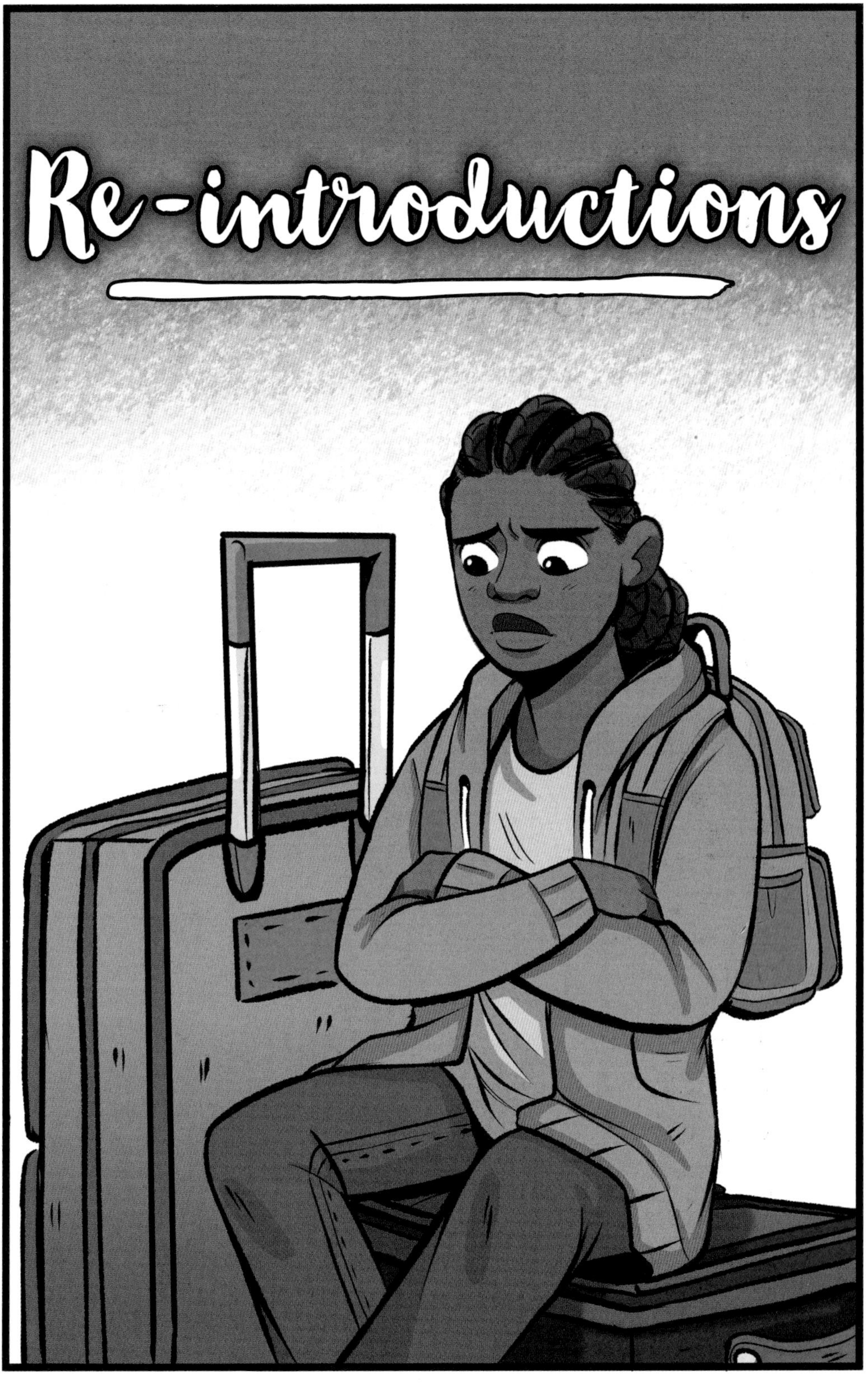
Re-introductions

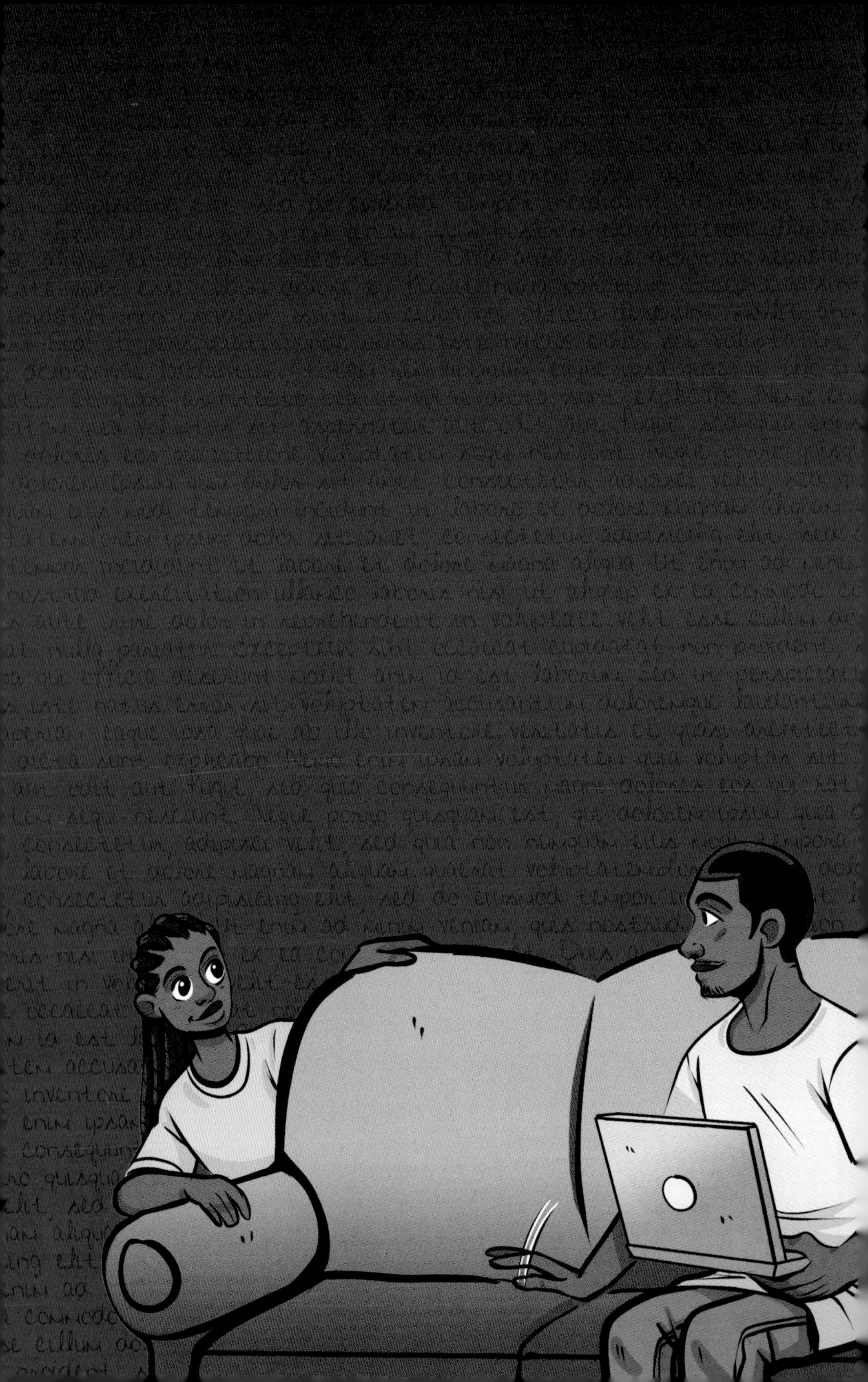

I DIDN'T LIKE BEING ON A PLANE, BUT AT LEAST THE WILD DAYS OF GOING THROUGH A LIFETIME OF JUNK AND MOVING HEAVY BOXES WERE OVER. THINGS WOULD BE EASIER NOW.

WHAT WAS THAT?

JUST SOME ROUGH WINDS.

BUT I WAS WRONG—BAD PLANE RIDES WERE SO MUCH WORSE.

I FEEL SICK.

ME TOO.

IT'LL END SOON. YOU BETTER TELL ME IF YOU ACTUALLY FEEL LIKE THROWING UP, THOUGH.

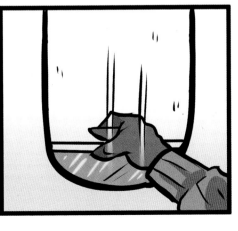

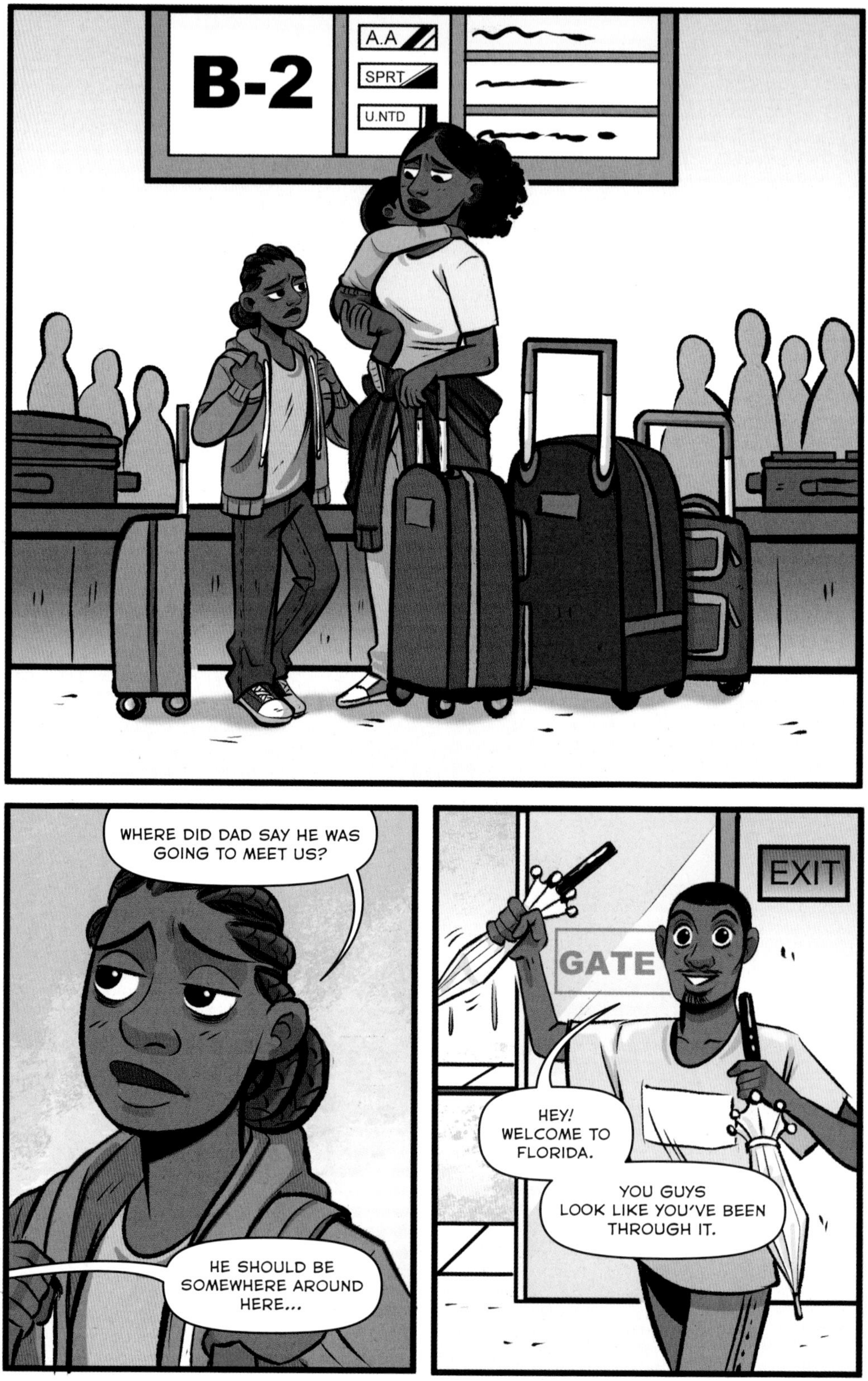
B-2
A.A
SPRT
U.NTD
WHERE DID DAD SAY HE WAS GOING TO MEET US?
HE SHOULD BE SOMEWHERE AROUND HERE...
EXIT
GATE
HEY! WELCOME TO FLORIDA.
YOU GUYS LOOK LIKE YOU'VE BEEN THROUGH IT.

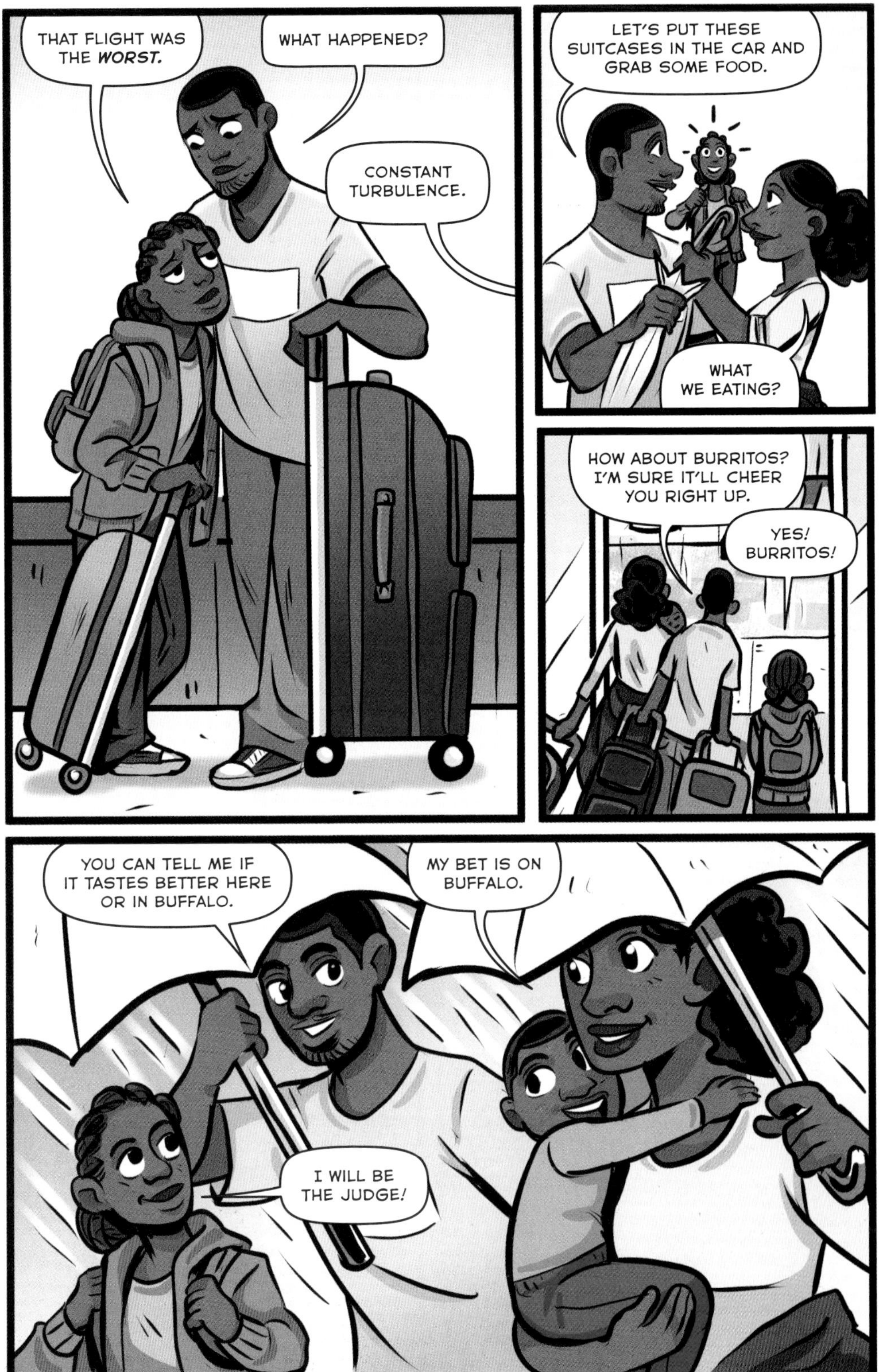
THAT FLIGHT WAS THE *WORST.*
WHAT HAPPENED?
CONSTANT TURBULENCE.
LET'S PUT THESE SUITCASES IN THE CAR AND GRAB SOME FOOD.
WHAT WE EATING?
HOW ABOUT BURRITOS? I'M SURE IT'LL CHEER YOU RIGHT UP.
YES! BURRITOS!
YOU CAN TELL ME IF IT TASTES BETTER HERE OR IN BUFFALO.
MY BET IS ON BUFFALO.
I WILL BE THE JUDGE!

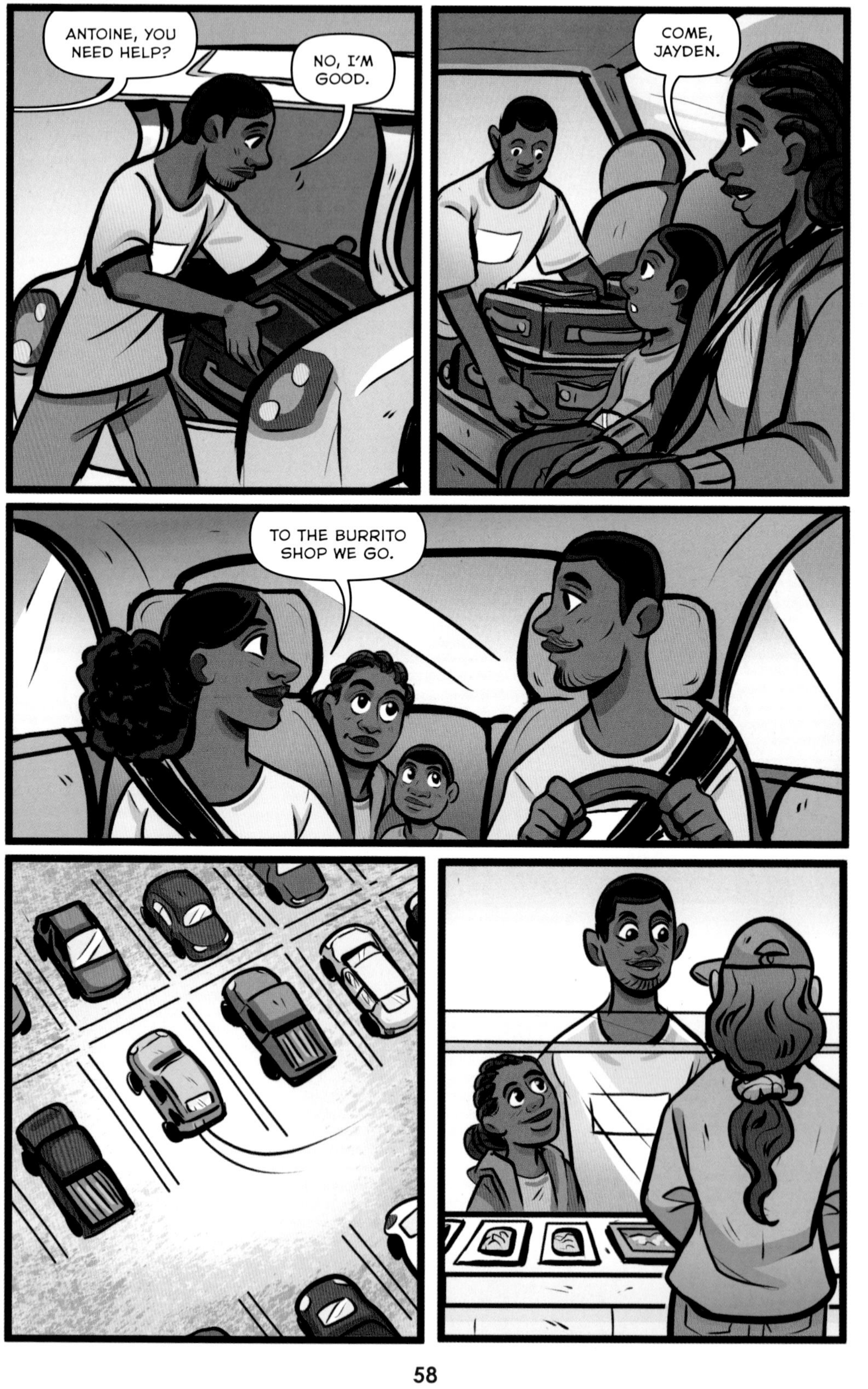
ANTOINE, YOU NEED HELP?
NO, I'M GOOD.
COME, JAYDEN.
TO THE BURRITO SHOP WE GO.

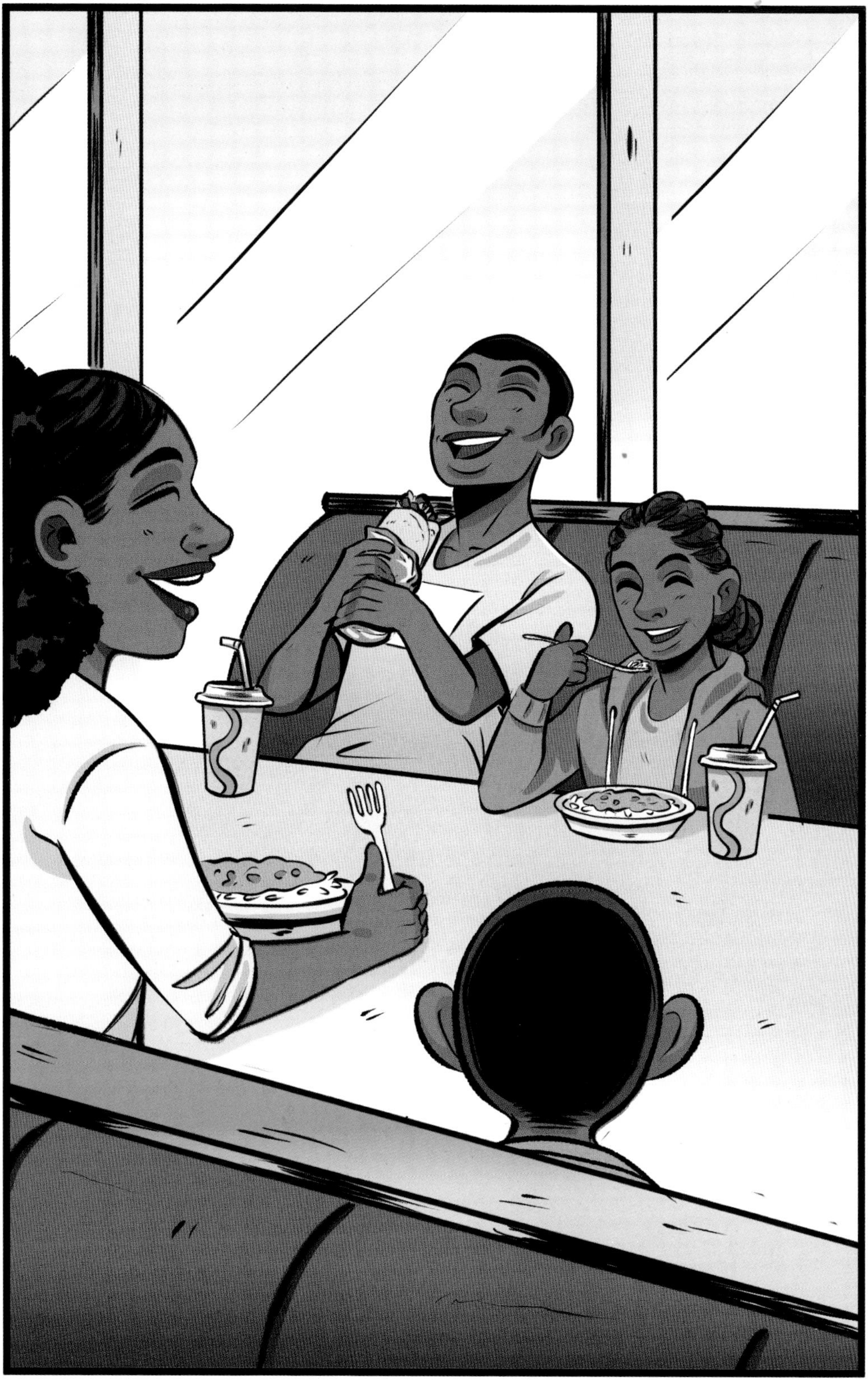

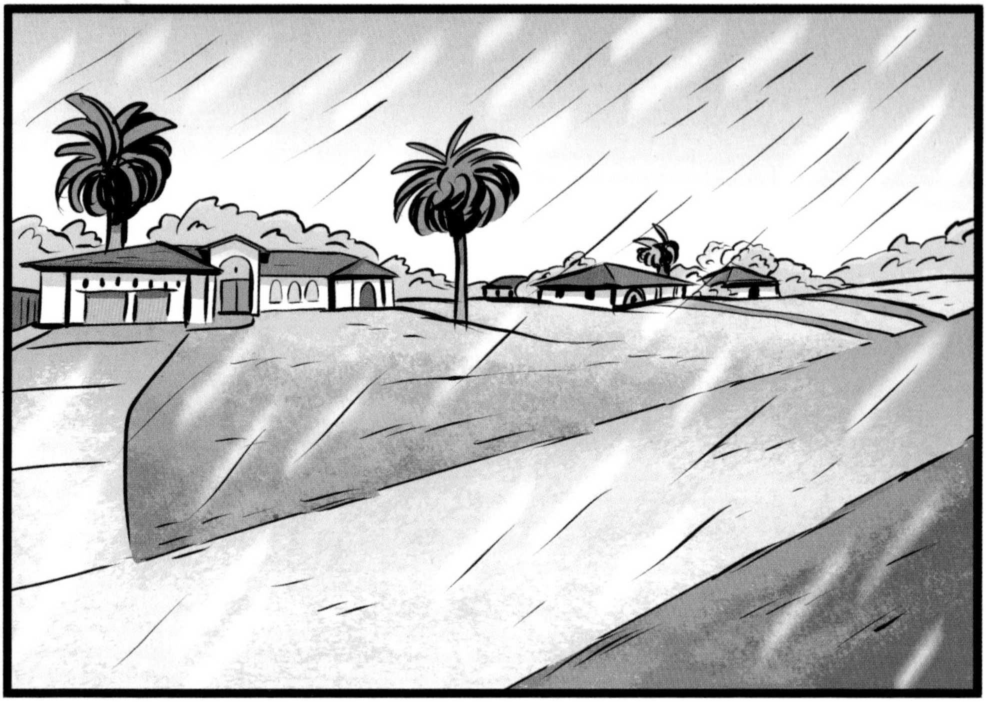

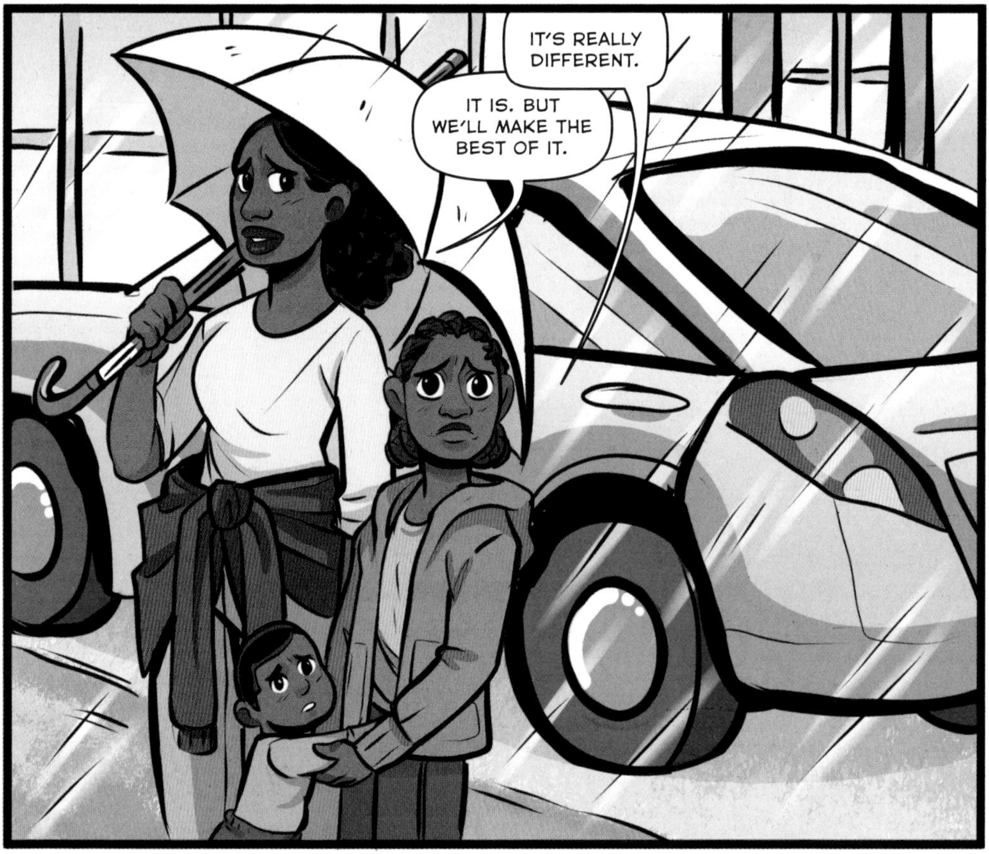
IT'S REALLY DIFFERENT.
IT IS. BUT WE'LL MAKE THE BEST OF IT.

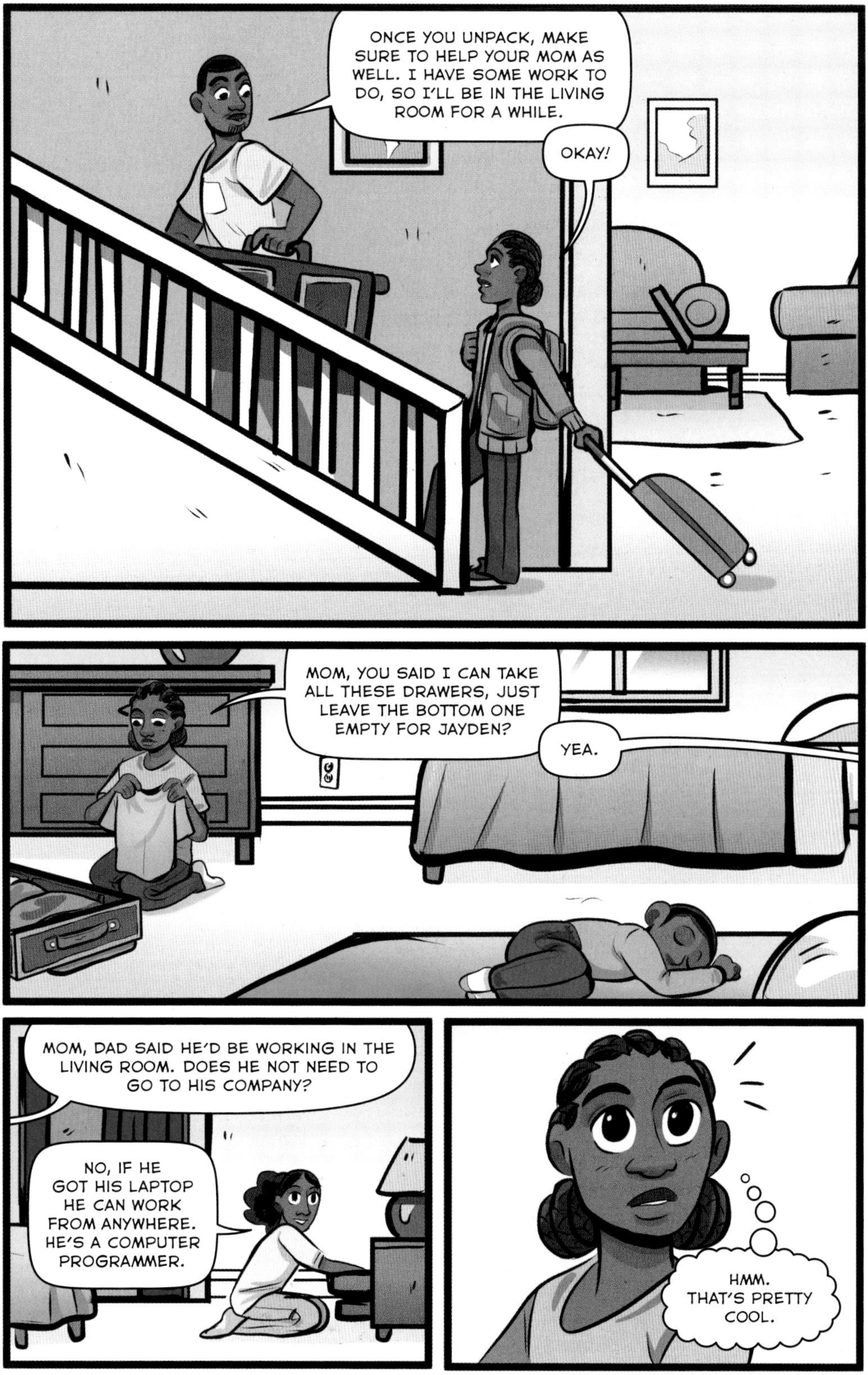
ONCE YOU UNPACK, MAKE SURE TO HELP YOUR MOM AS WELL. I HAVE SOME WORK TO DO, SO I'LL BE IN THE LIVING ROOM FOR A WHILE.
OKAY!
MOM, YOU SAID I CAN TAKE ALL THESE DRAWERS, JUST LEAVE THE BOTTOM ONE EMPTY FOR JAYDEN?
YEA.
MOM, DAD SAID HE'D BE WORKING IN THE LIVING ROOM. DOES HE NOT NEED TO GO TO HIS COMPANY?
NO, IF HE GOT HIS LAPTOP HE CAN WORK FROM ANYWHERE. HE'S A COMPUTER PROGRAMMER.
HMM. THAT'S PRETTY COOL.

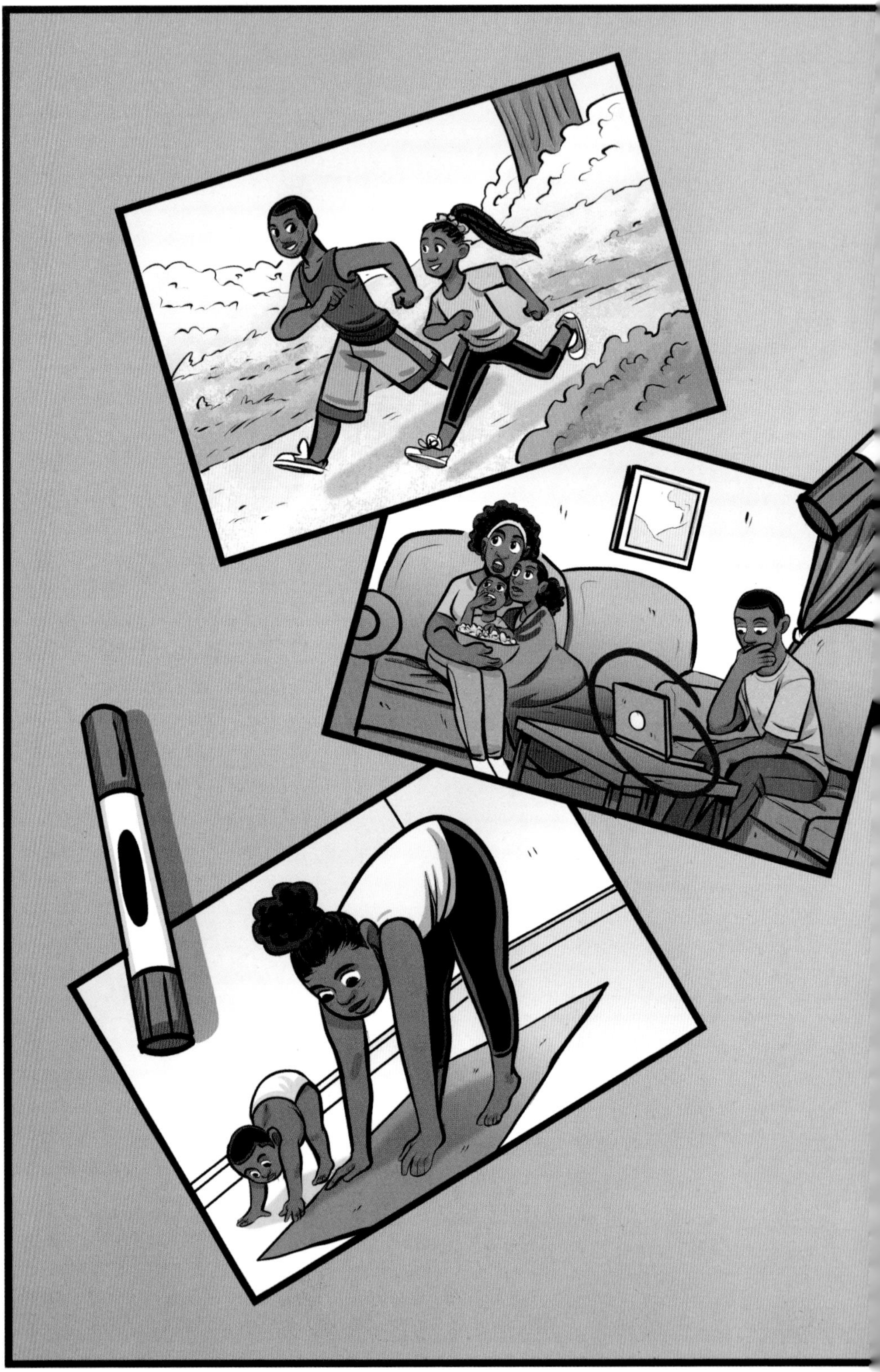

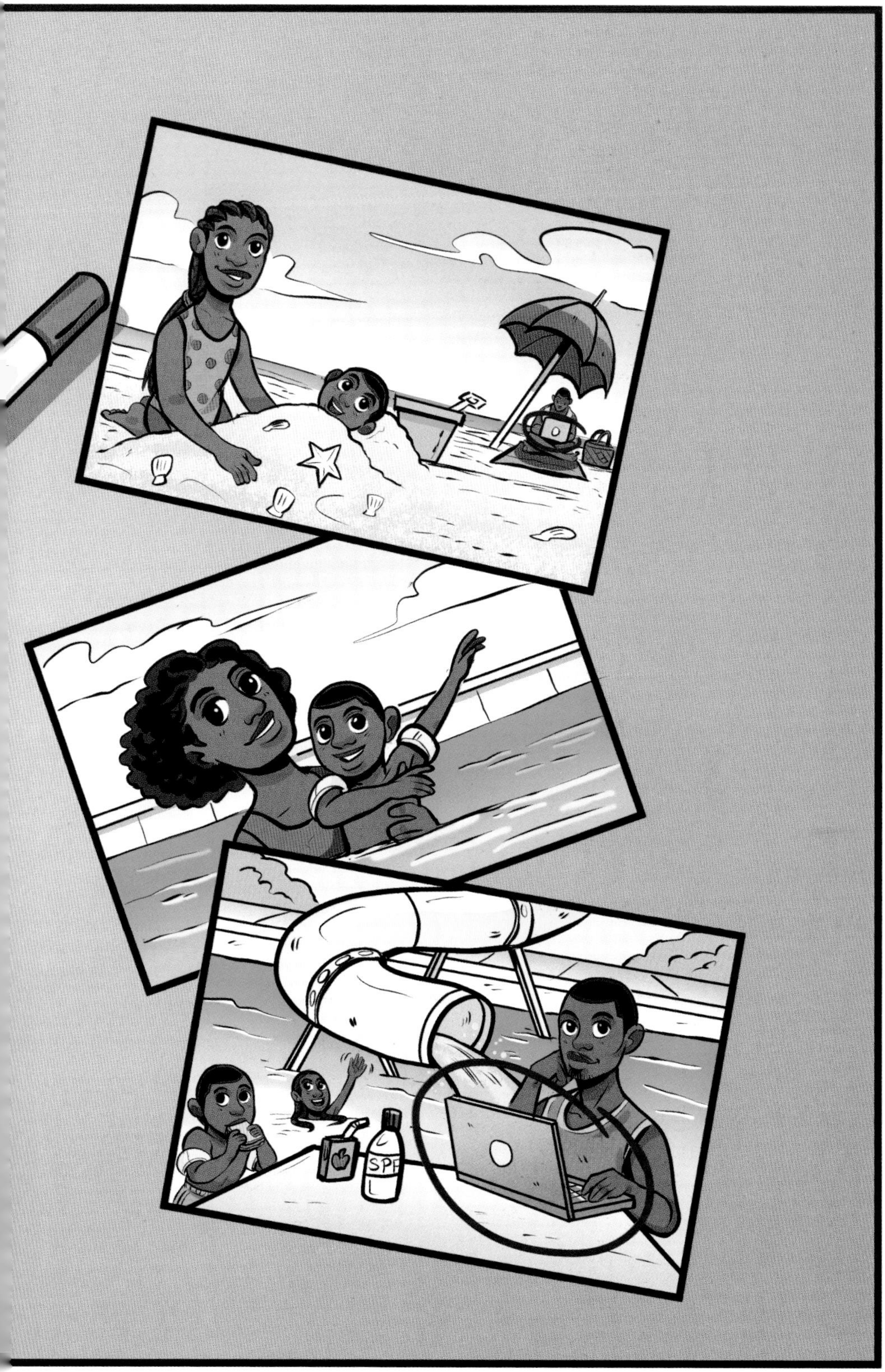
SPF

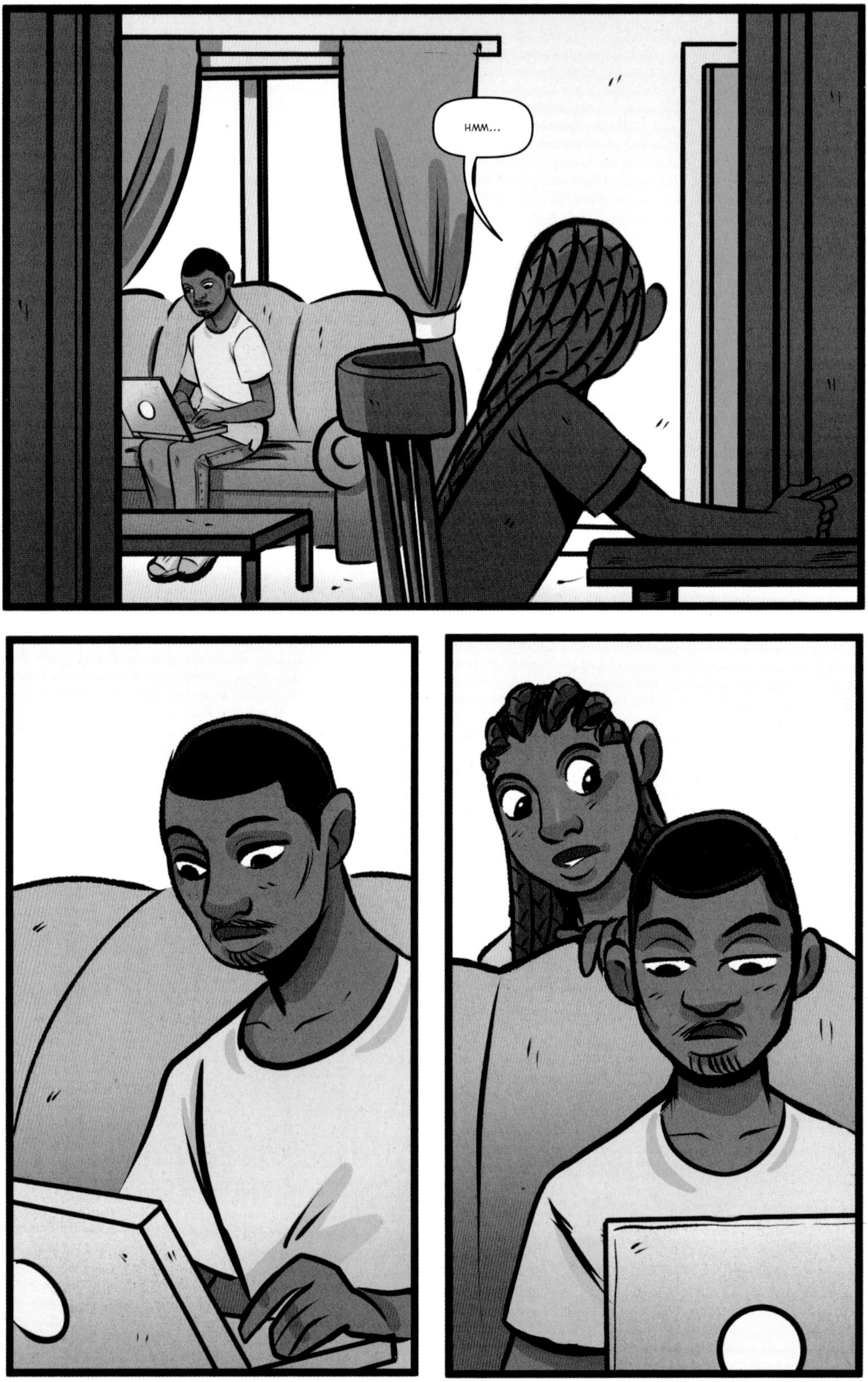
HMM...

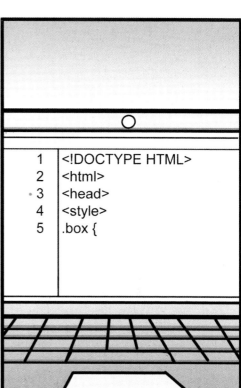

```
1   <!DOCTYPE HTML>
2   <html>
3   <head>
4   <style>
5   .box {
```

```
1  <!DOCTYPE HTML>
2  <html>
3  <head>
4  <style>
5  .box {
```

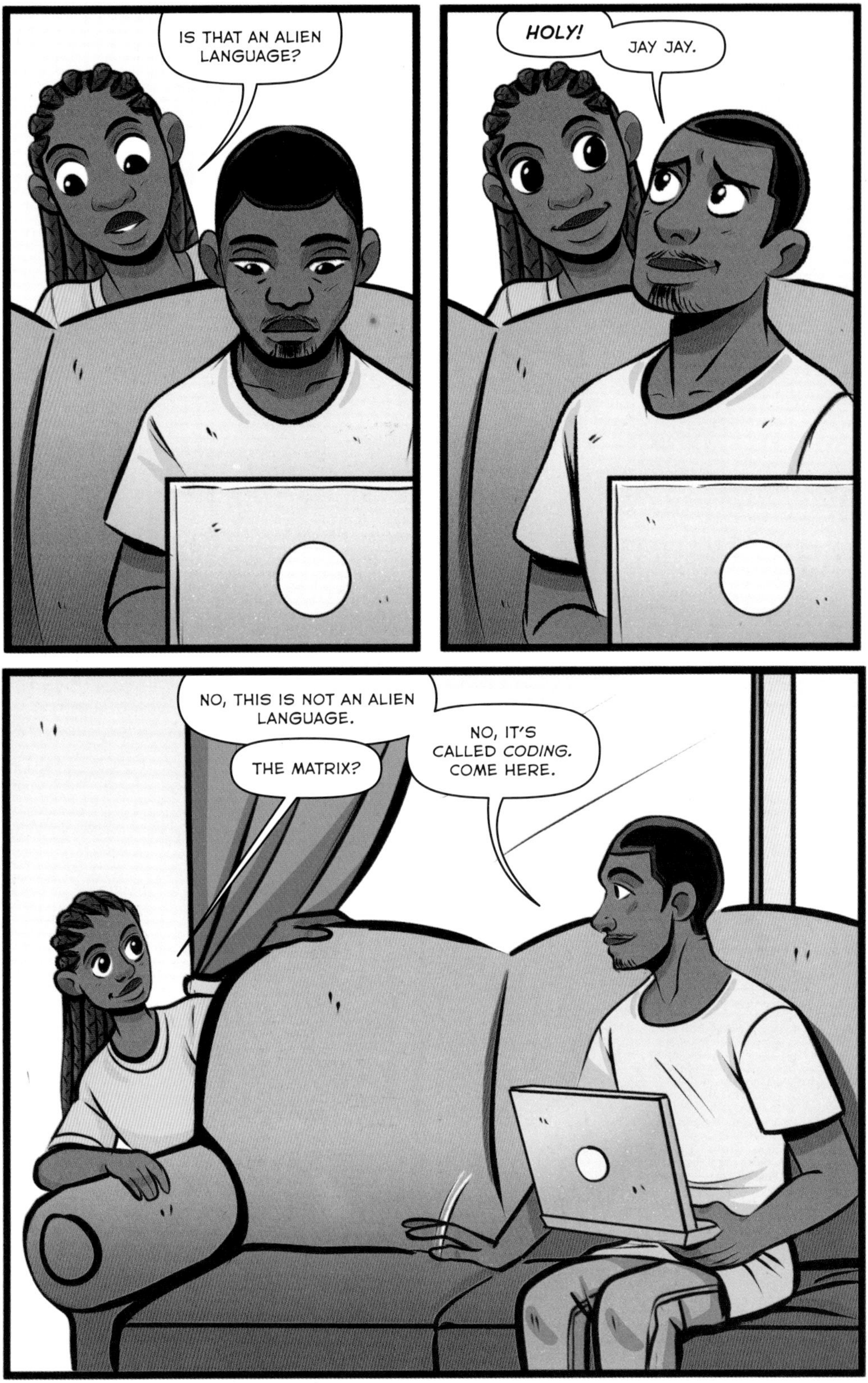
IS THAT AN ALIEN LANGUAGE?
HOLY!
JAY JAY.
NO, THIS IS NOT AN ALIEN LANGUAGE.
THE MATRIX?
NO, IT'S CALLED *CODING.* COME HERE.

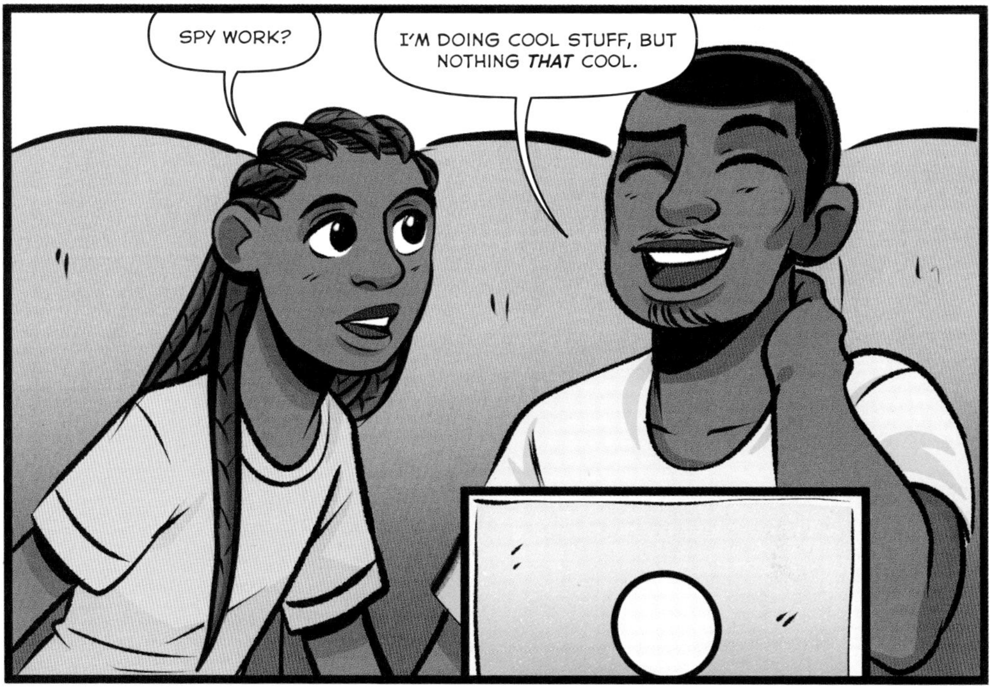
SPY WORK?
I'M DOING COOL STUFF, BUT NOTHING *THAT* COOL.

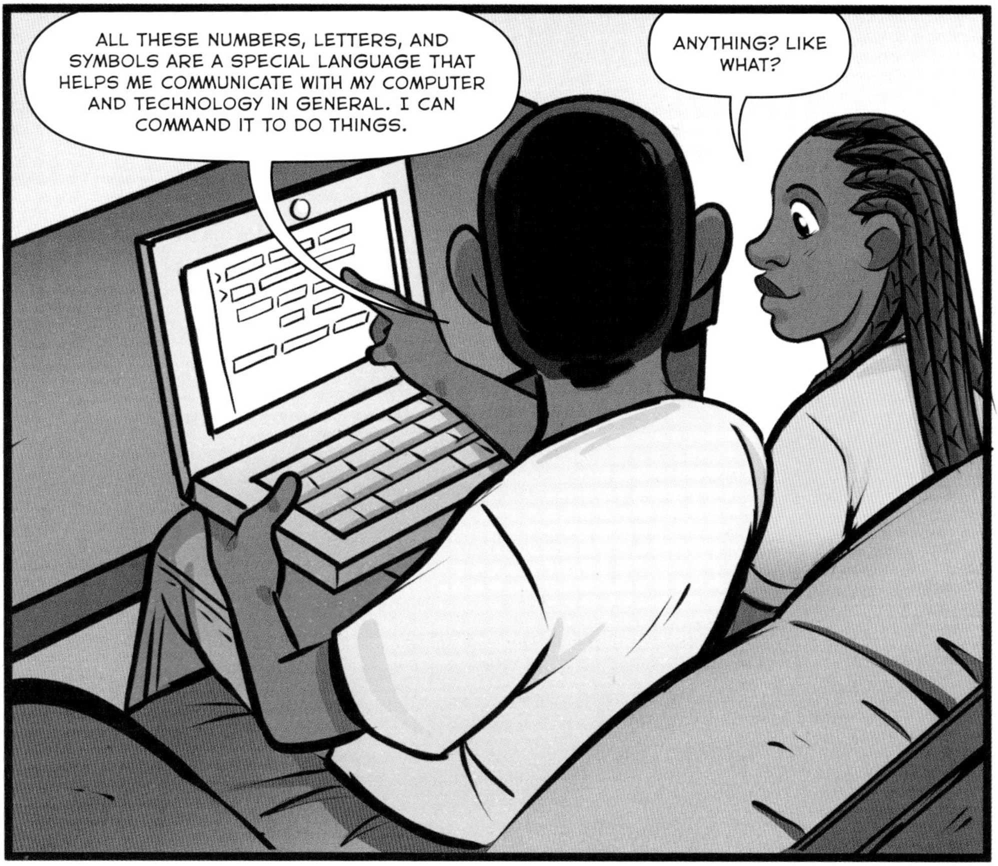
ALL THESE NUMBERS, LETTERS, AND SYMBOLS ARE A SPECIAL LANGUAGE THAT HELPS ME COMMUNICATE WITH MY COMPUTER AND TECHNOLOGY IN GENERAL. I CAN COMMAND IT TO DO THINGS.
ANYTHING? LIKE WHAT?

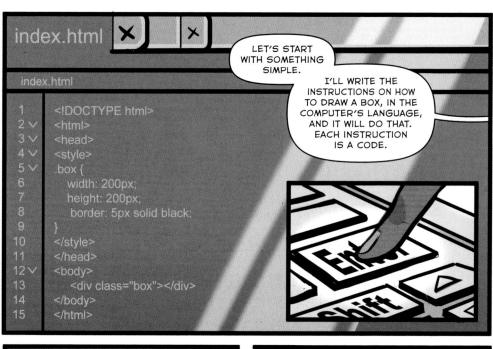

index.html
index.html
<!DOCTYPE html>
<html>
<head>
<style>
.box {
width: 200px;
height: 200px;
border: 5px solid black;
}
</style>
</head>
<body>
<div class="box"></div>
</body>
</html>
LET'S START WITH SOMETHING SIMPLE.
I'LL WRITE THE INSTRUCTIONS ON HOW TO DRAW A BOX, IN THE COMPUTER'S LANGUAGE, AND IT WILL DO THAT. EACH INSTRUCTION IS A CODE.
Enter
Shift
WHOA!
THAT'S **SO** COOL! WHAT OTHER STUFF CAN CODE DO?
THERE IS CODE ALL AROUND YOU WITHOUT YOU REALIZING.

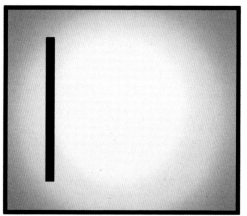

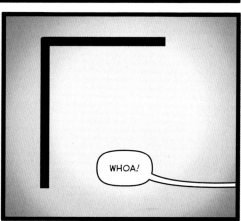

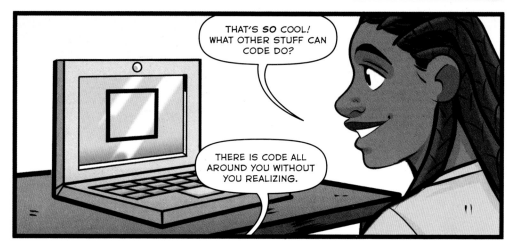

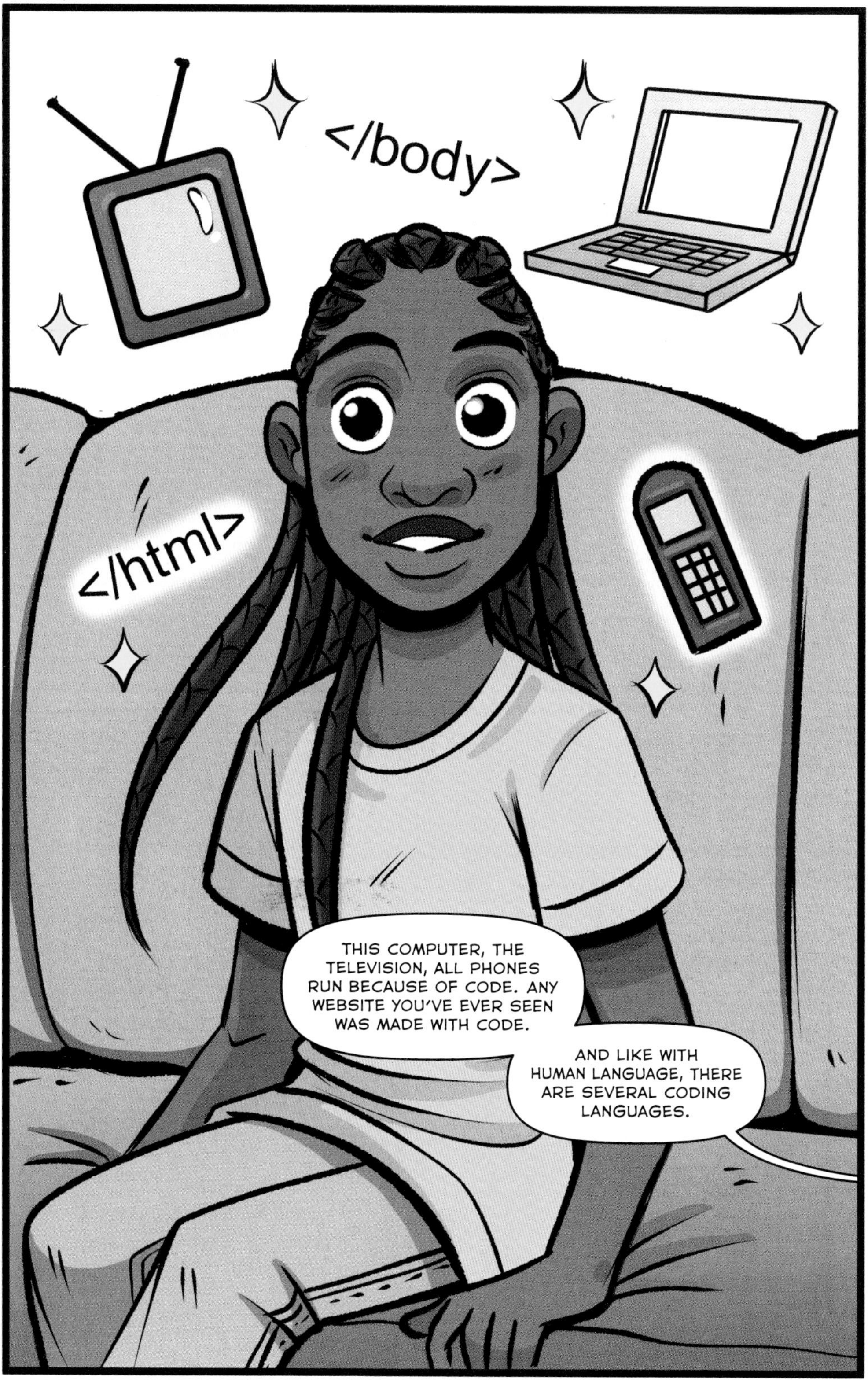
</body>
</html>
THIS COMPUTER, THE TELEVISION, ALL PHONES RUN BECAUSE OF CODE. ANY WEBSITE YOU'VE EVER SEEN WAS MADE WITH CODE.
AND LIKE WITH HUMAN LANGUAGE, THERE ARE SEVERAL CODING LANGUAGES.

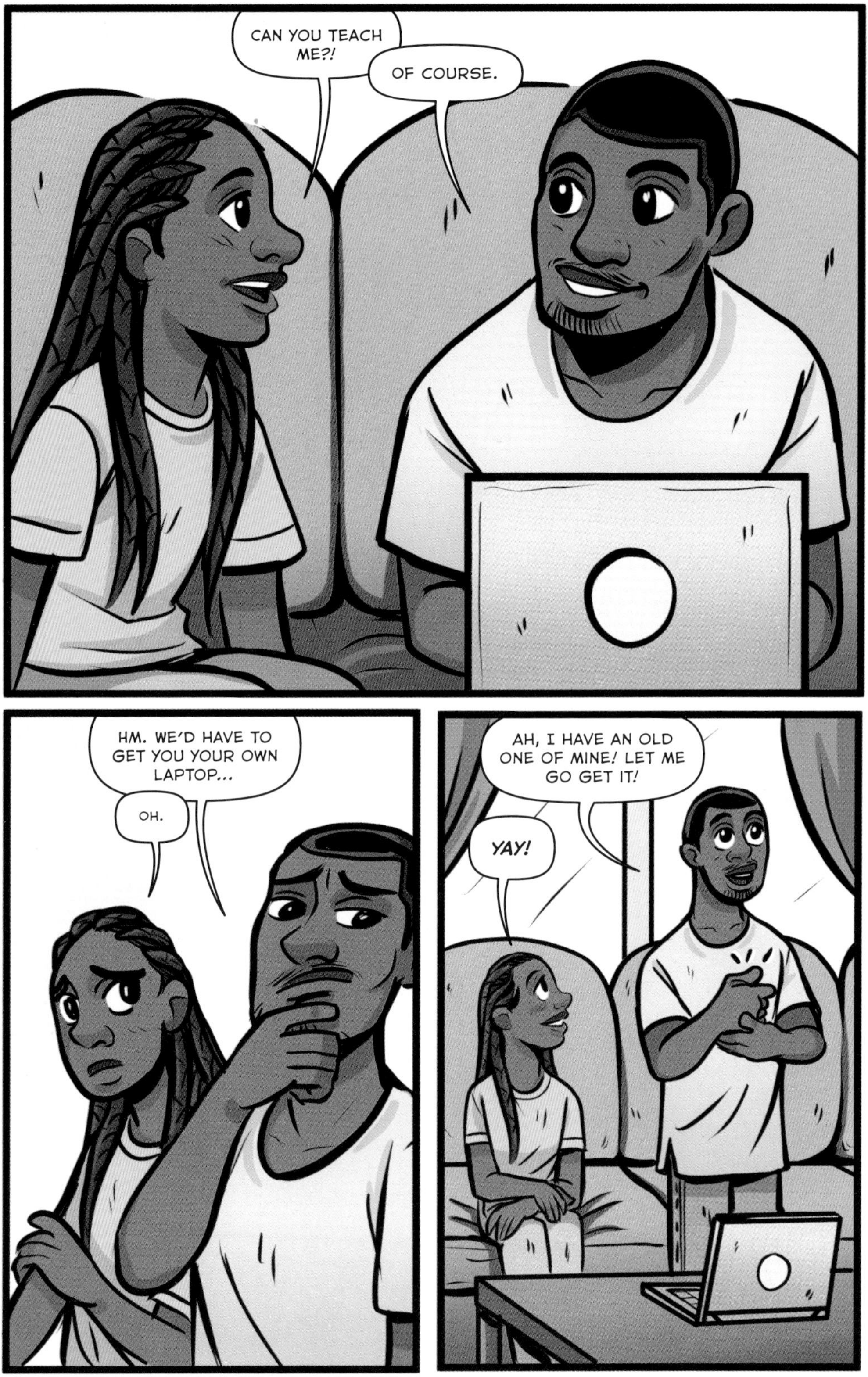
CAN YOU TEACH ME?!
OF COURSE.
HM. WE'D HAVE TO GET YOU YOUR OWN LAPTOP...
OH.
AH, I HAVE AN OLD ONE OF MINE! LET ME GO GET IT!
YAY!

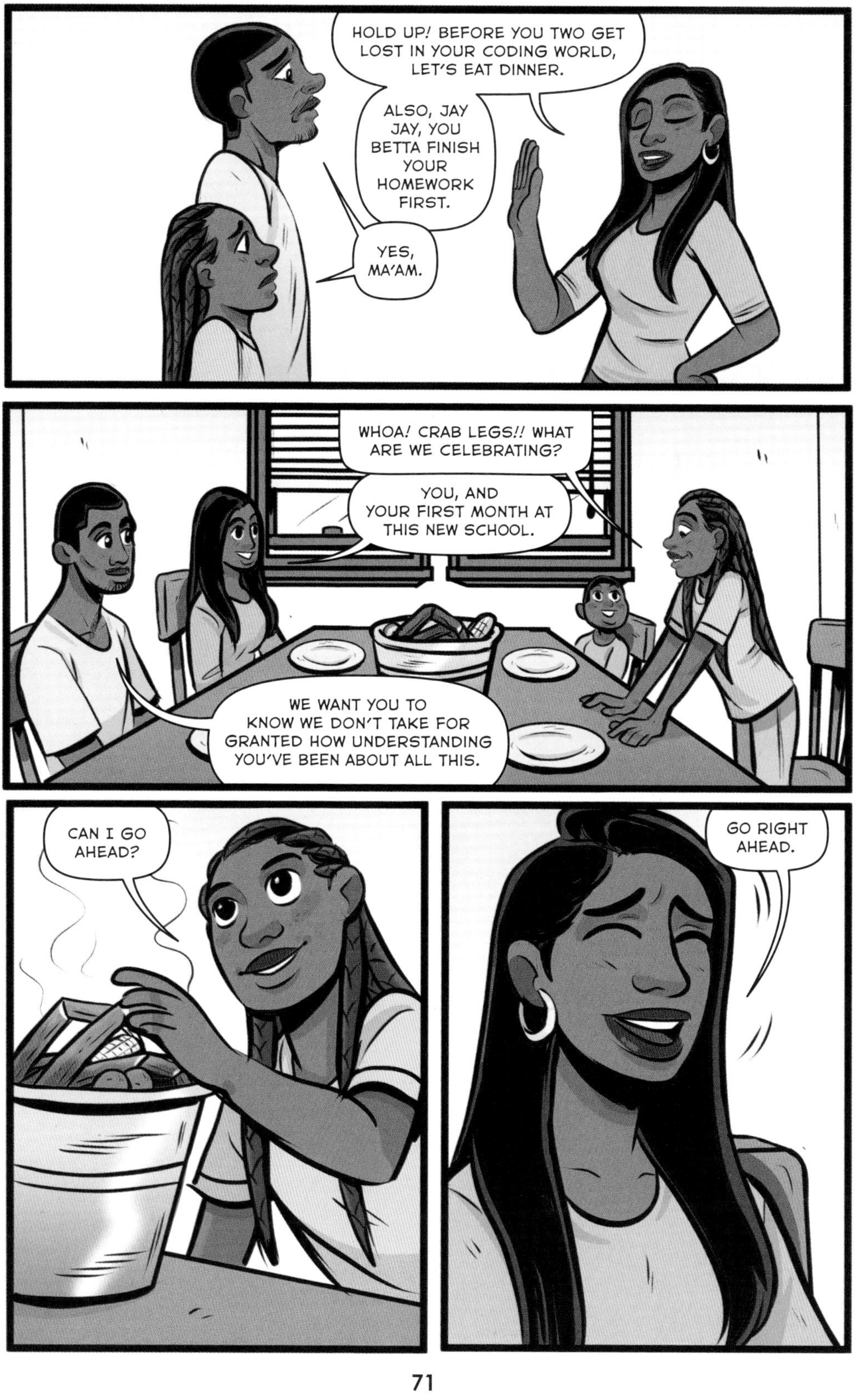
HOLD UP! BEFORE YOU TWO GET LOST IN YOUR CODING WORLD, LET'S EAT DINNER.
ALSO, JAY JAY, YOU BETTA FINISH YOUR HOMEWORK FIRST.
YES, MA'AM.
WHOA! CRAB LEGS!! WHAT ARE WE CELEBRATING?
YOU, AND YOUR FIRST MONTH AT THIS NEW SCHOOL.
WE WANT YOU TO KNOW WE DON'T TAKE FOR GRANTED HOW UNDERSTANDING YOU'VE BEEN ABOUT ALL THIS.
CAN I GO AHEAD?
GO RIGHT AHEAD.

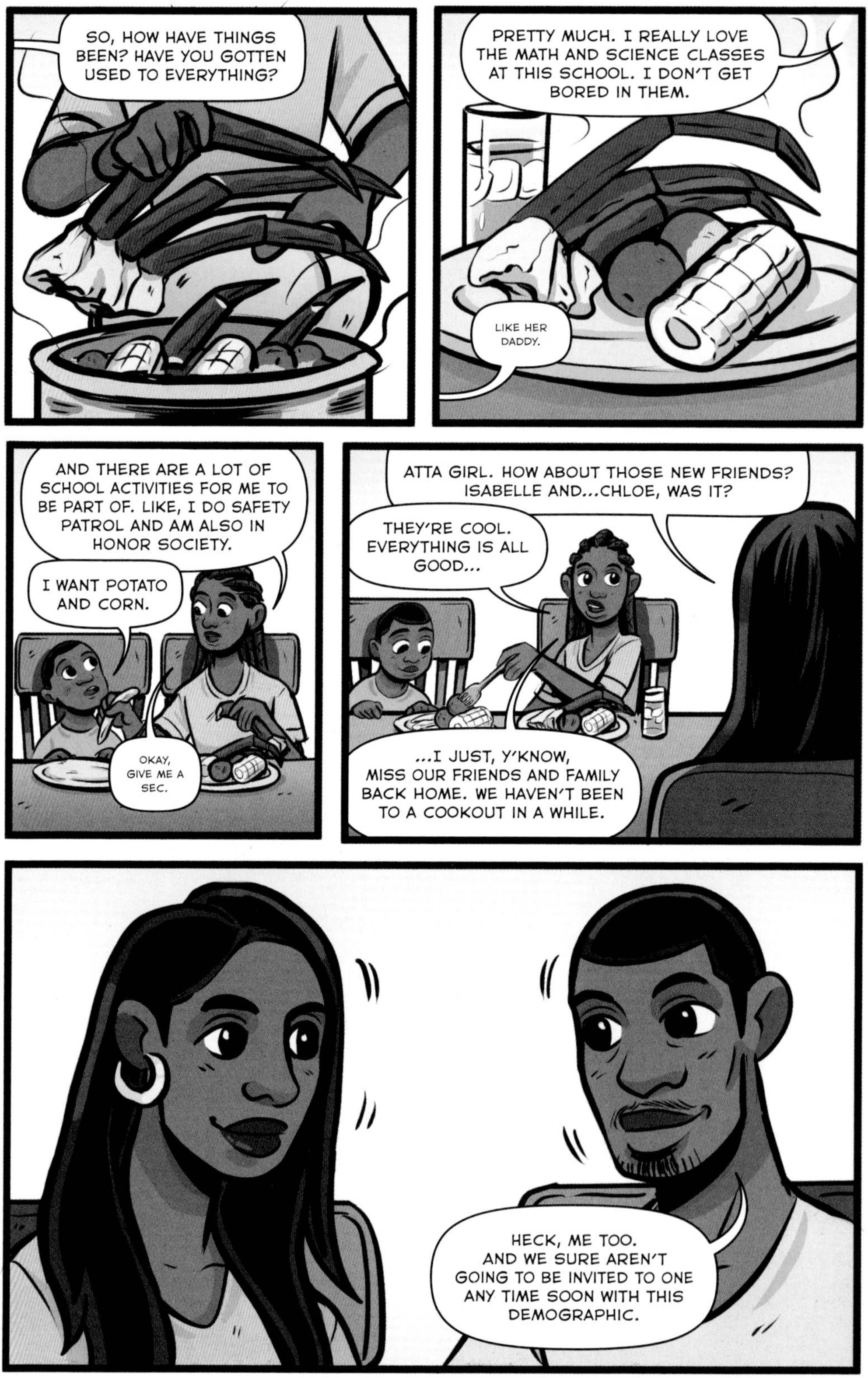
SO, HOW HAVE THINGS BEEN? HAVE YOU GOTTEN USED TO EVERYTHING?
PRETTY MUCH. I REALLY LOVE THE MATH AND SCIENCE CLASSES AT THIS SCHOOL. I DON'T GET BORED IN THEM.
LIKE HER DADDY.
AND THERE ARE A LOT OF SCHOOL ACTIVITIES FOR ME TO BE PART OF. LIKE, I DO SAFETY PATROL AND AM ALSO IN HONOR SOCIETY.
I WANT POTATO AND CORN.
OKAY, GIVE ME A SEC.
ATTA GIRL. HOW ABOUT THOSE NEW FRIENDS? ISABELLE AND...CHLOE, WAS IT?
THEY'RE COOL. EVERYTHING IS ALL GOOD...
...I JUST, Y'KNOW, MISS OUR FRIENDS AND FAMILY BACK HOME. WE HAVEN'T BEEN TO A COOKOUT IN A WHILE.
HECK, ME TOO. AND WE SURE AREN'T GOING TO BE INVITED TO ONE ANY TIME SOON WITH THIS DEMOGRAPHIC.

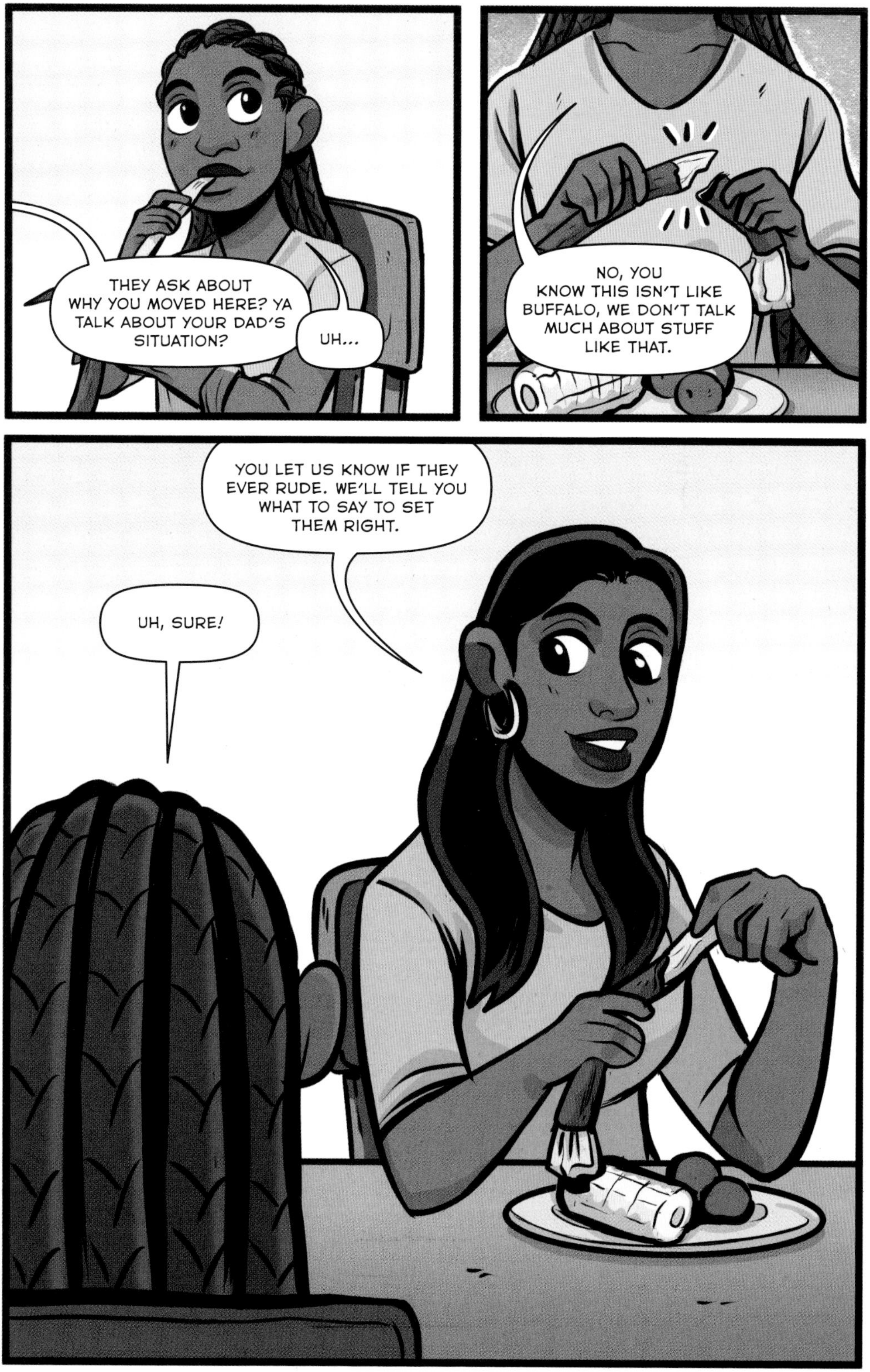
THEY ASK ABOUT WHY YOU MOVED HERE? YA TALK ABOUT YOUR DAD'S SITUATION?
UH...
NO, YOU KNOW THIS ISN'T LIKE BUFFALO, WE DON'T TALK MUCH ABOUT STUFF LIKE THAT.
YOU LET US KNOW IF THEY EVER RUDE. WE'LL TELL YOU WHAT TO SAY TO SET THEM RIGHT.
UH, SURE!

[illegible]

consectetur, adipisci velit, sed quia non numquam eius modi tempora
labore et dolore magnam aliquam quaerat voluptatem. dolorem ipsum do
consectetur adipiscing elit, sed do eiusmod tempor incididunt ut
dolore magna aliqua. Ut enim ad minim veniam, quis nostrud exercitation
oris nisi ut aliquip ex ea commodo consequat. Duis aute irure dolor i
erit in voluptate velit esse cillum dolore eu fugiat nulla pariatur. E
nt occaecat cupidatat non proident, sunt in culpa qui officia deserun
nim id est laborum. Sed ut perspiciatis unde omnis iste natus error
tatem accusantium doloremque laudantium, totam rem aperiam, eaque ip
lo inventore veritatis et quasi architecto beatae vitae dicta sunt e
mo enim ipsam voluptatem quia voluptas sit aspernatur aut odit aut
ia consequuntur magni dolores eos qui ratione voluptatem sequi nesciun
orro quisquam est, qui dolorem ipsum quia dolor sit amet, consectetur,
velit, sed quia non numquam eius modi tempora incidunt ut labore et
gnam aliquam quaerat voluptatem. dolorem ipsum dolor sit amet, consecte
icing elit, sed do eiusmod tempor incididunt ut labore et dolore mag
enim ad minim veniam, quis nostrud exercitation ullamco laboris nisi
ea commodo consequat. Duis aute irure dolor in reprehenderit in volup
sse cillum dolore eu fugiat nulla pariatur. Excepteur sint occaecat c
n proident, sunt in culpa qui officia deserunt mollit anim id est lab

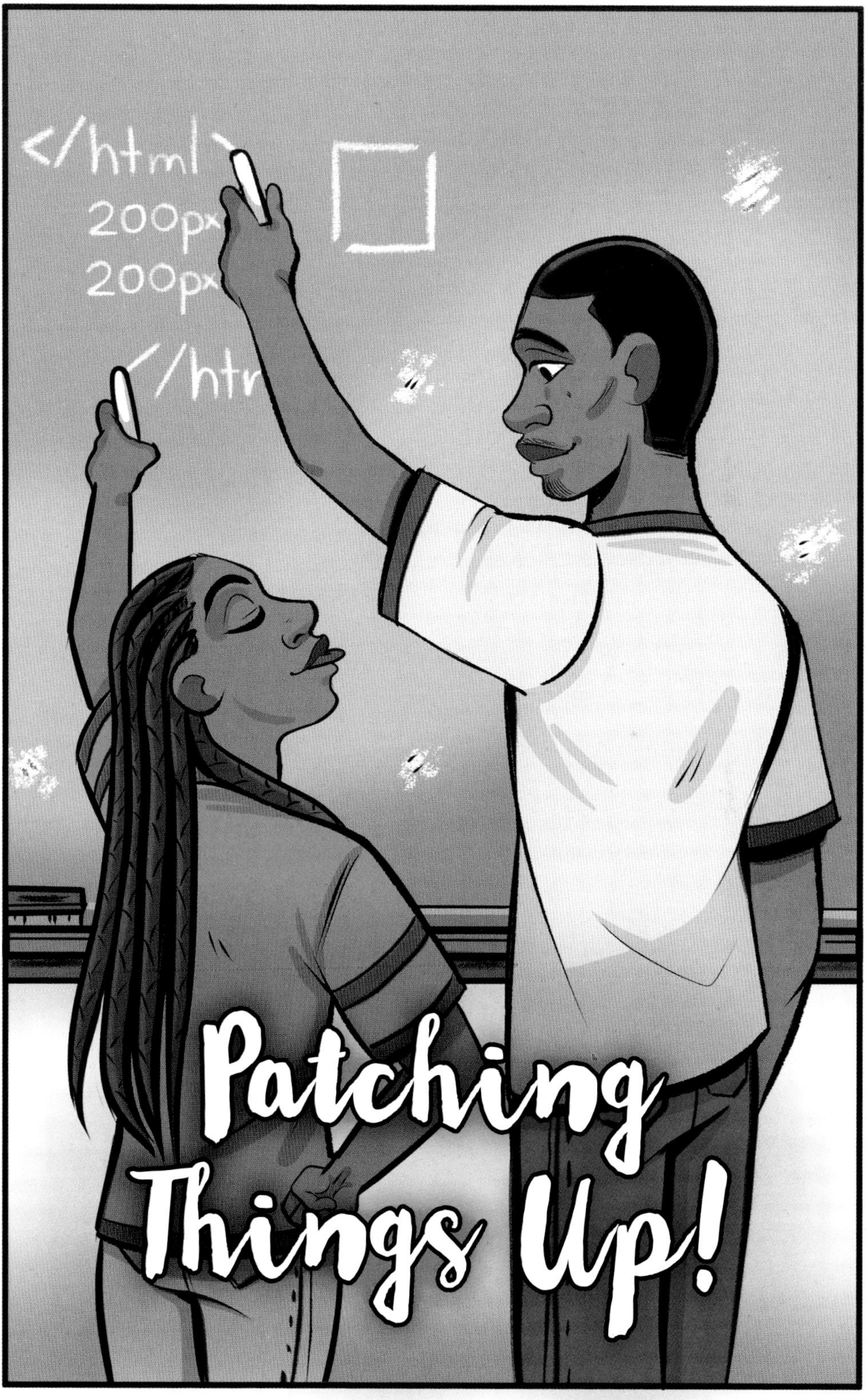
</html>
200px
200px
Patching
Things Up!

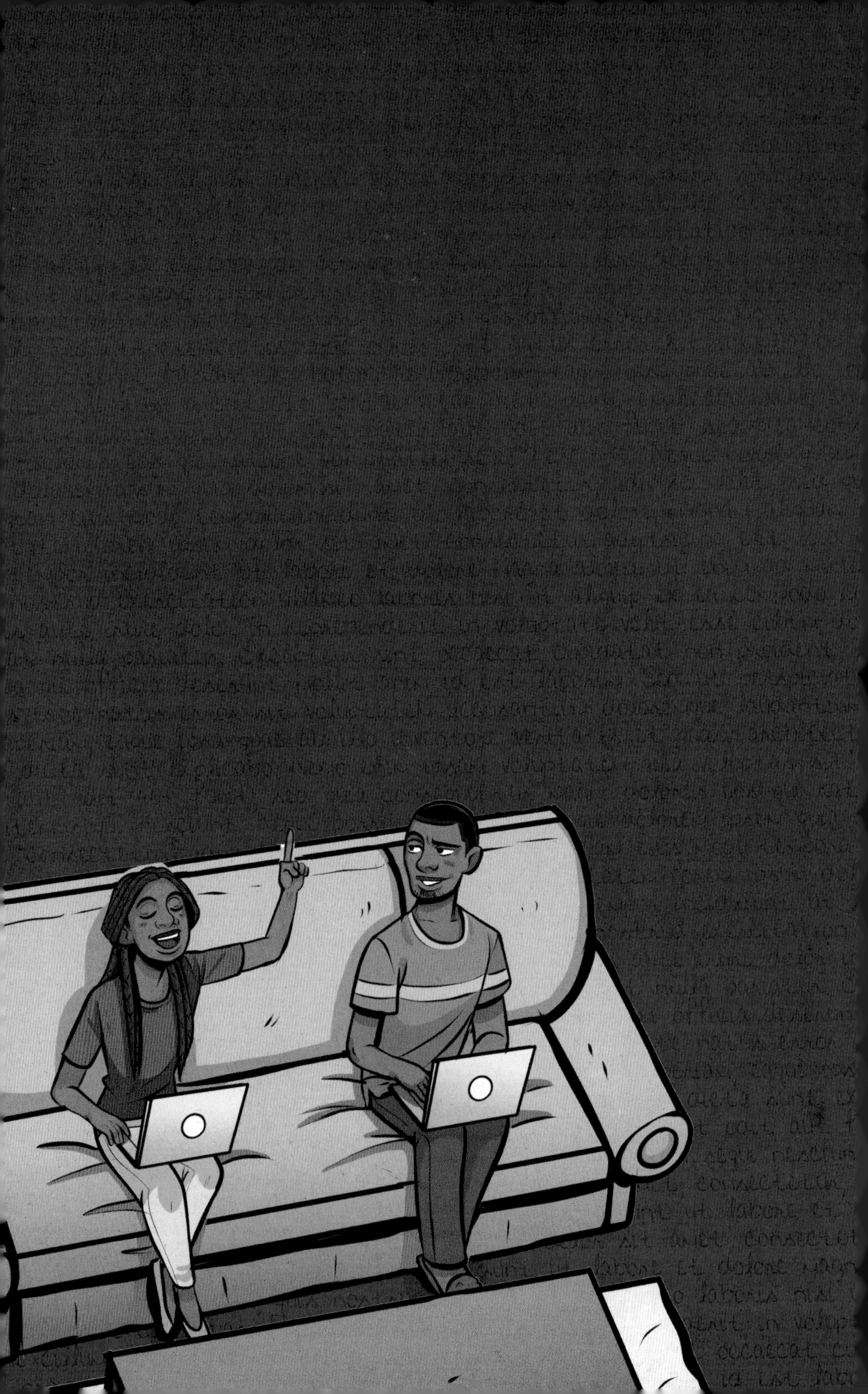

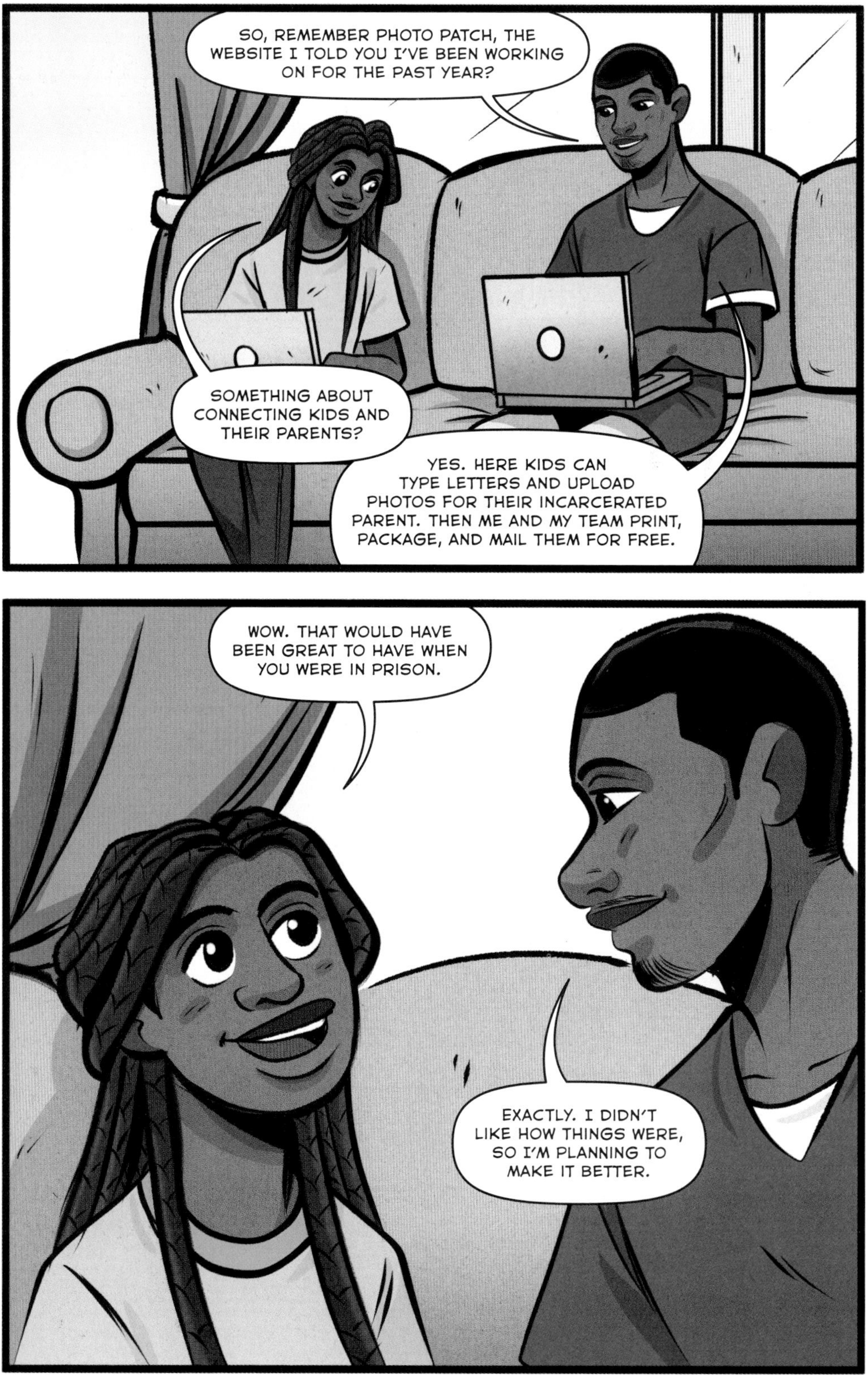
SO, REMEMBER PHOTO PATCH, THE WEBSITE I TOLD YOU I'VE BEEN WORKING ON FOR THE PAST YEAR?
SOMETHING ABOUT CONNECTING KIDS AND THEIR PARENTS?
YES. HERE KIDS CAN TYPE LETTERS AND UPLOAD PHOTOS FOR THEIR INCARCERATED PARENT. THEN ME AND MY TEAM PRINT, PACKAGE, AND MAIL THEM FOR FREE.
WOW. THAT WOULD HAVE BEEN GREAT TO HAVE WHEN YOU WERE IN PRISON.
EXACTLY. I DIDN'T LIKE HOW THINGS WERE, SO I'M PLANNING TO MAKE IT BETTER.

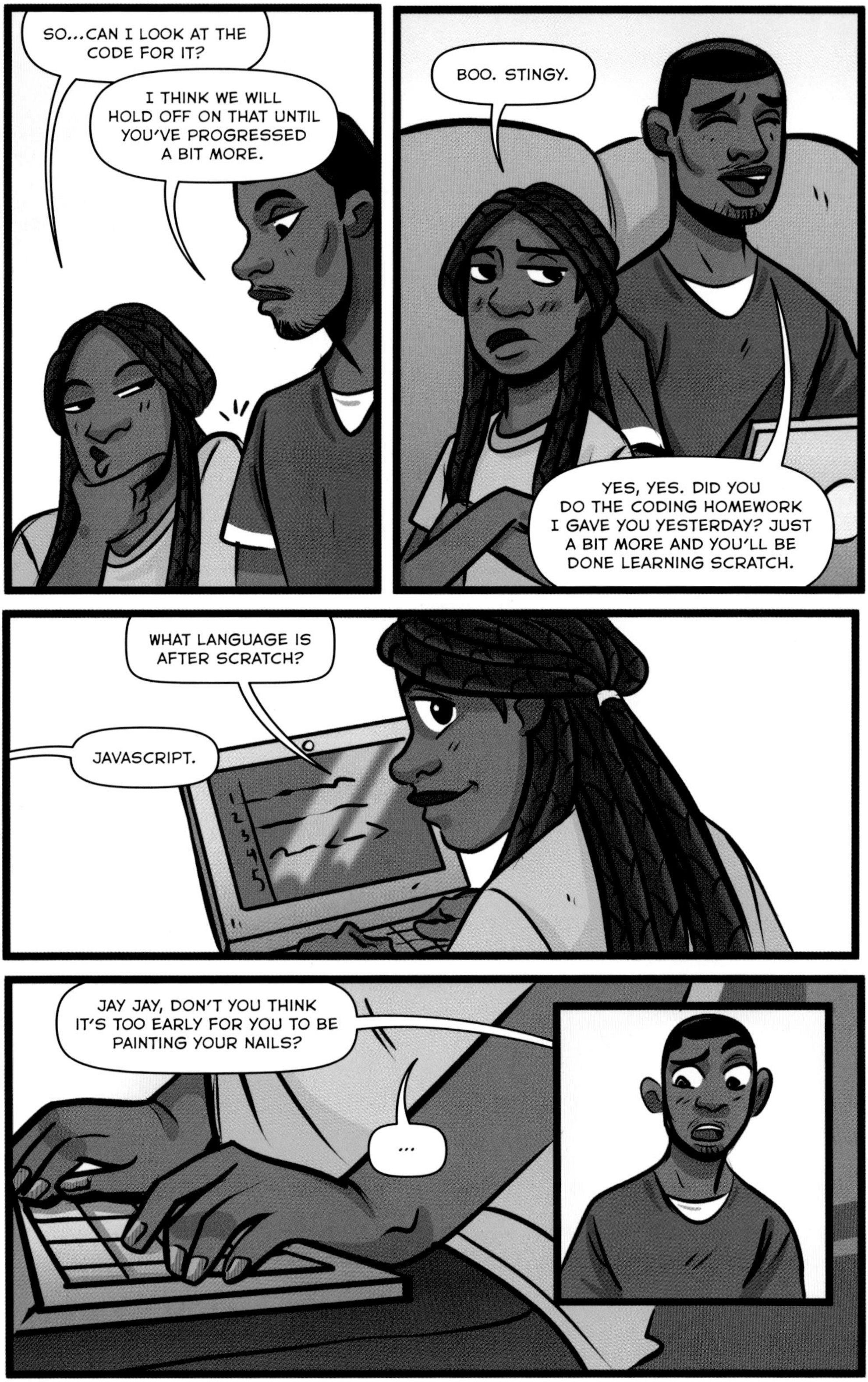
SO...CAN I LOOK AT THE CODE FOR IT?
I THINK WE WILL HOLD OFF ON THAT UNTIL YOU'VE PROGRESSED A BIT MORE.
BOO. STINGY.
YES, YES. DID YOU DO THE CODING HOMEWORK I GAVE YOU YESTERDAY? JUST A BIT MORE AND YOU'LL BE DONE LEARNING SCRATCH.
WHAT LANGUAGE IS AFTER SCRATCH?
JAVASCRIPT.
JAY JAY, DON'T YOU THINK IT'S TOO EARLY FOR YOU TO BE PAINTING YOUR NAILS?
...

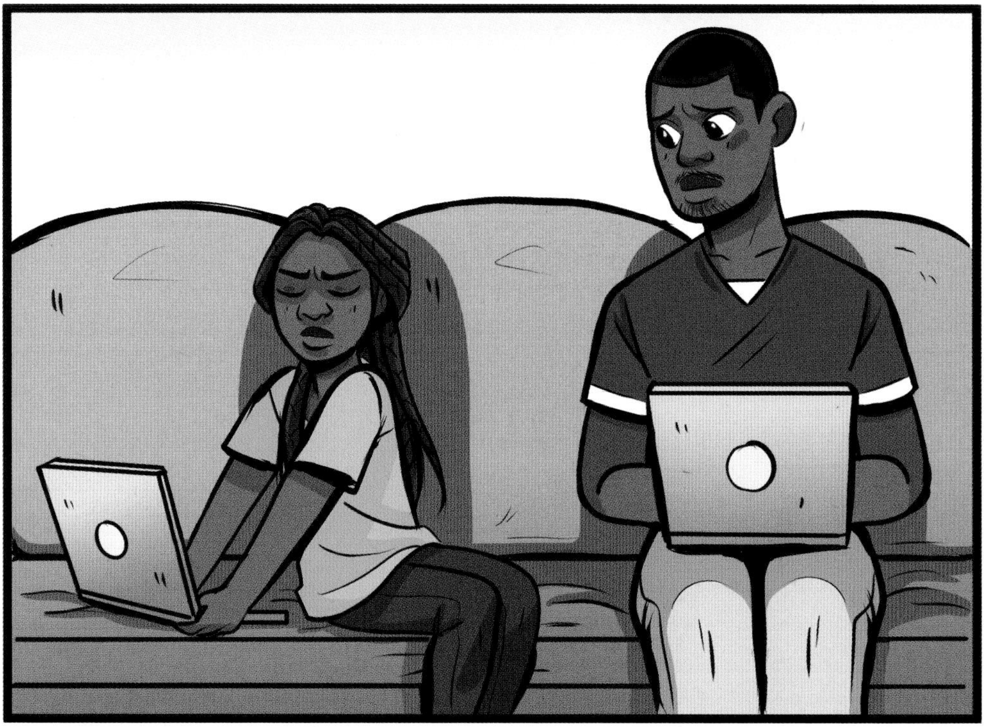

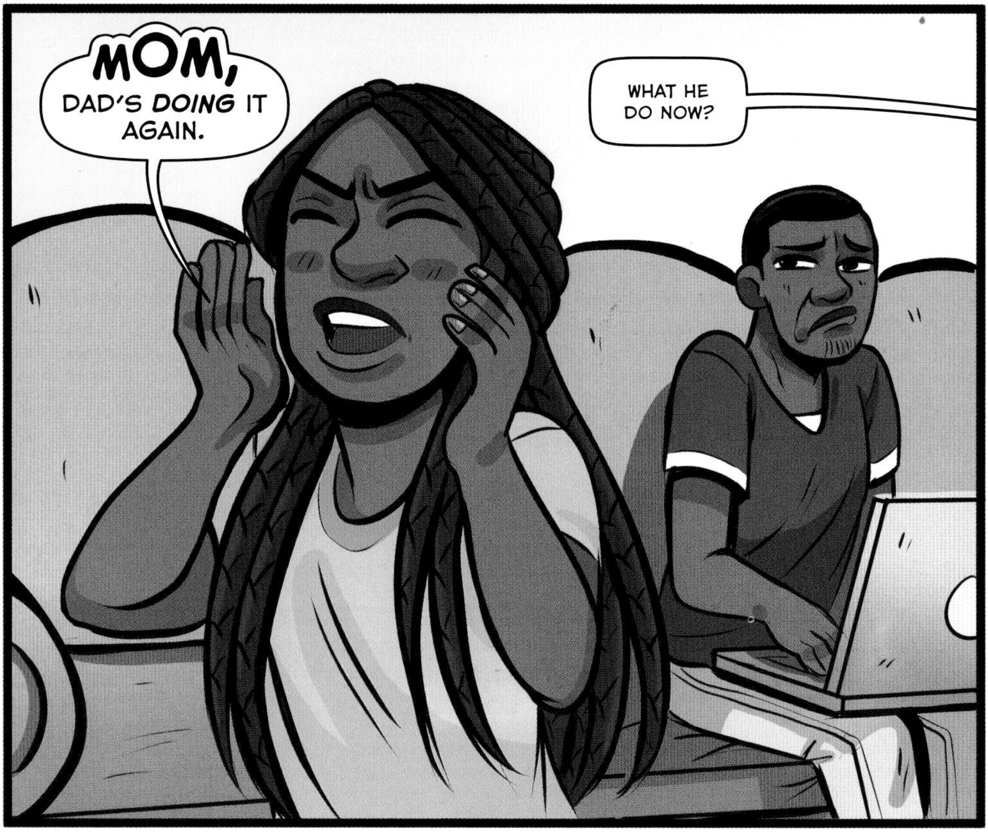
MOM, DAD'S *DOING* IT AGAIN.
WHAT HE DO NOW?

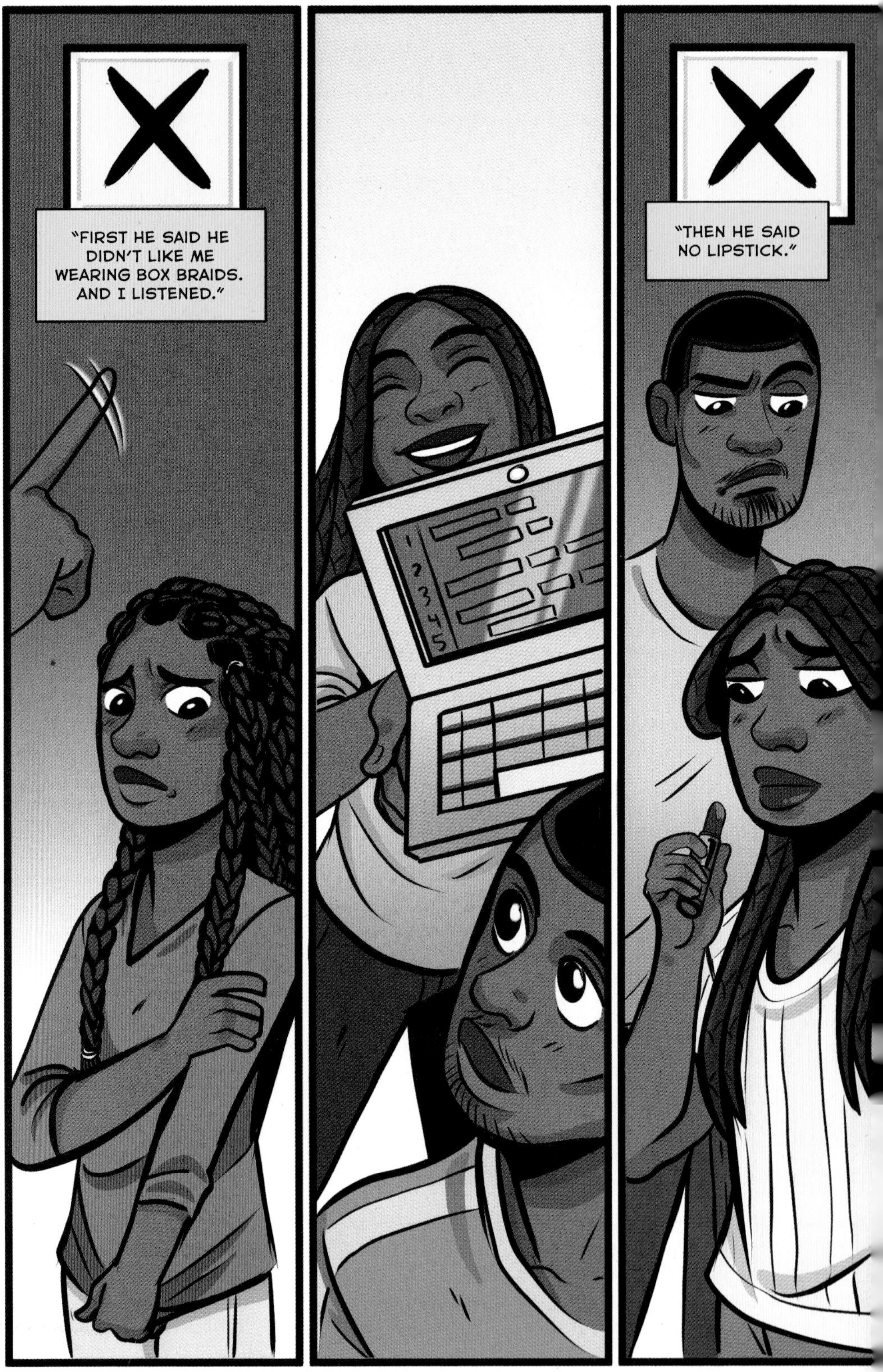
"FIRST HE SAID HE DIDN'T LIKE ME WEARING BOX BRAIDS. AND I LISTENED."
1
2
3
4
5
"THEN HE SAID NO LIPSTICK."

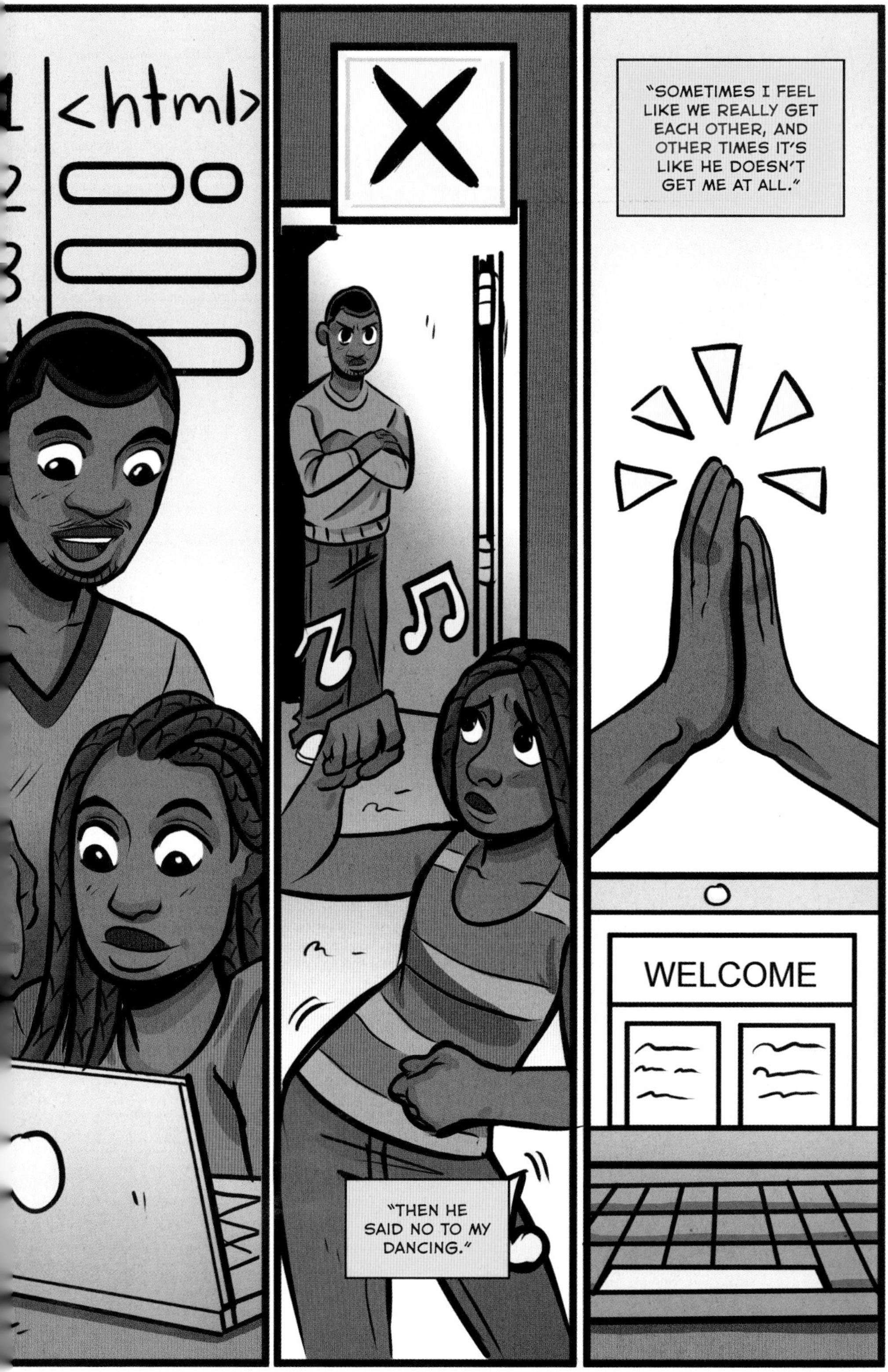
<html>
"THEN HE SAID NO TO MY DANCING."
"SOMETIMES I FEEL LIKE WE REALLY GET EACH OTHER, AND OTHER TIMES IT'S LIKE HE DOESN'T GET ME AT ALL."
WELCOME

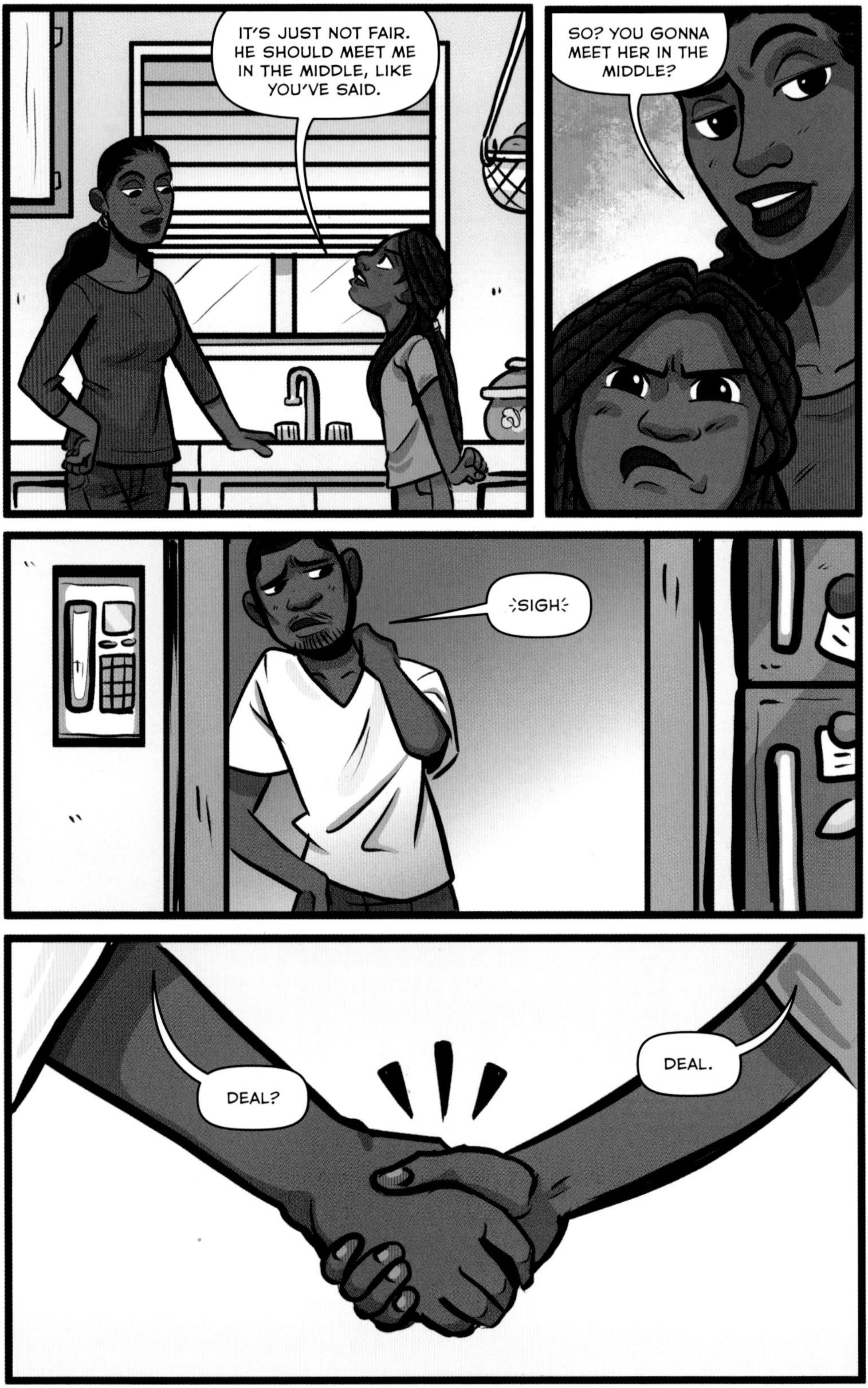
IT'S JUST NOT FAIR. HE SHOULD MEET ME IN THE MIDDLE, LIKE YOU'VE SAID.
SO? YOU GONNA MEET HER IN THE MIDDLE?
SIGH
DEAL?
DEAL.

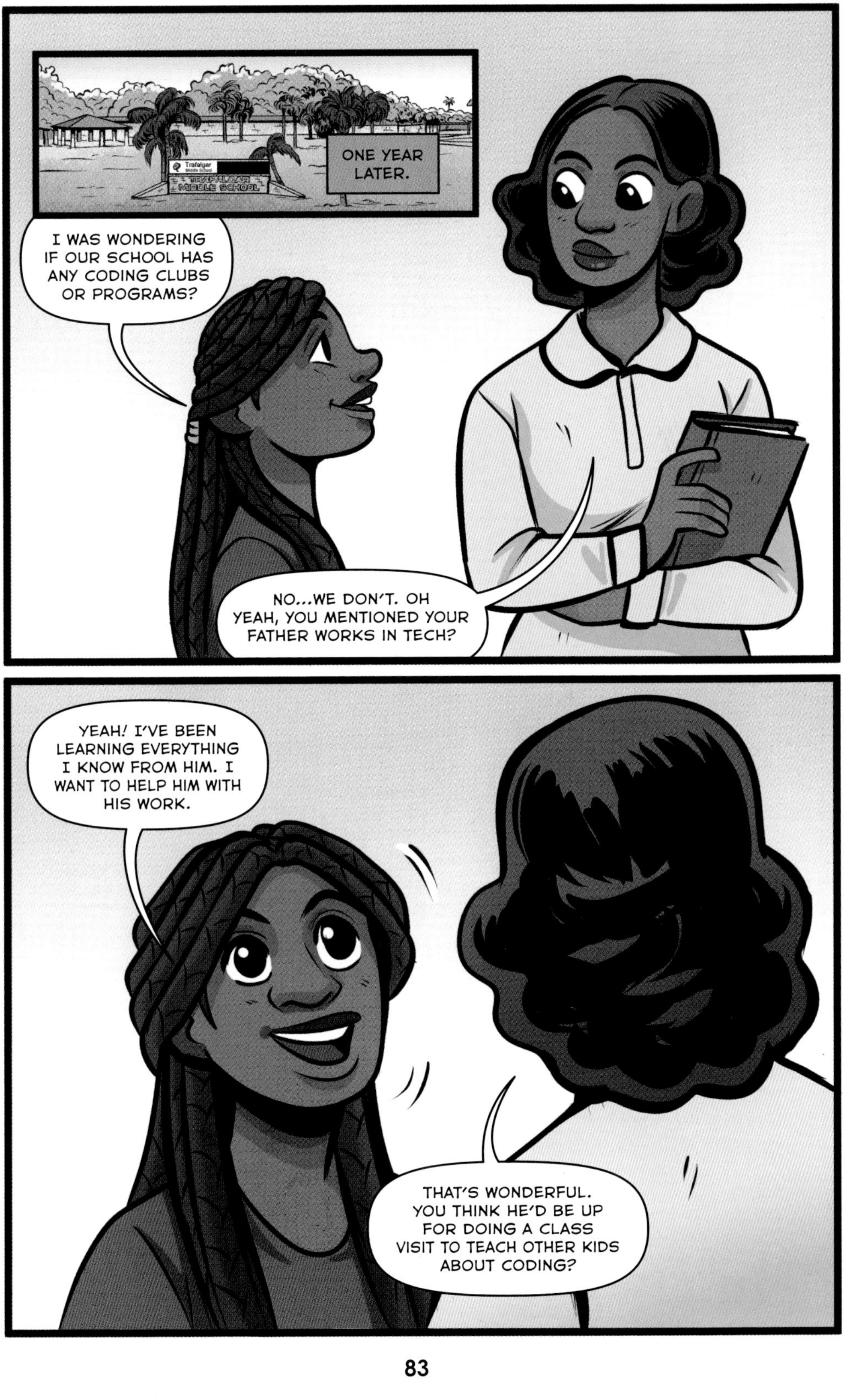
ONE YEAR LATER.
I WAS WONDERING IF OUR SCHOOL HAS ANY CODING CLUBS OR PROGRAMS?
NO...WE DON'T. OH YEAH, YOU MENTIONED YOUR FATHER WORKS IN TECH?
YEAH! I'VE BEEN LEARNING EVERYTHING I KNOW FROM HIM. I WANT TO HELP HIM WITH HIS WORK.
THAT'S WONDERFUL. YOU THINK HE'D BE UP FOR DOING A CLASS VISIT TO TEACH OTHER KIDS ABOUT CODING?

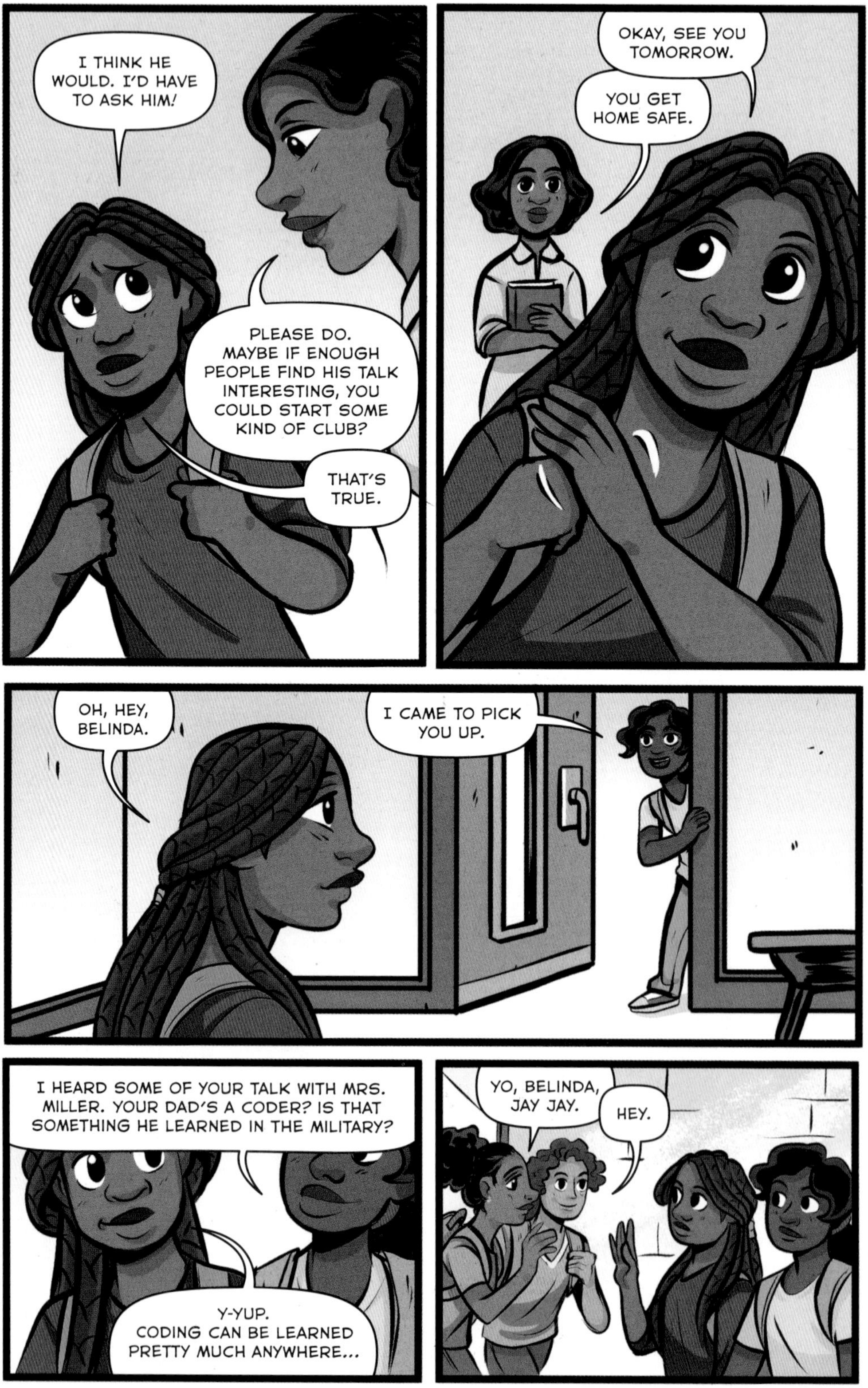
I THINK HE WOULD. I'D HAVE TO ASK HIM!
PLEASE DO. MAYBE IF ENOUGH PEOPLE FIND HIS TALK INTERESTING, YOU COULD START SOME KIND OF CLUB?
THAT'S TRUE.
OKAY, SEE YOU TOMORROW.
YOU GET HOME SAFE.
OH, HEY, BELINDA.
I CAME TO PICK YOU UP.
I HEARD SOME OF YOUR TALK WITH MRS. MILLER. YOUR DAD'S A CODER? IS THAT SOMETHING HE LEARNED IN THE MILITARY?
Y-YUP. CODING CAN BE LEARNED PRETTY MUCH ANYWHERE...
YO, BELINDA, JAY JAY.
HEY.

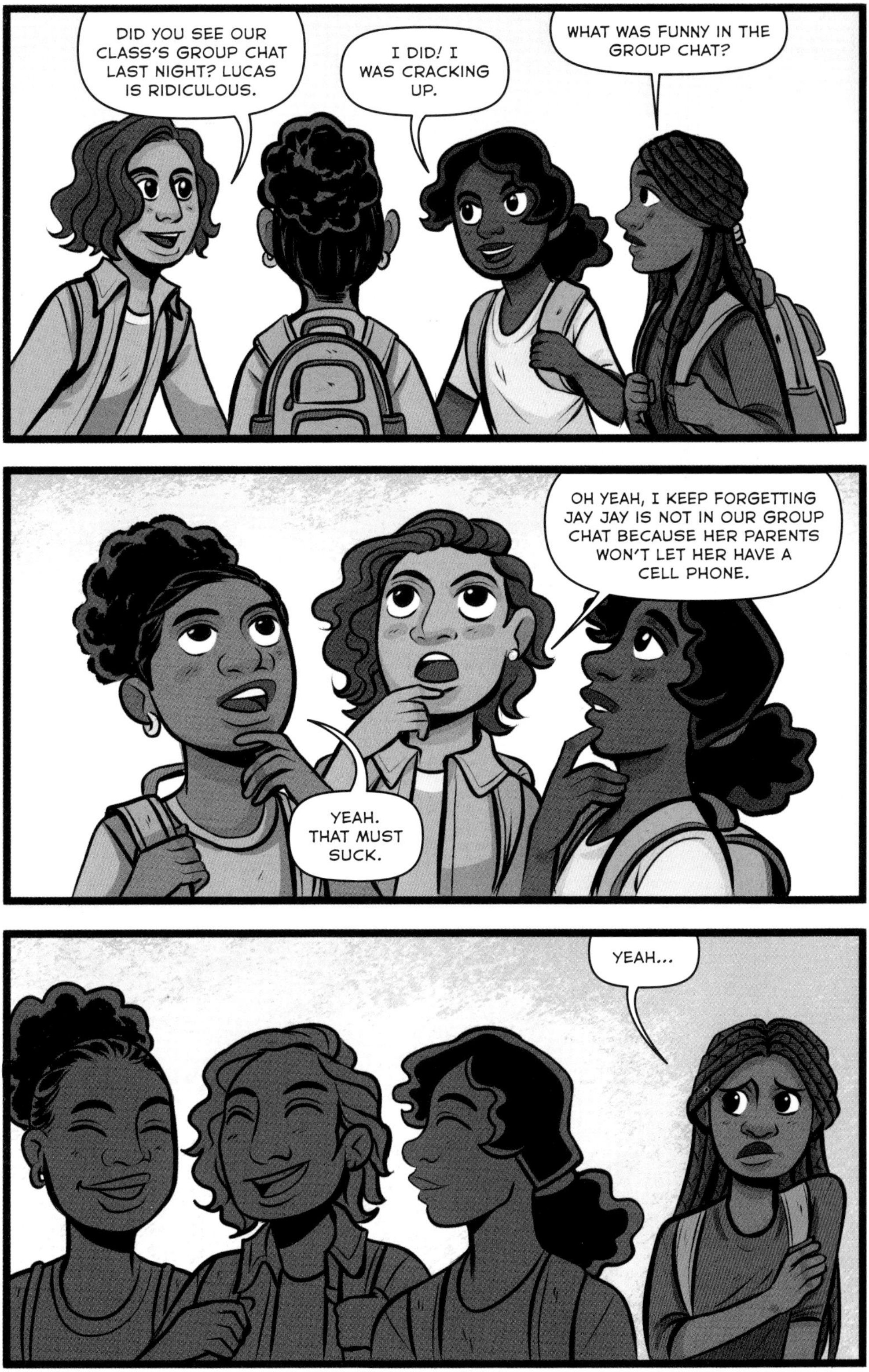
DID YOU SEE OUR CLASS'S GROUP CHAT LAST NIGHT? LUCAS IS RIDICULOUS.
I DID! I WAS CRACKING UP.
WHAT WAS FUNNY IN THE GROUP CHAT?
OH YEAH, I KEEP FORGETTING JAY JAY IS NOT IN OUR GROUP CHAT BECAUSE HER PARENTS WON'T LET HER HAVE A CELL PHONE.
YEAH. THAT MUST SUCK.
YEAH...

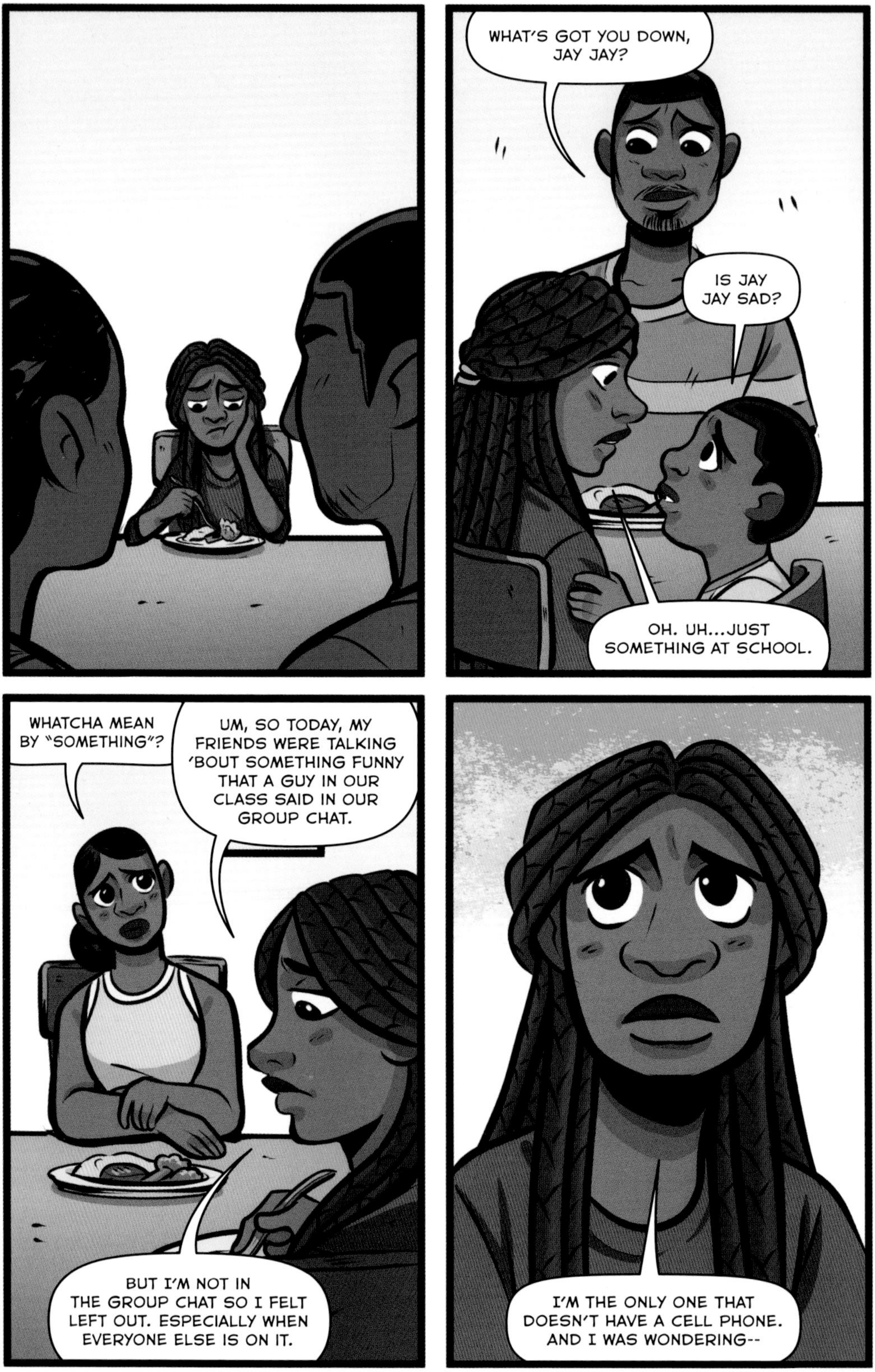
WHAT'S GOT YOU DOWN, JAY JAY?
IS JAY JAY SAD?
OH. UH...JUST SOMETHING AT SCHOOL.
WHATCHA MEAN BY "SOMETHING"?
UM, SO TODAY, MY FRIENDS WERE TALKING 'BOUT SOMETHING FUNNY THAT A GUY IN OUR CLASS SAID IN OUR GROUP CHAT.
BUT I'M NOT IN THE GROUP CHAT SO I FELT LEFT OUT. ESPECIALLY WHEN EVERYONE ELSE IS ON IT.
I'M THE ONLY ONE THAT DOESN'T HAVE A CELL PHONE. AND I WAS WONDERING--

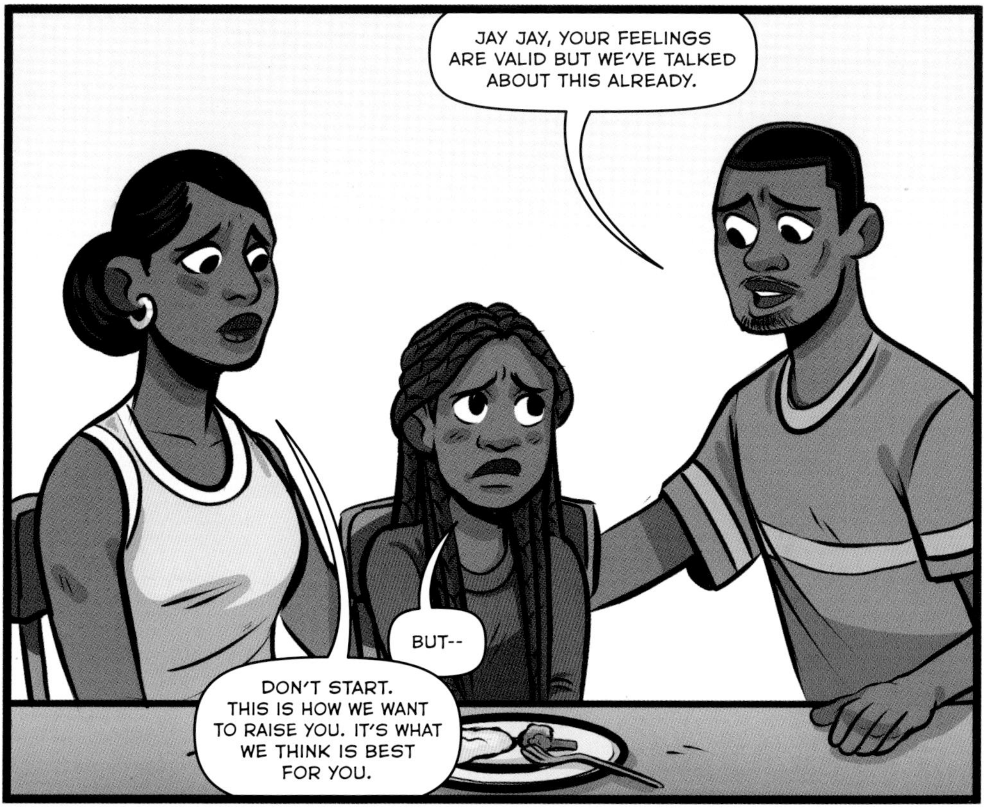
JAY JAY, YOUR FEELINGS ARE VALID BUT WE'VE TALKED ABOUT THIS ALREADY.
BUT--
DON'T START. THIS IS HOW WE WANT TO RAISE YOU. IT'S WHAT WE THINK IS BEST FOR YOU.

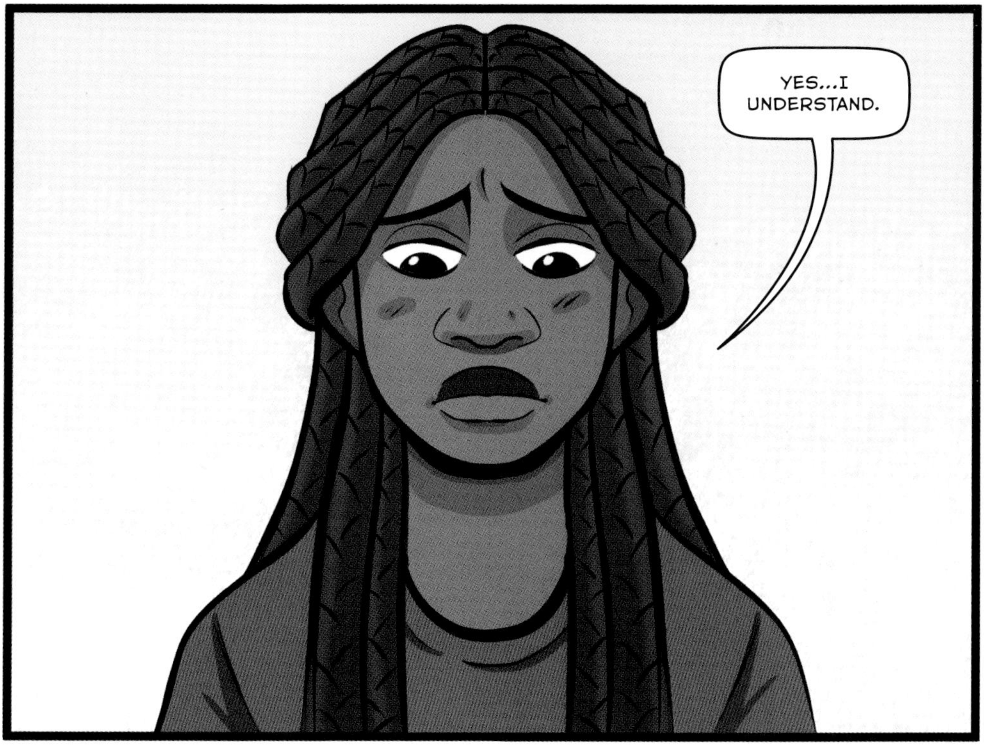
YES...I UNDERSTAND.

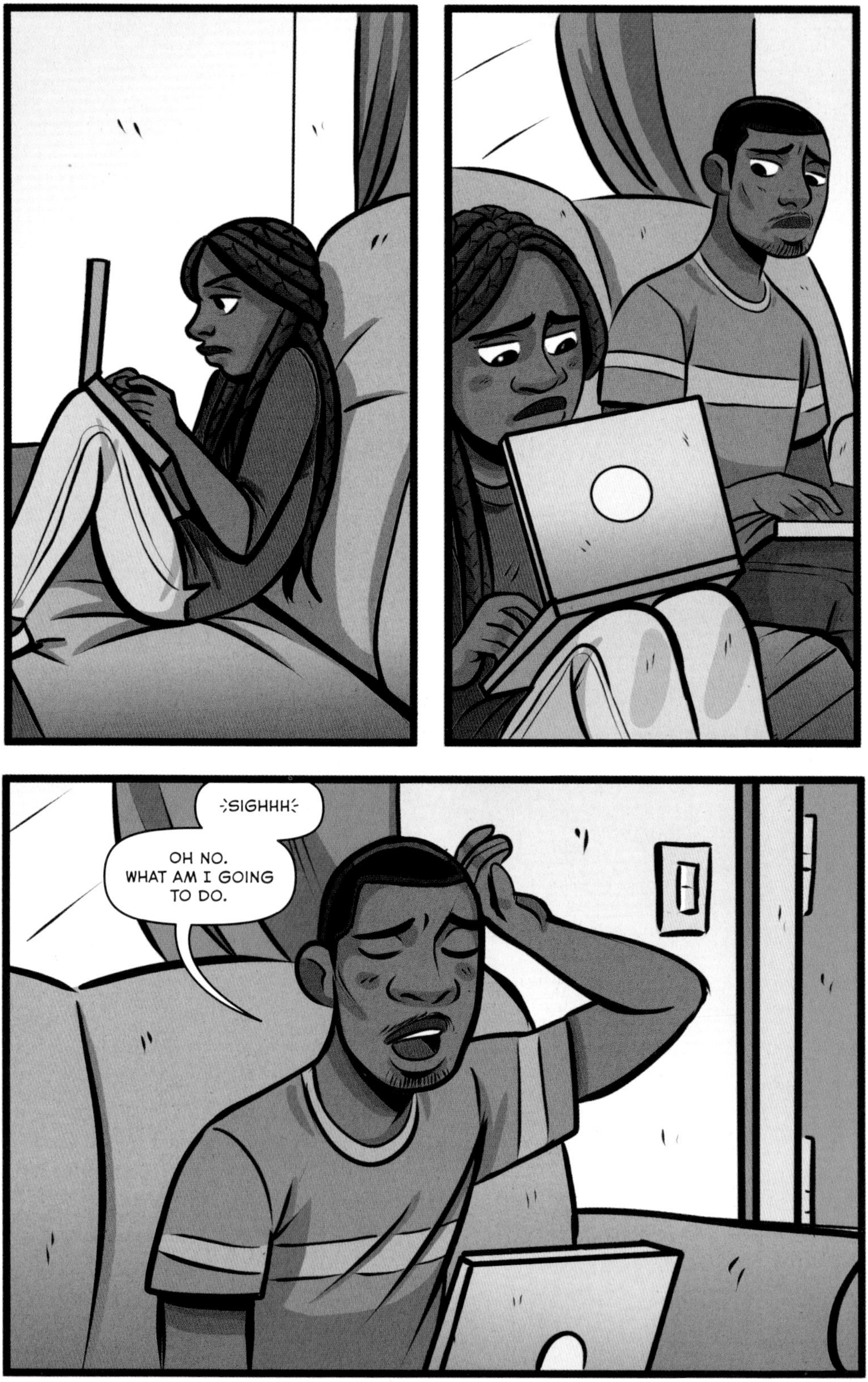

-SIGHHH-
OH NO. WHAT AM I GOING TO DO.

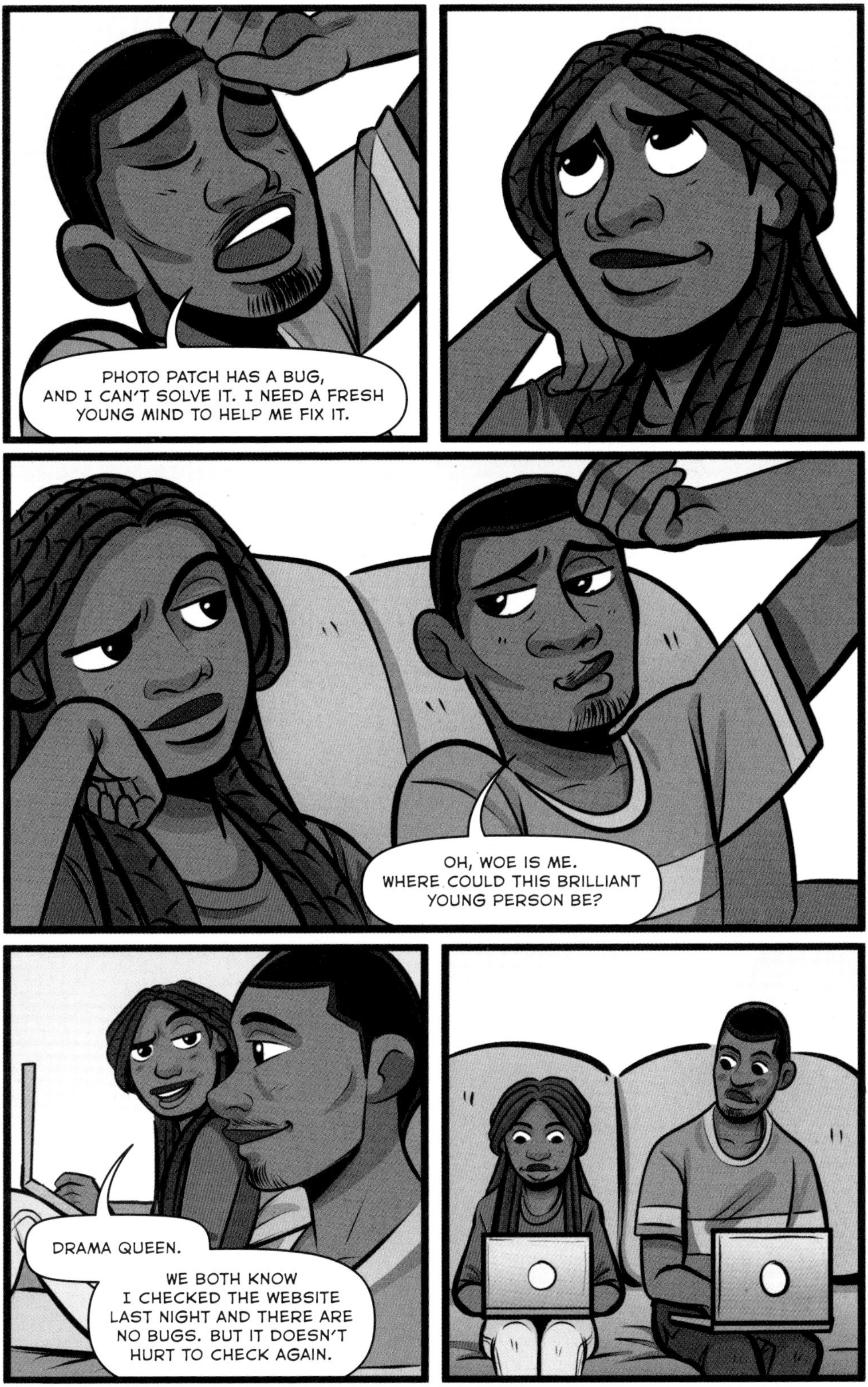
PHOTO PATCH HAS A BUG, AND I CAN'T SOLVE IT. I NEED A FRESH YOUNG MIND TO HELP ME FIX IT.
OH, WOE IS ME. WHERE COULD THIS BRILLIANT YOUNG PERSON BE?
DRAMA QUEEN.
WE BOTH KNOW I CHECKED THE WEBSITE LAST NIGHT AND THERE ARE NO BUGS. BUT IT DOESN'T HURT TO CHECK AGAIN.

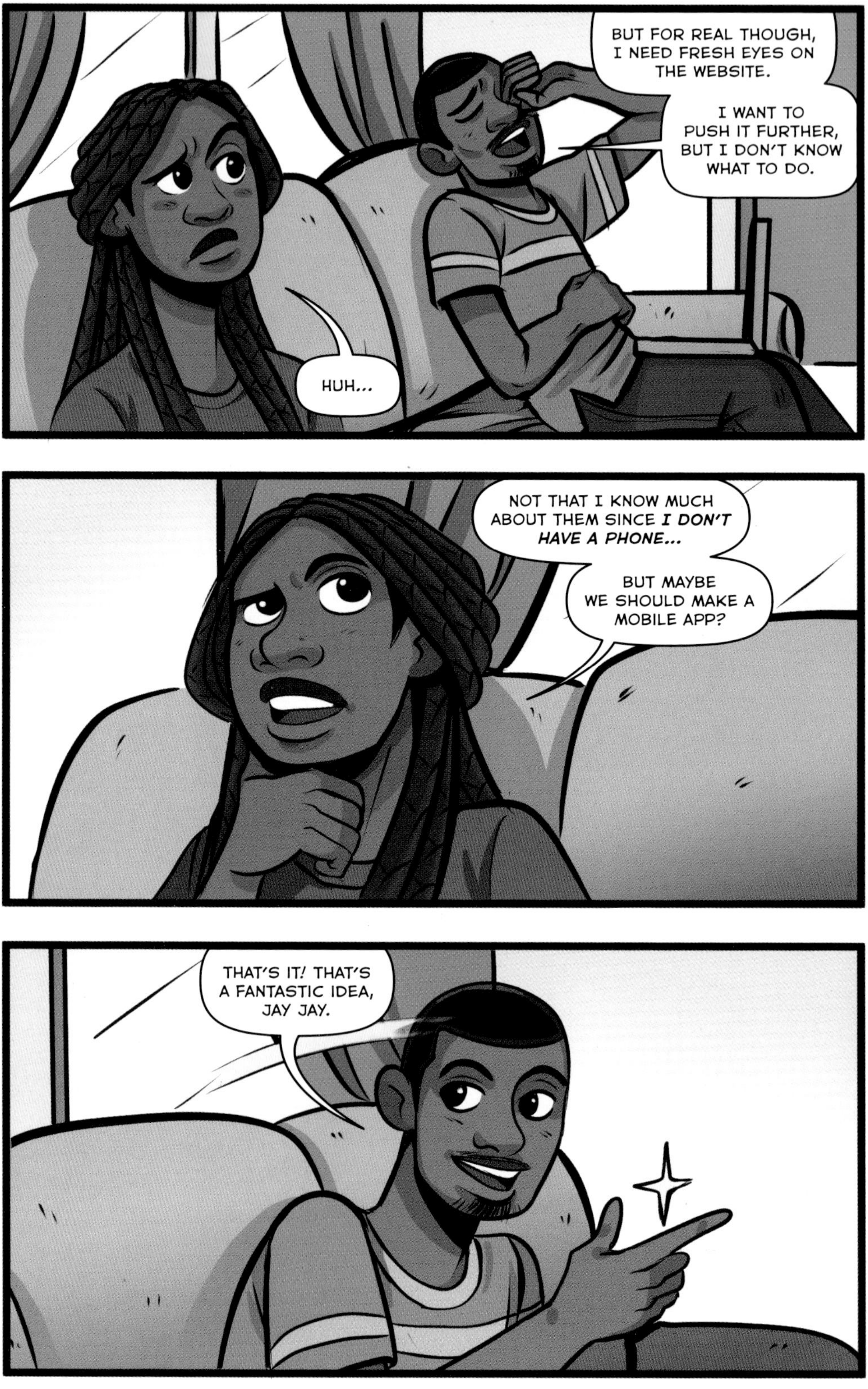
BUT FOR REAL THOUGH, I NEED FRESH EYES ON THE WEBSITE.
I WANT TO PUSH IT FURTHER, BUT I DON'T KNOW WHAT TO DO.
HUH...
NOT THAT I KNOW MUCH ABOUT THEM SINCE *I DON'T HAVE A PHONE...*
BUT MAYBE WE SHOULD MAKE A MOBILE APP?
THAT'S IT! THAT'S A FANTASTIC IDEA, JAY JAY.

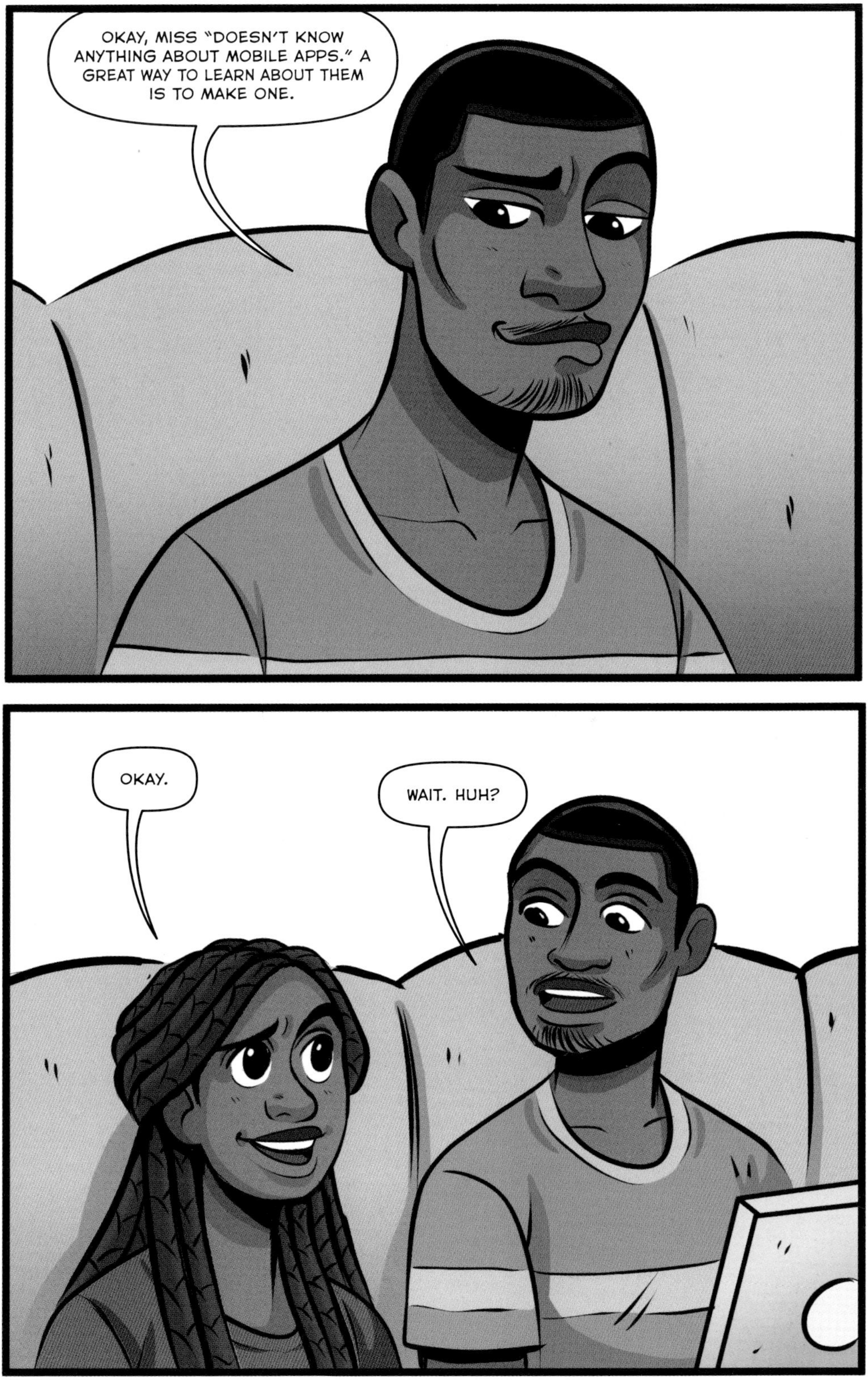
OKAY, MISS "DOESN'T KNOW ANYTHING ABOUT MOBILE APPS." A GREAT WAY TO LEARN ABOUT THEM IS TO MAKE ONE.
OKAY.
WAIT. HUH?

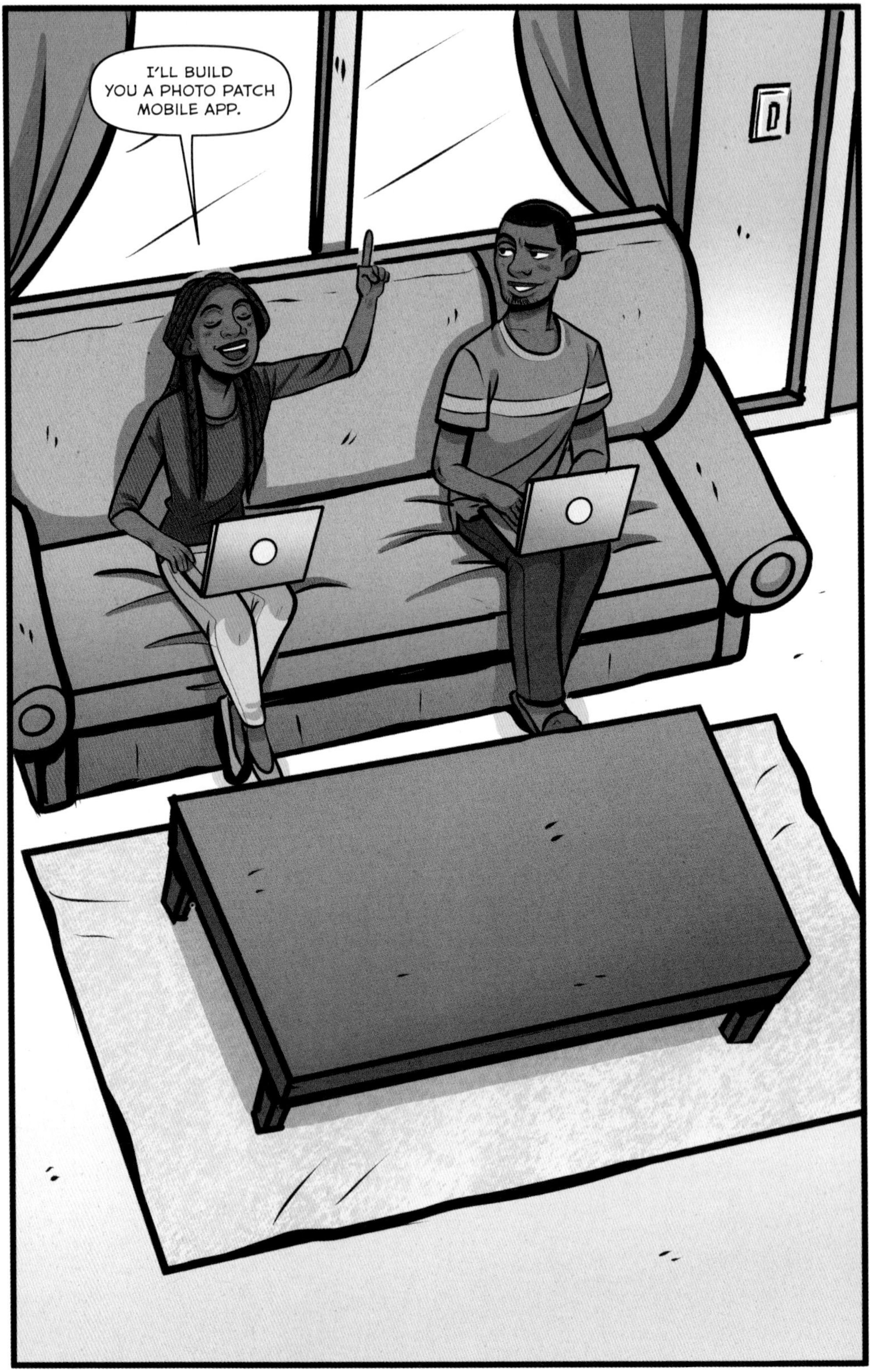
I'LL BUILD YOU A PHOTO PATCH MOBILE APP.

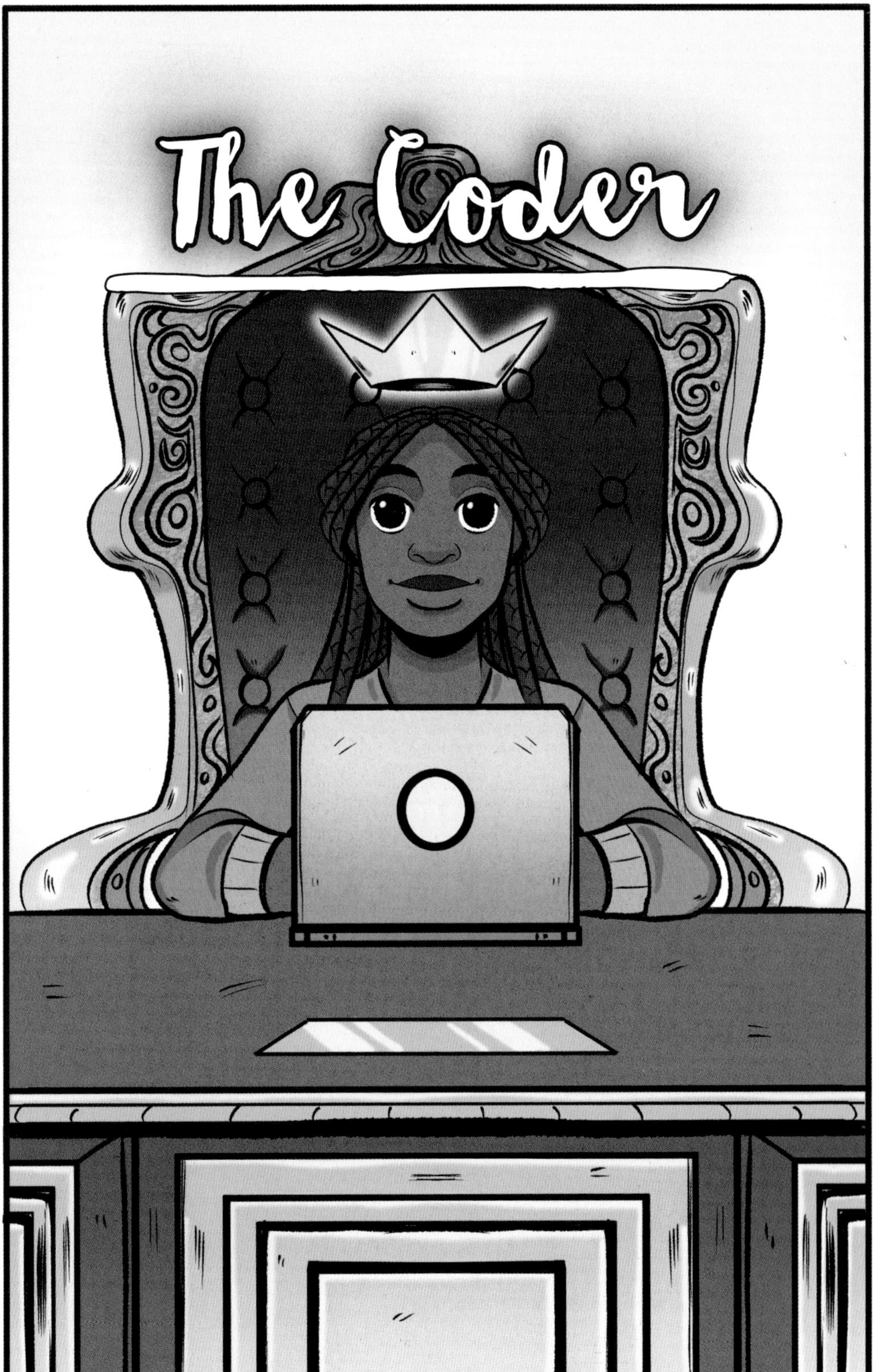
The Coder

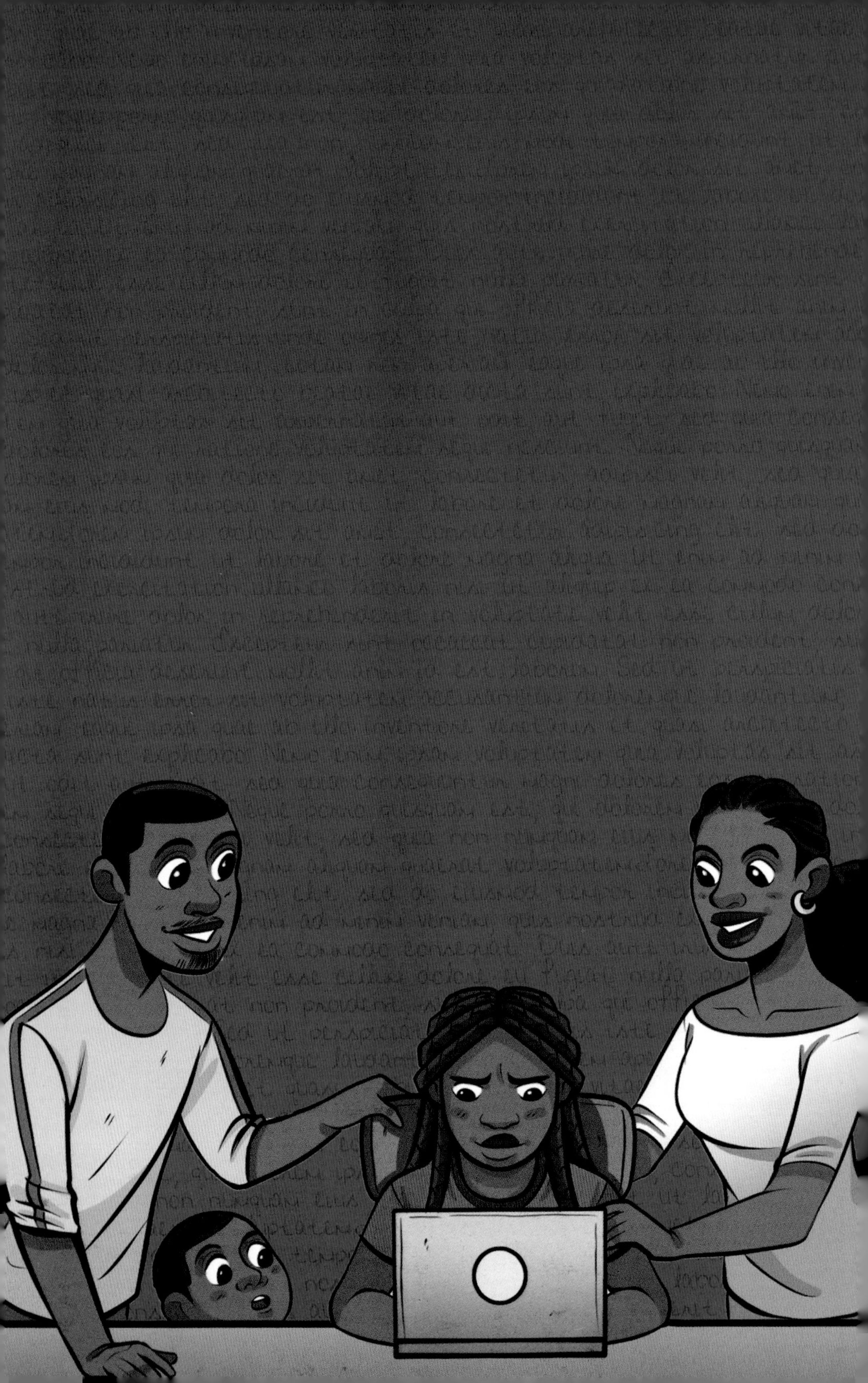

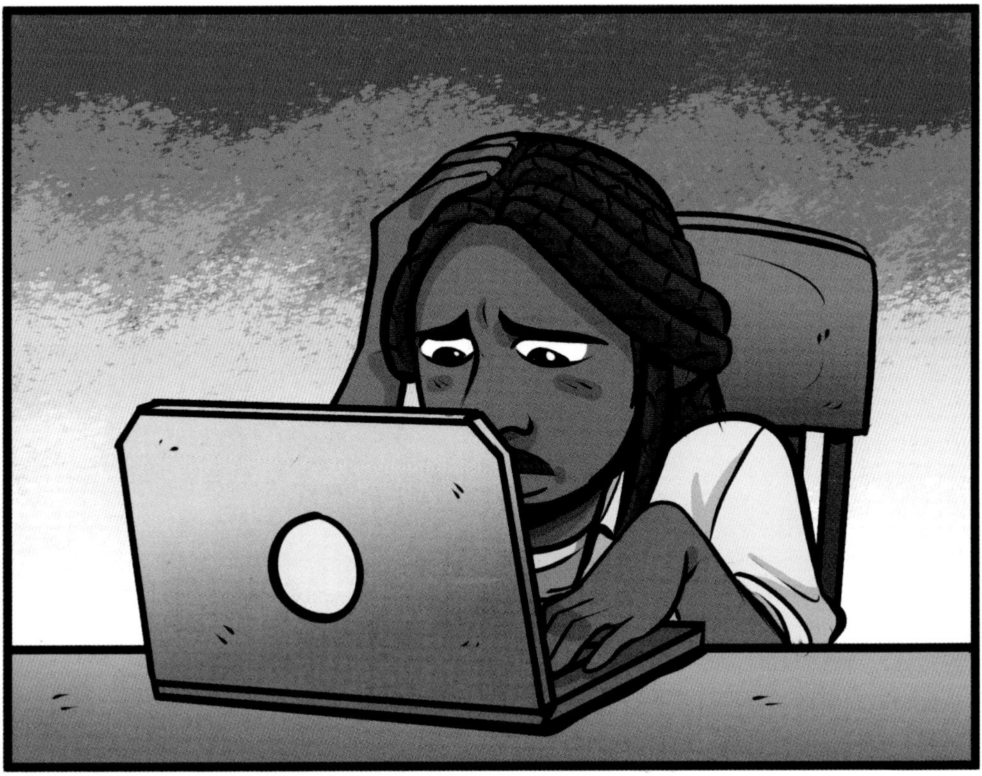

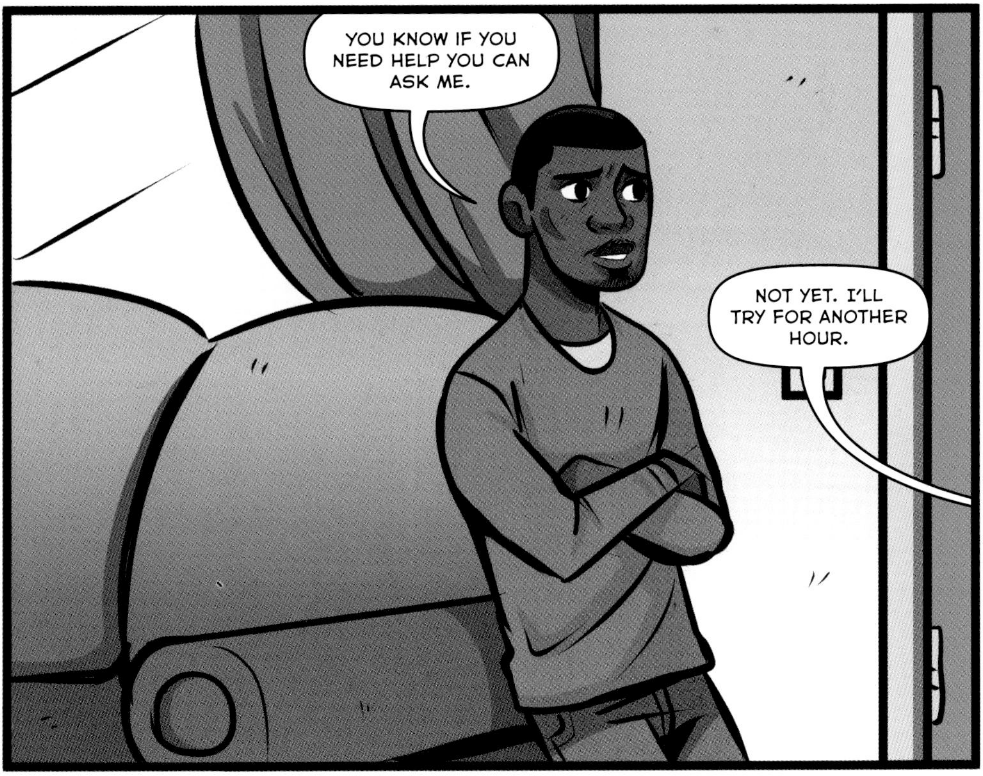
YOU KNOW IF YOU NEED HELP YOU CAN ASK ME.
NOT YET. I'LL TRY FOR ANOTHER HOUR.

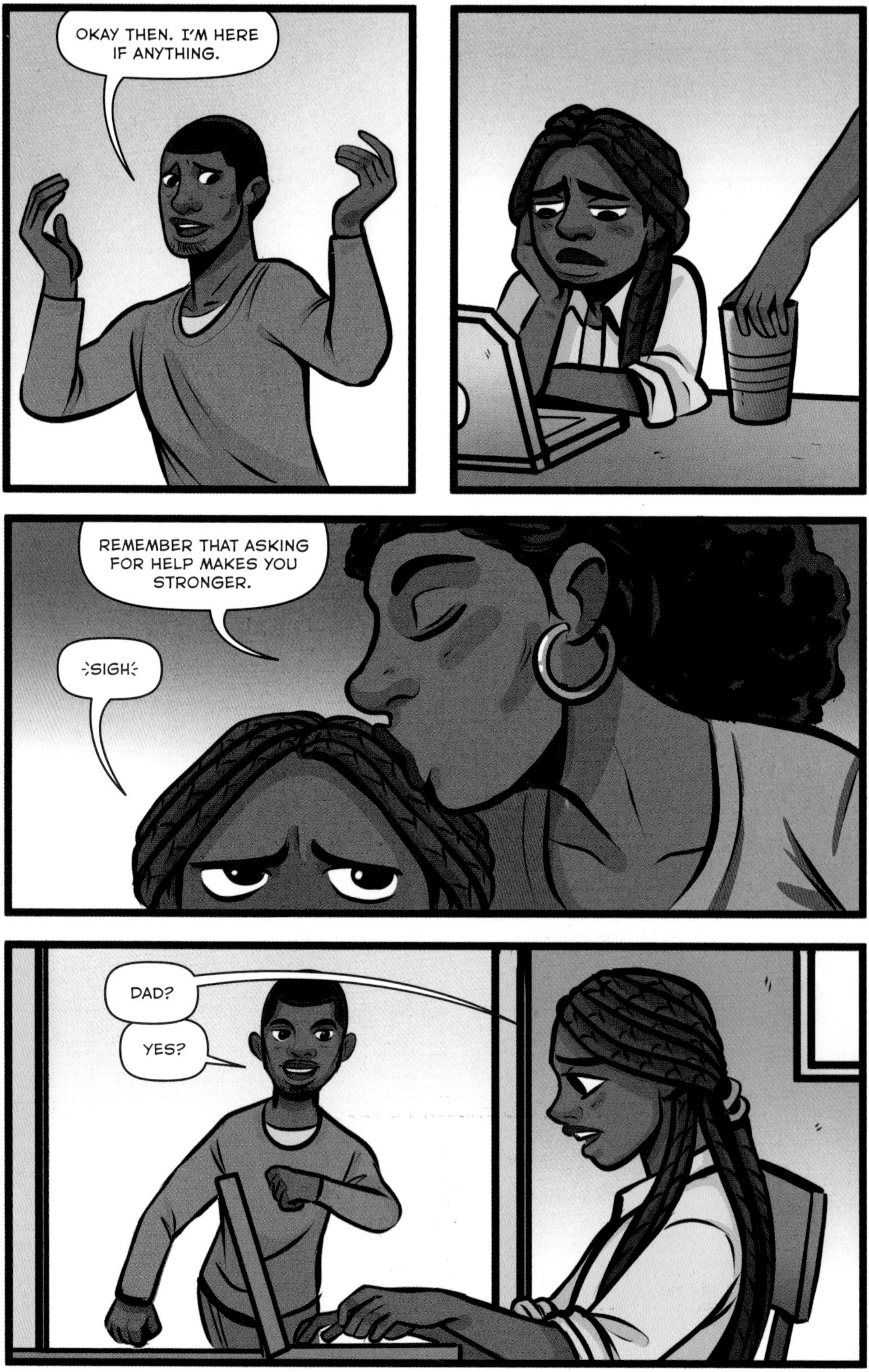
OKAY THEN. I'M HERE IF ANYTHING.
REMEMBER THAT ASKING FOR HELP MAKES YOU STRONGER.
SIGH
DAD?
YES?

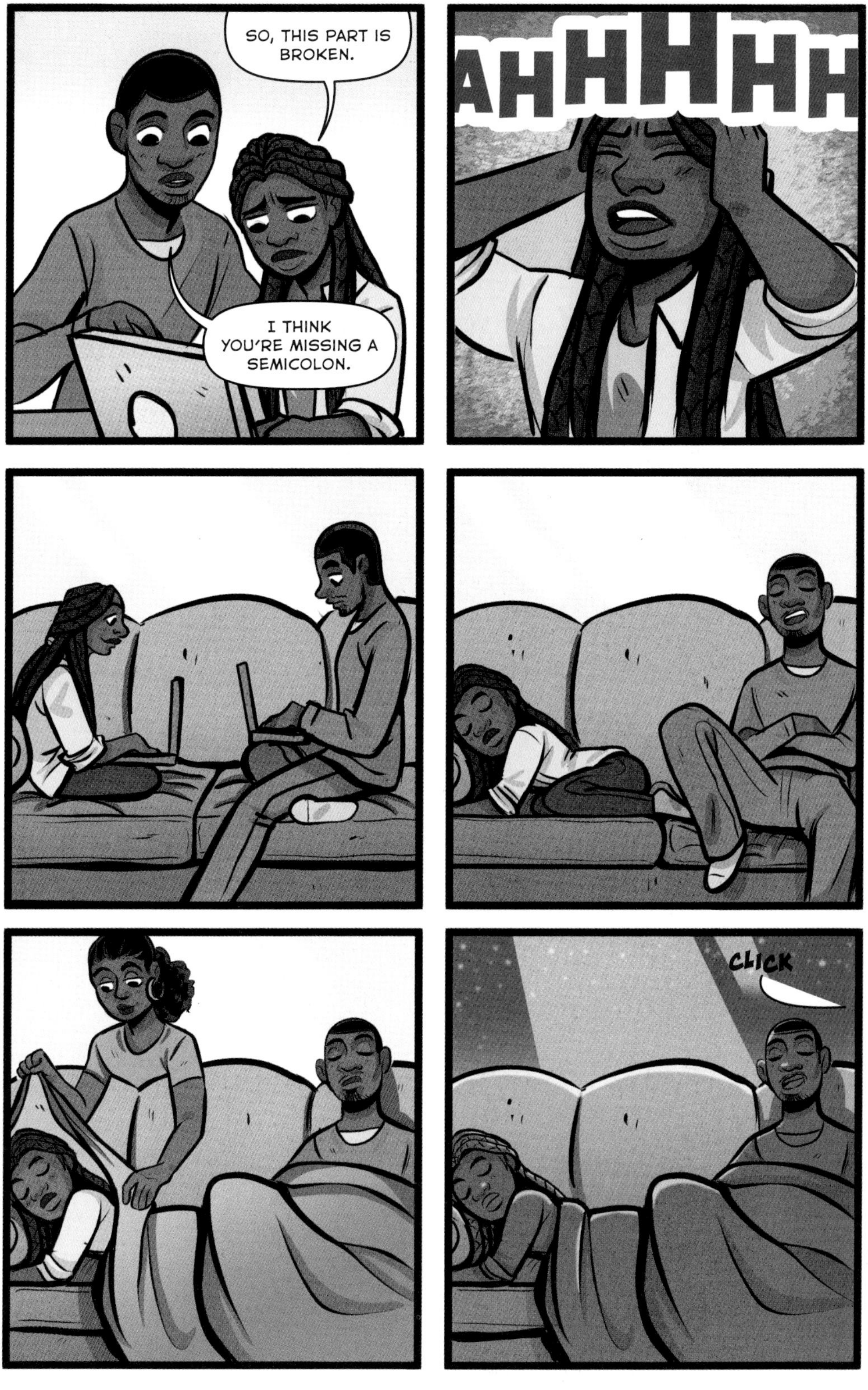
SO, THIS PART IS BROKEN.
I THINK YOU'RE MISSING A SEMICOLON.
AHHHHHH
CLICK

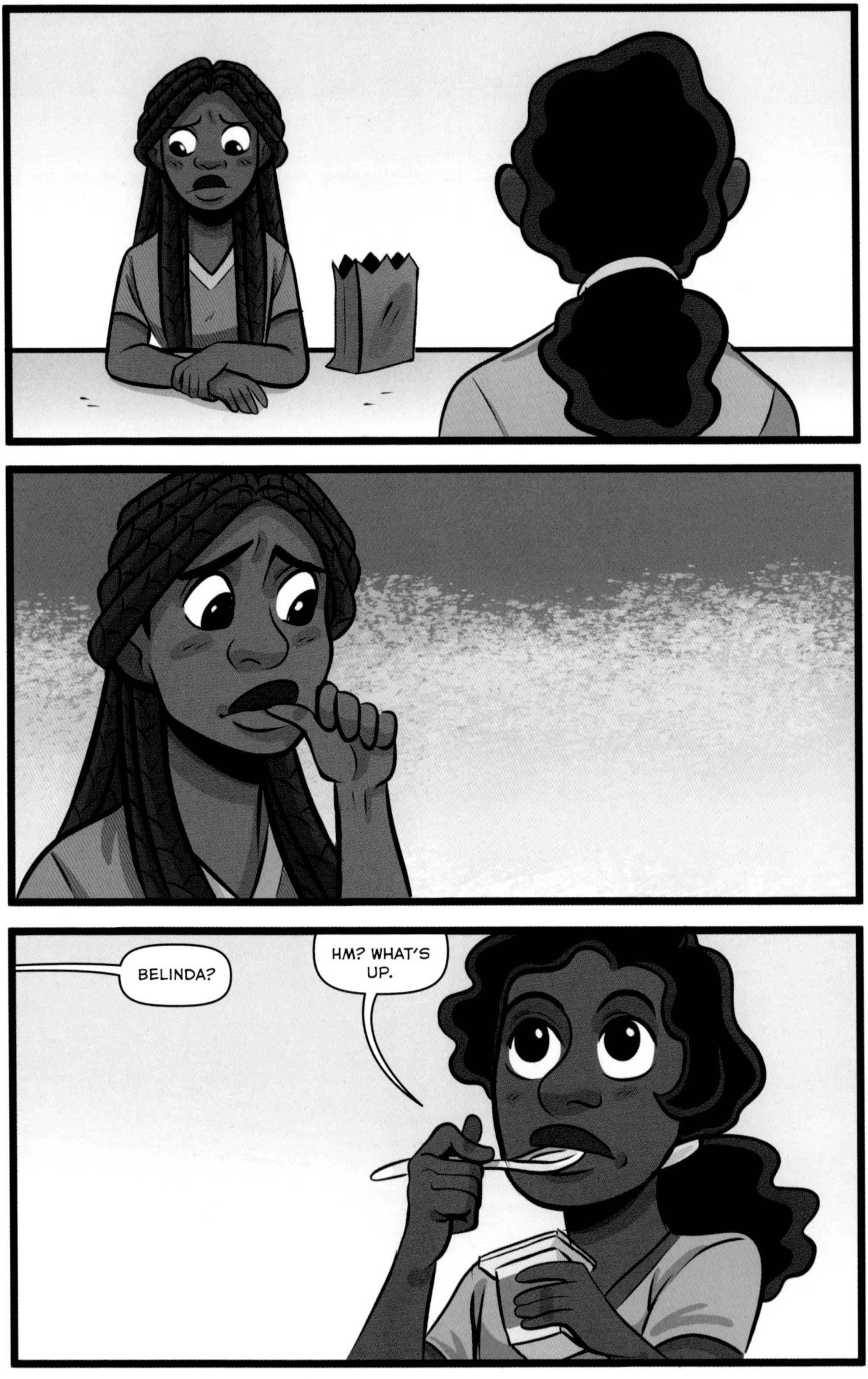
BELINDA?
HM? WHAT'S UP.

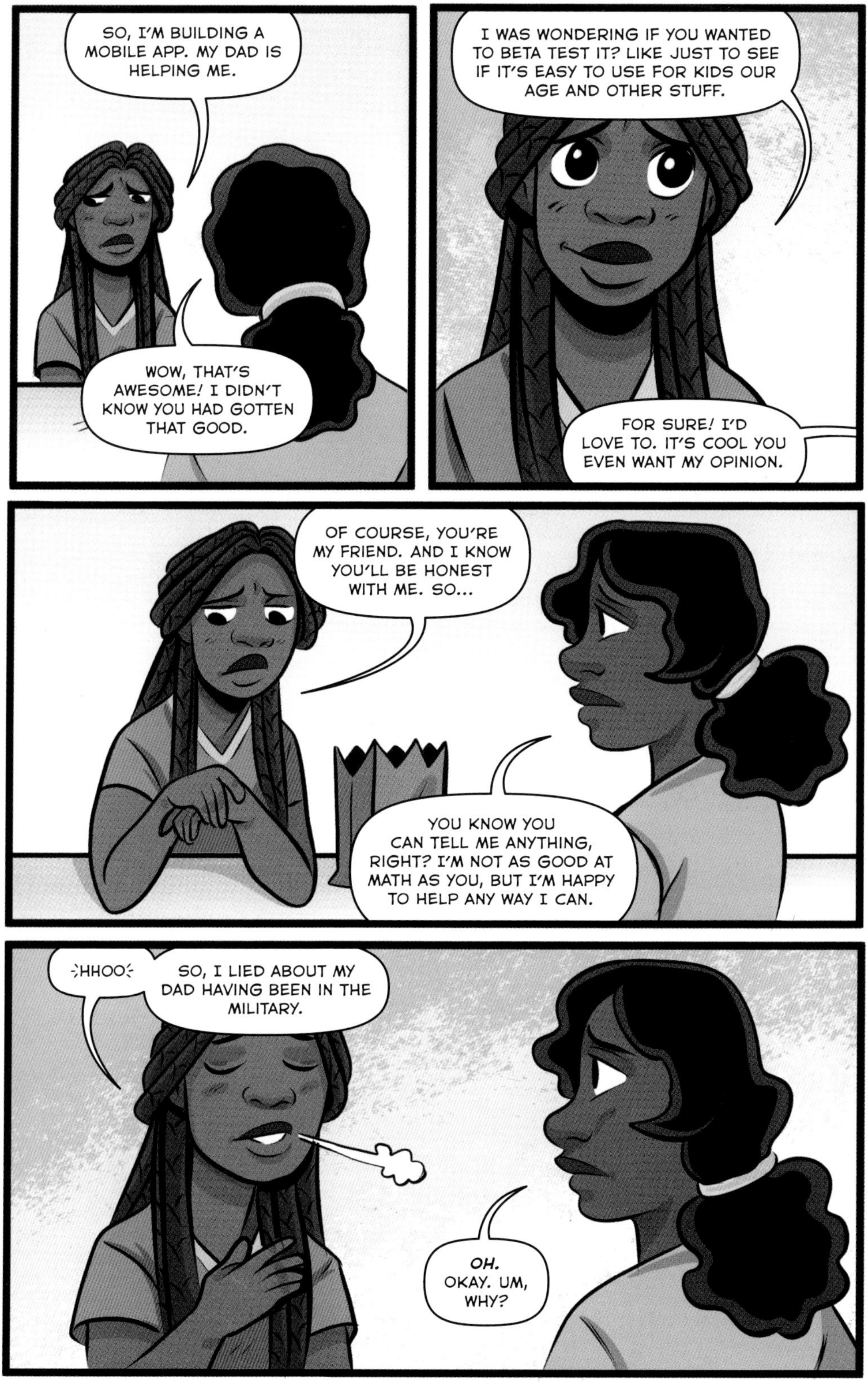
SO, I'M BUILDING A MOBILE APP. MY DAD IS HELPING ME.
WOW, THAT'S AWESOME! I DIDN'T KNOW YOU HAD GOTTEN THAT GOOD.
I WAS WONDERING IF YOU WANTED TO BETA TEST IT? LIKE JUST TO SEE IF IT'S EASY TO USE FOR KIDS OUR AGE AND OTHER STUFF.
FOR SURE! I'D LOVE TO. IT'S COOL YOU EVEN WANT MY OPINION.
OF COURSE, YOU'RE MY FRIEND. AND I KNOW YOU'LL BE HONEST WITH ME. SO...
YOU KNOW YOU CAN TELL ME ANYTHING, RIGHT? I'M NOT AS GOOD AT MATH AS YOU, BUT I'M HAPPY TO HELP ANY WAY I CAN.
HHOO
SO, I LIED ABOUT MY DAD HAVING BEEN IN THE MILITARY.
OH. OKAY. UM, WHY?

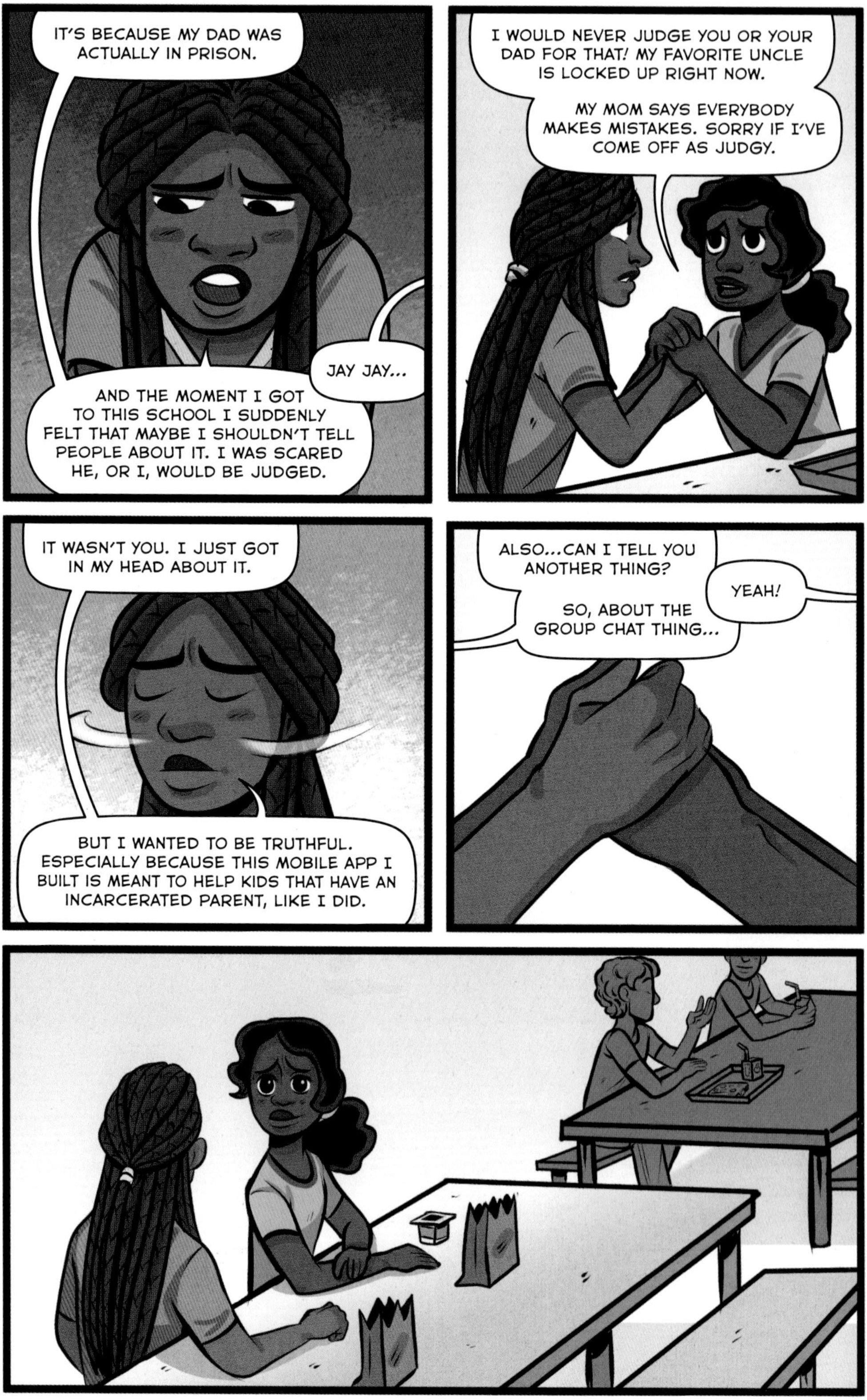
IT'S BECAUSE MY DAD WAS ACTUALLY IN PRISON.
AND THE MOMENT I GOT TO THIS SCHOOL I SUDDENLY FELT THAT MAYBE I SHOULDN'T TELL PEOPLE ABOUT IT. I WAS SCARED HE, OR I, WOULD BE JUDGED.
JAY JAY...
I WOULD NEVER JUDGE YOU OR YOUR DAD FOR THAT! MY FAVORITE UNCLE IS LOCKED UP RIGHT NOW.
MY MOM SAYS EVERYBODY MAKES MISTAKES. SORRY IF I'VE COME OFF AS JUDGY.
IT WASN'T YOU. I JUST GOT IN MY HEAD ABOUT IT.
BUT I WANTED TO BE TRUTHFUL. ESPECIALLY BECAUSE THIS MOBILE APP I BUILT IS MEANT TO HELP KIDS THAT HAVE AN INCARCERATED PARENT, LIKE I DID.
ALSO...CAN I TELL YOU ANOTHER THING?
YEAH!
SO, ABOUT THE GROUP CHAT THING...

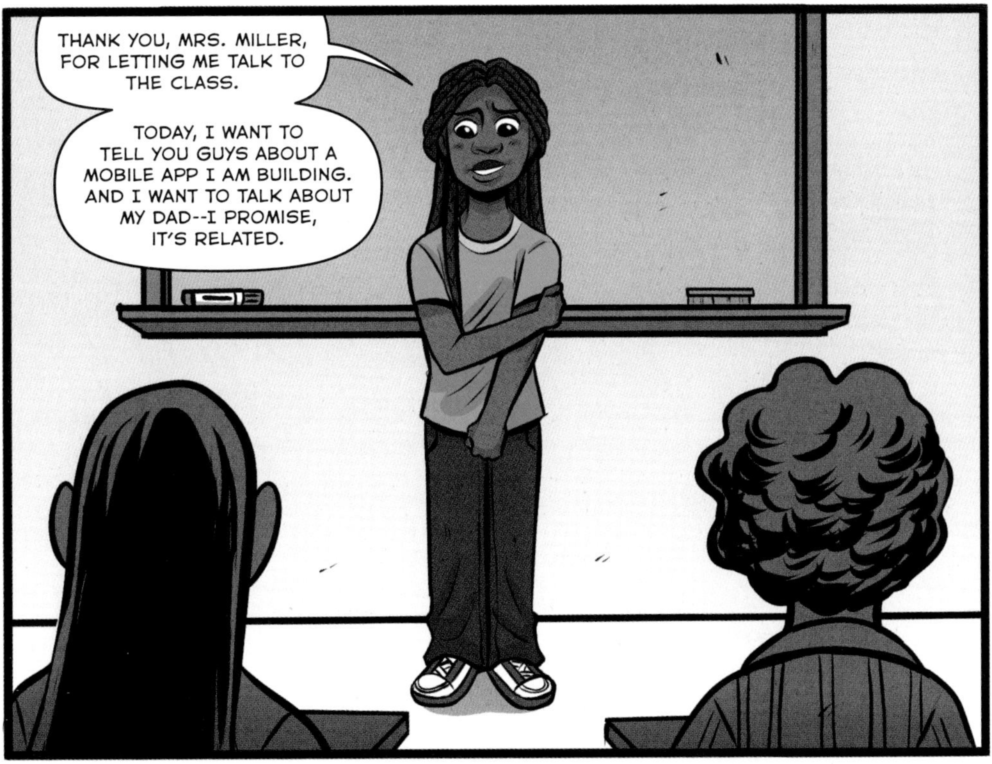
THANK YOU, MRS. MILLER, FOR LETTING ME TALK TO THE CLASS.
TODAY, I WANT TO TELL YOU GUYS ABOUT A MOBILE APP I AM BUILDING. AND I WANT TO TALK ABOUT MY DAD--I PROMISE, IT'S RELATED.

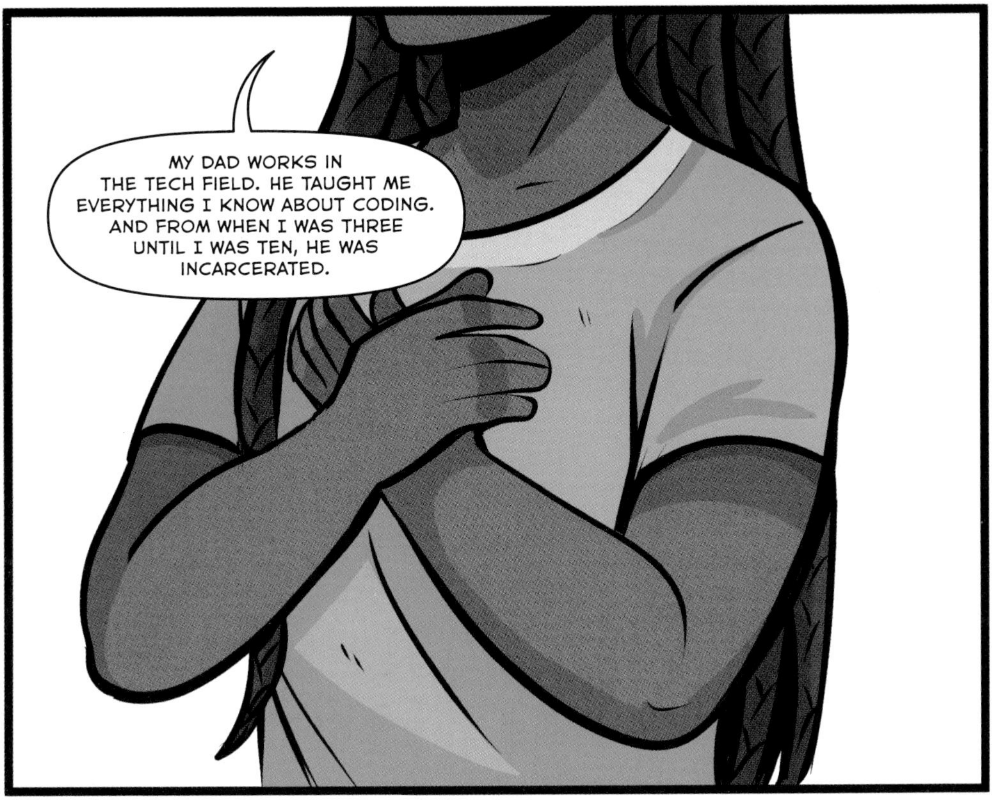
MY DAD WORKS IN THE TECH FIELD. HE TAUGHT ME EVERYTHING I KNOW ABOUT CODING. AND FROM WHEN I WAS THREE UNTIL I WAS TEN, HE WAS INCARCERATED.

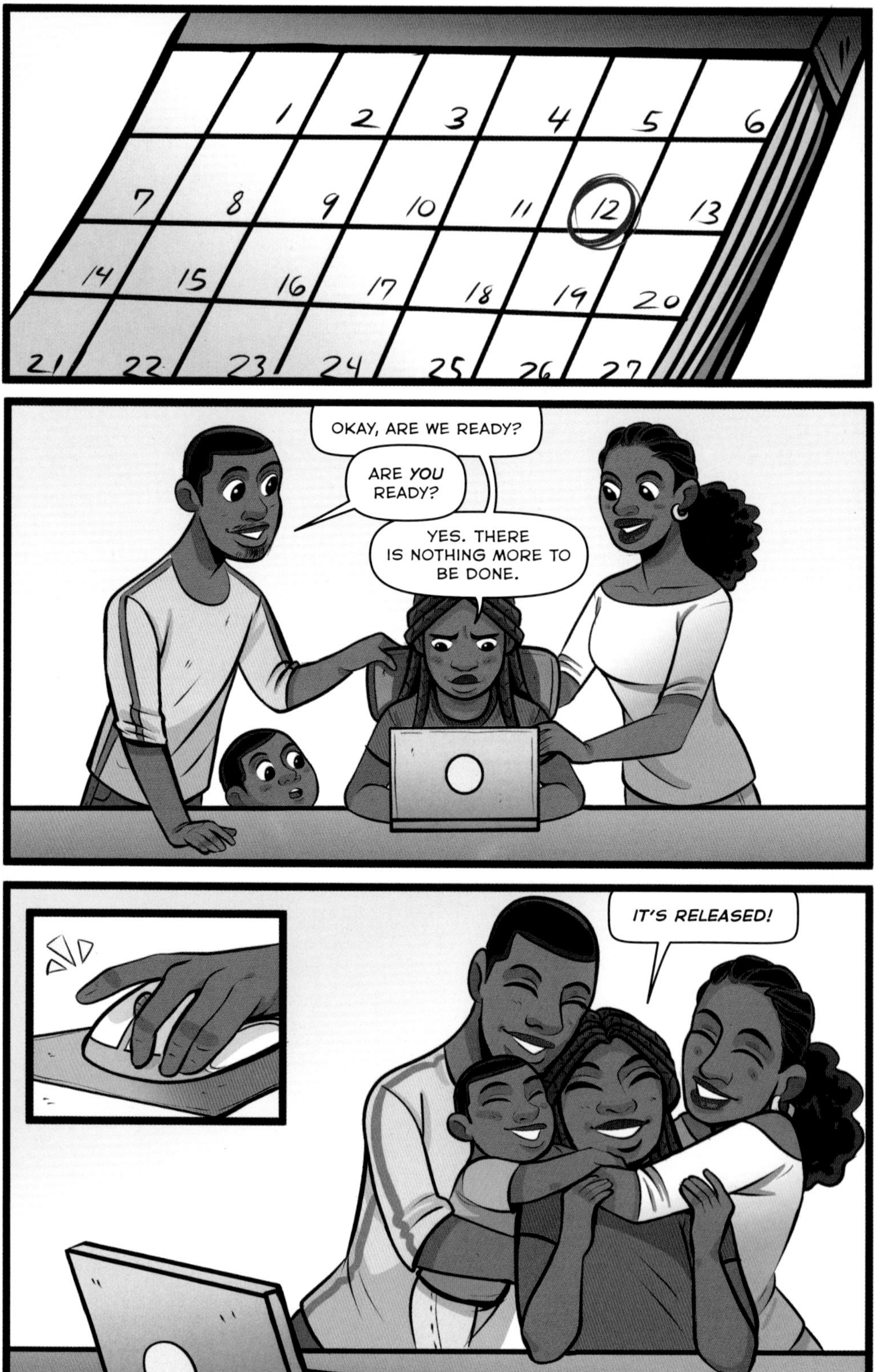
1 2 3 4 5 6
7 8 9 10 11 12 13
14 15 16 17 18 19 20
21 22 23 24 25 26 27
OKAY, ARE WE READY?
ARE *YOU* READY?
YES. THERE IS NOTHING MORE TO BE DONE.
IT'S RELEASED!

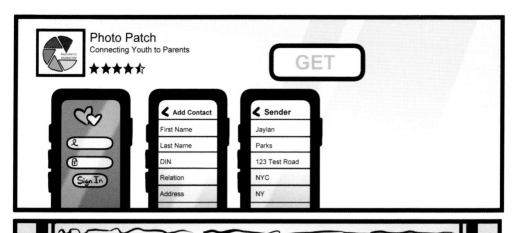

Photo Patch
Connecting Youth to Parents
GET
Sign In
Add Contact
First Name
Last Name
DIN
Relation
Address
Sender
Jaylan
Parks
123 Test Road
NYC
NY
A NEW REVOLUTIONARY MOBILE APP: PHOTO PATCH
Connecting incarcerated people with their families for free.
Available on all app stores.
For more information visit: photopatch.org
Search
Photo Patch Foundation
Sponsored •
Connecting incarcerated people with their families for free.
Start reaching out today!
Learn More
"This is absolutely fantastic. Had my daughter teach me how to use this and we've been able to have more steady communication with her dad. It's life changing." -- Sarah B.
"I didn't think I'd actually need something like this but it makes talking to my mother much easier." -- Kayla J.

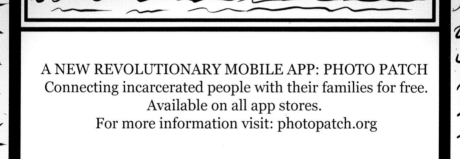

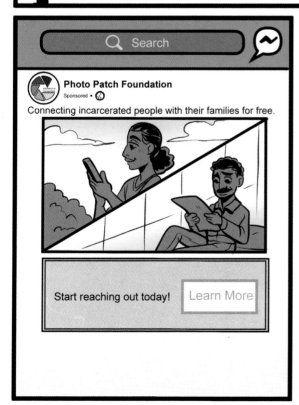

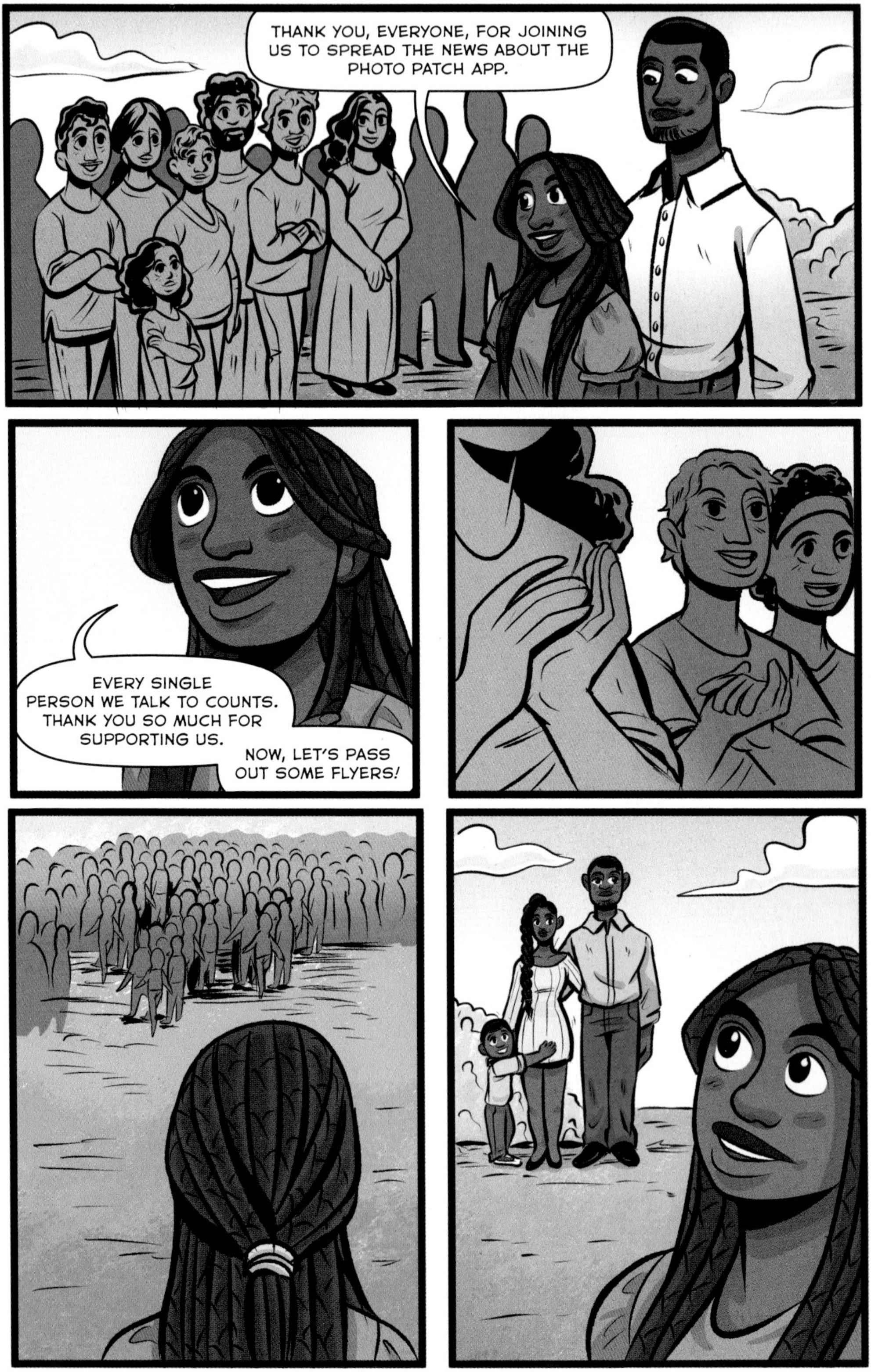
THANK YOU, EVERYONE, FOR JOINING US TO SPREAD THE NEWS ABOUT THE PHOTO PATCH APP.
EVERY SINGLE PERSON WE TALK TO COUNTS. THANK YOU SO MUCH FOR SUPPORTING US.
NOW, LET'S PASS OUT SOME FLYERS!

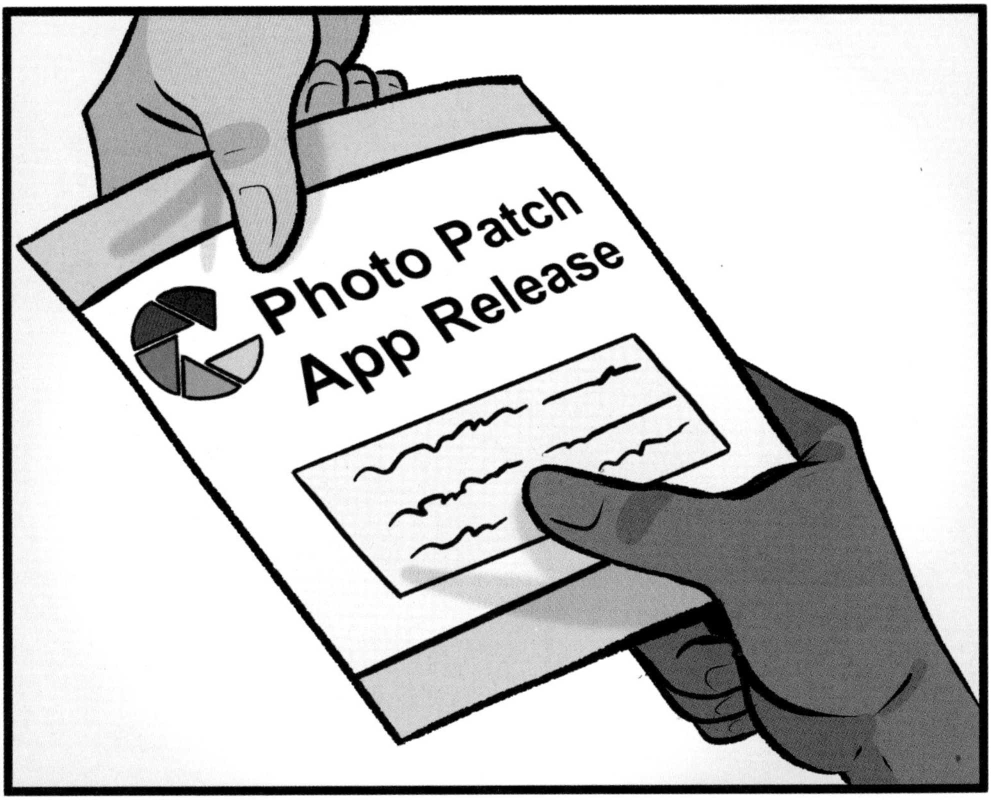
Photo Patch
App Release

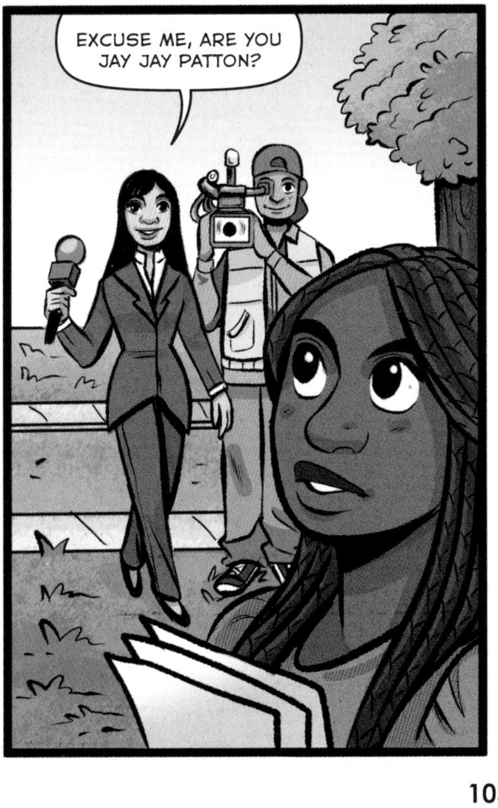
EXCUSE ME, ARE YOU JAY JAY PATTON?

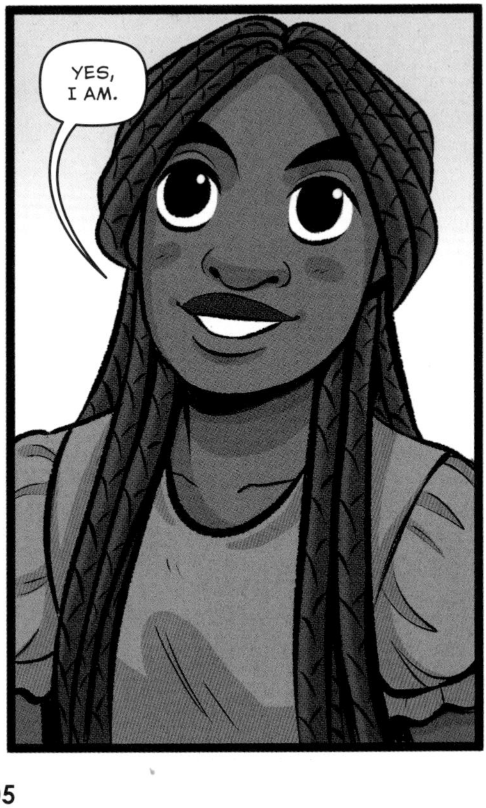
YES, I AM.

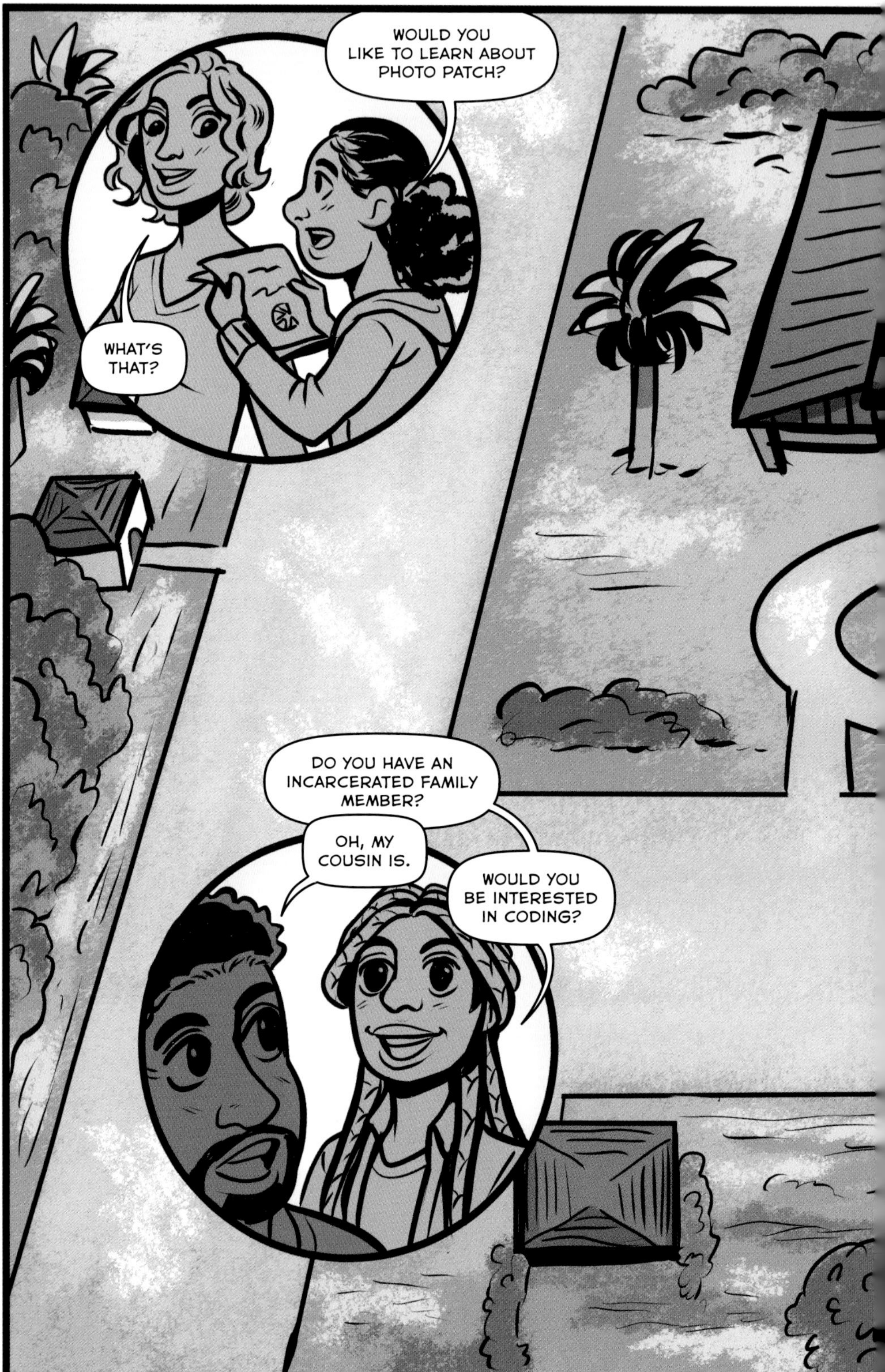
WOULD YOU LIKE TO LEARN ABOUT PHOTO PATCH?
WHAT'S THAT?
DO YOU HAVE AN INCARCERATED FAMILY MEMBER?
OH, MY COUSIN IS.
WOULD YOU BE INTERESTED IN CODING?

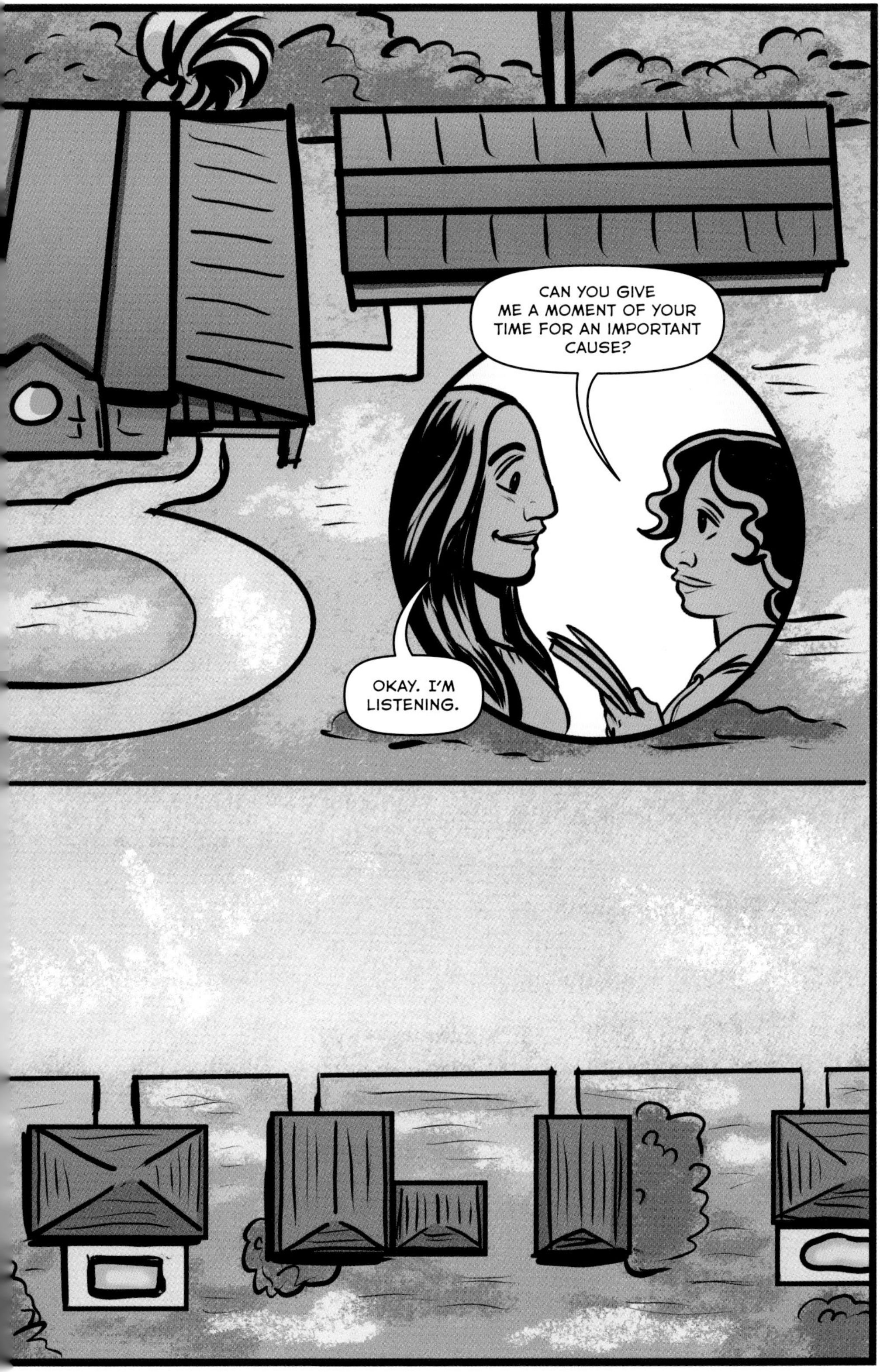
CAN YOU GIVE ME A MOMENT OF YOUR TIME FOR AN IMPORTANT CAUSE?
OKAY. I'M LISTENING.

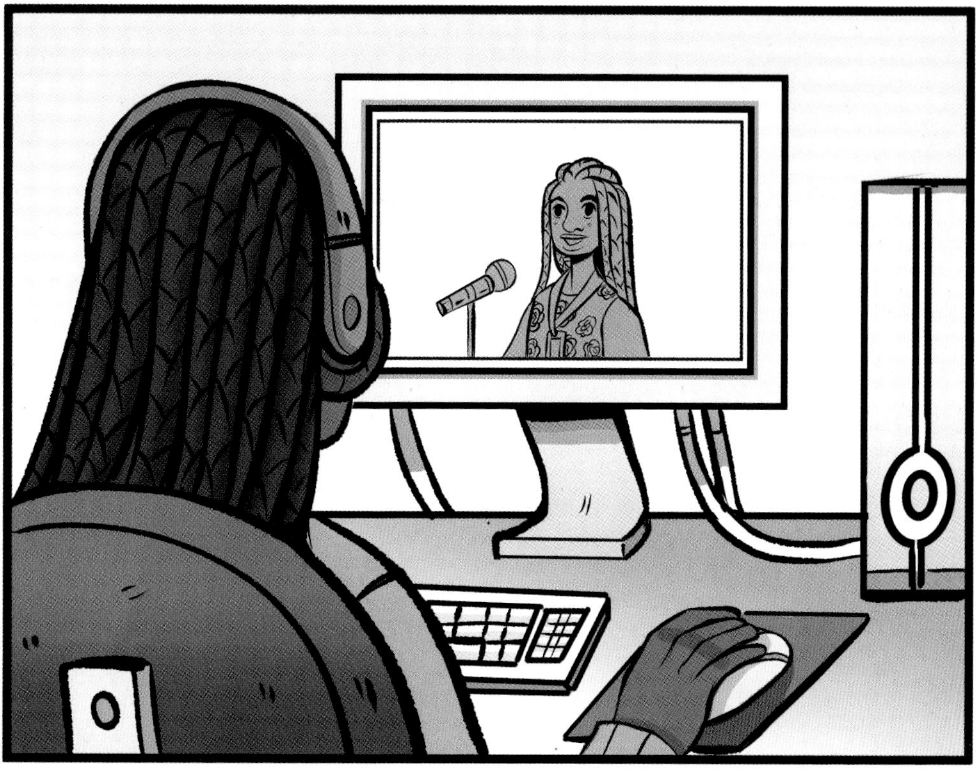

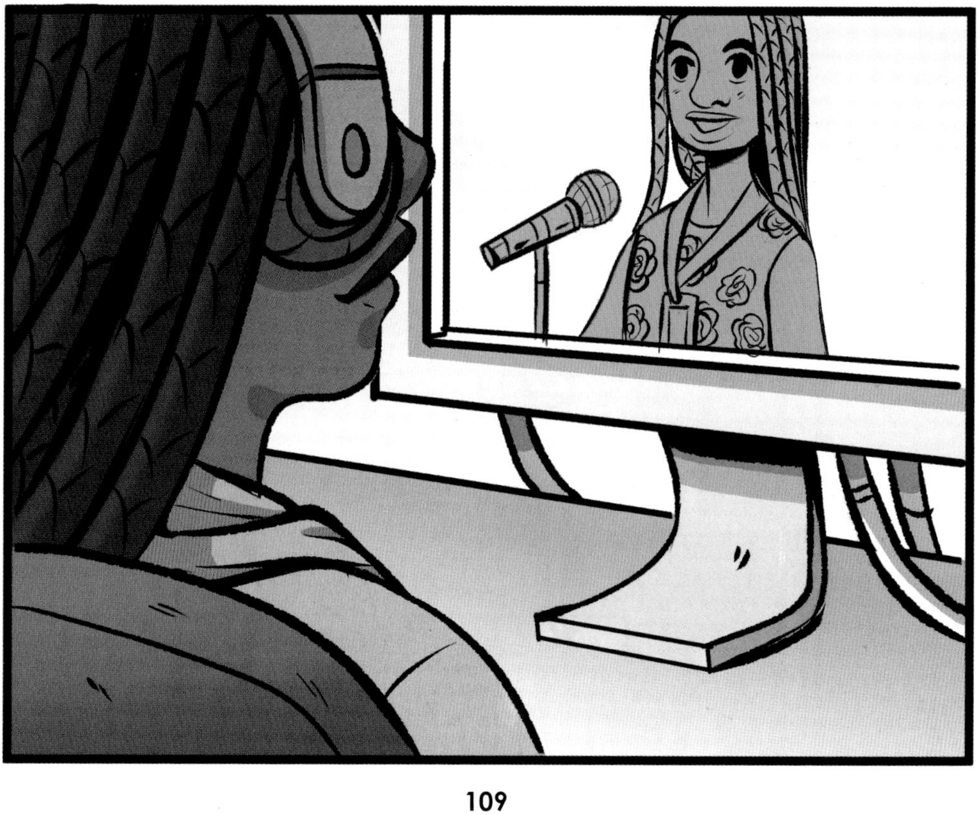

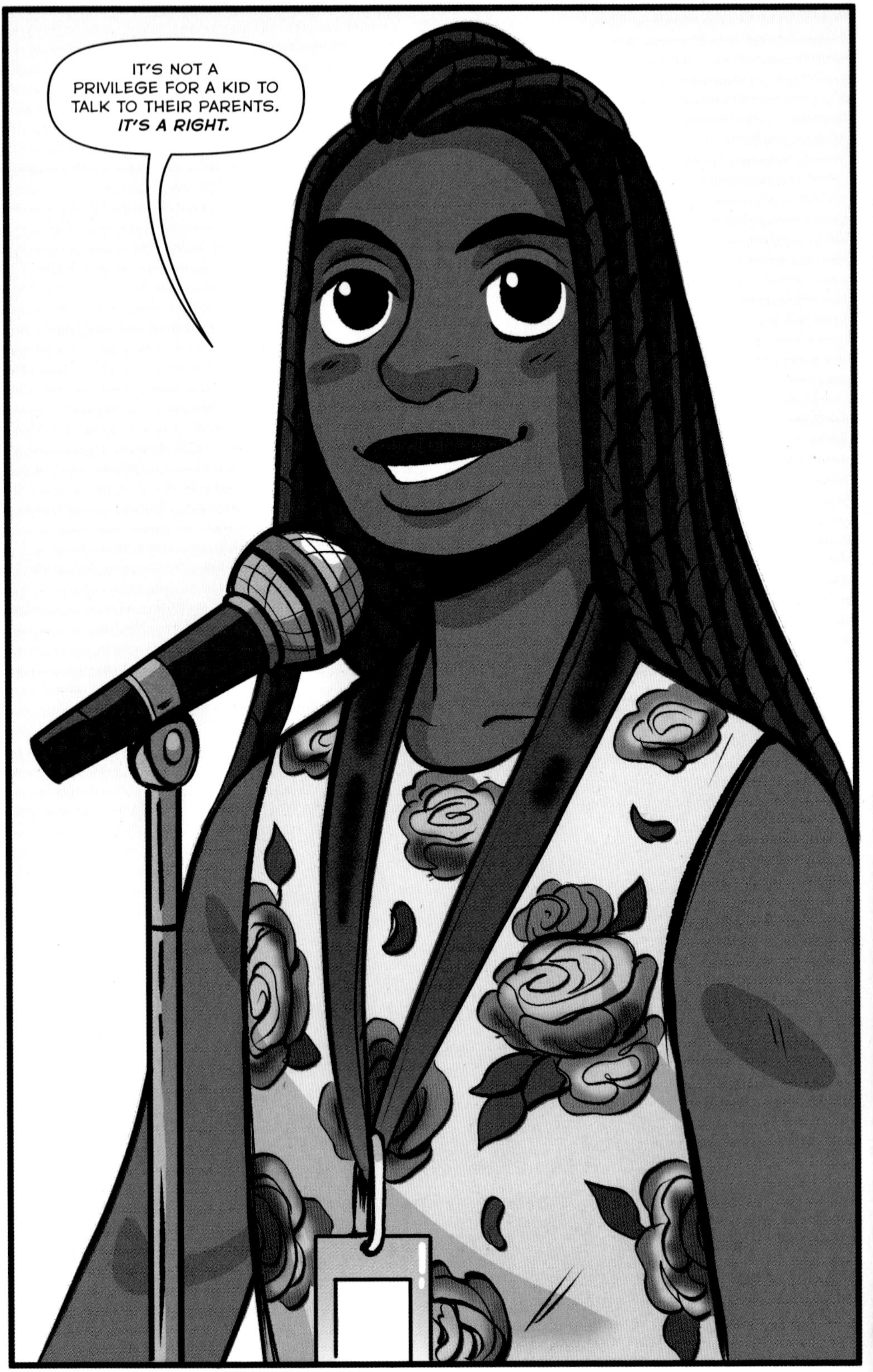
IT'S NOT A PRIVILEGE FOR A KID TO TALK TO THEIR PARENTS. *IT'S A RIGHT.*

2010

Antoine teaches himself how to build websites and apps in prison, graduating as class valedictorian.

Antoine giving his valedictorian speech and holding up his diploma

2014

Antoine is released from prison and moves to Florida

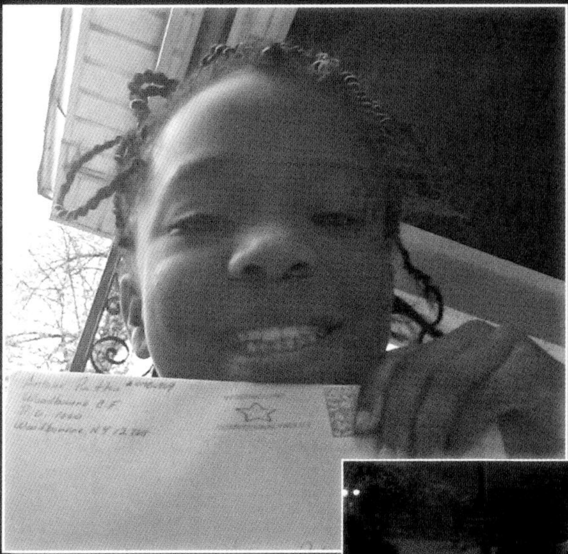

Jay Jay with a letter from Antoine

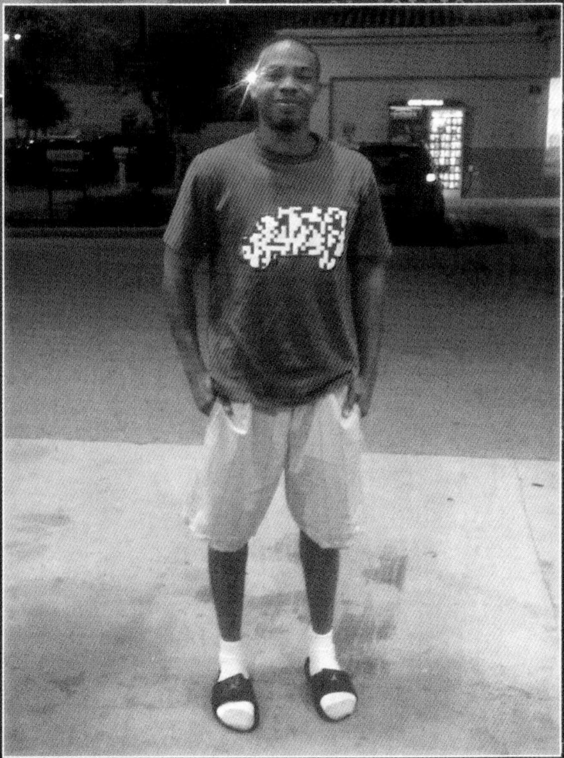

Antoine after his first tech interview

2015

Gina and Jay'Aina move to Florida
with Antoine

Gina, Jay'Aina, and Antoine traveling

**Jay'Aina's first
day of school**

2015

Antoine and Jay'Aina create the Photo Patch Foundation

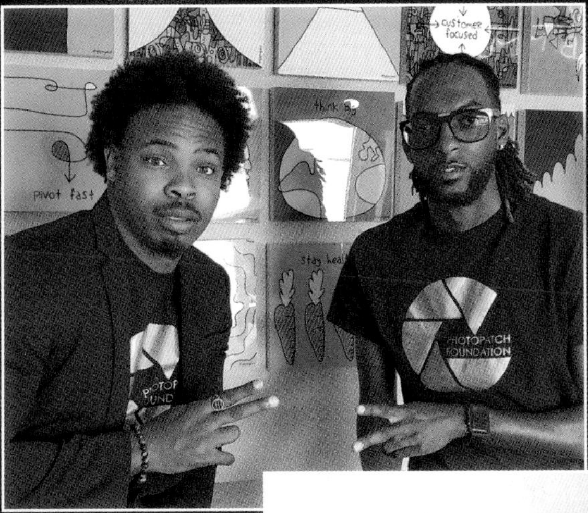
customer focused
pivot fast
PHOTOPATCH FOUNDATION

Antoine with Photo Patch Operations Director Greg Bryant

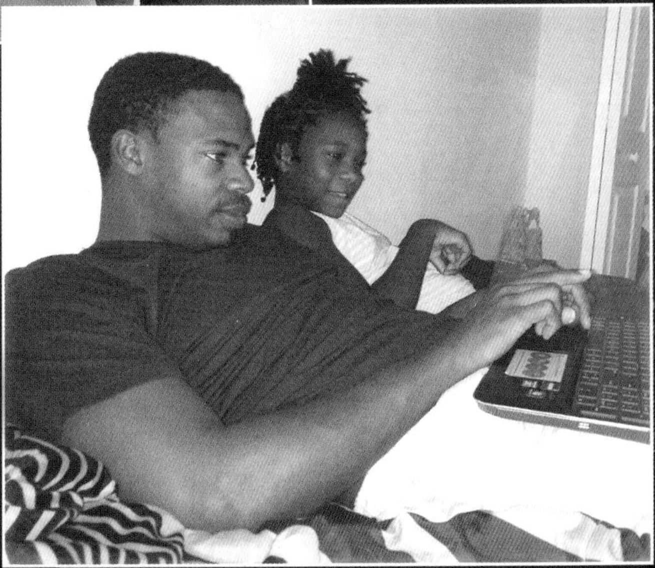

Jay Jay and Antoine coding together

Antoine and Jay'Aina create the Photo Patch Foundation

TODAY

Since its launch in 2017, the Photo Patch app has been used by more than 60,000 families. Jay'Aina and Antoine have been able to share their story on international stages, podcasts, and publications. They have partnered with local and national organizations like Boys & Girls Clubs https://www.bgca.org/ and Big Brothers, Big Sisters.

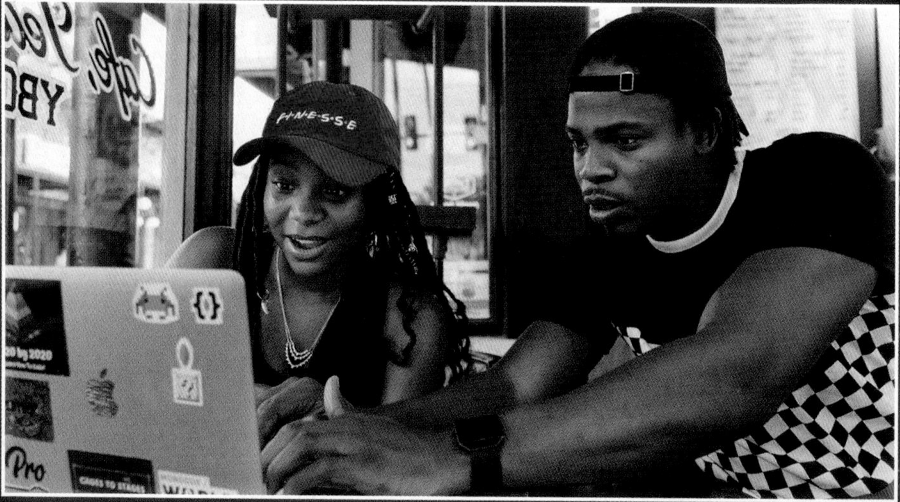
F-I-N-E-S-S-E

Antoine and Jay'Aina working together, present day

Antoine at a presentation for Photo Patch

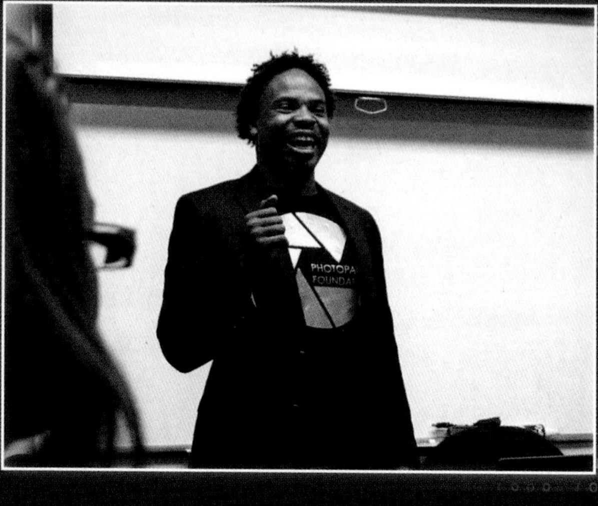

Antoine, Jay'Aina,
and Gina
attending a gala

Jay'Aina teaching at Microsoft

The Photo Patch foundation has sent more than one
million pictures and letters between incarcerated
parents and their children.

The Photo Patch foundation not only works to bring families together through its app, but also hosts workshops and outreach events through its Unlock Academy program to empower those impacted by incarceration through teaching skills like coding, game development, cyber security, résumé development, and much more. Jay'Aina and Antoine continue to build their foundation and its app, with the aim of reaching families across the United States.

Jay'Aina giving a keynote address in Oklahoma

Antoine asking Jay'Aina a question while she teaches a class to young people at Microsoft

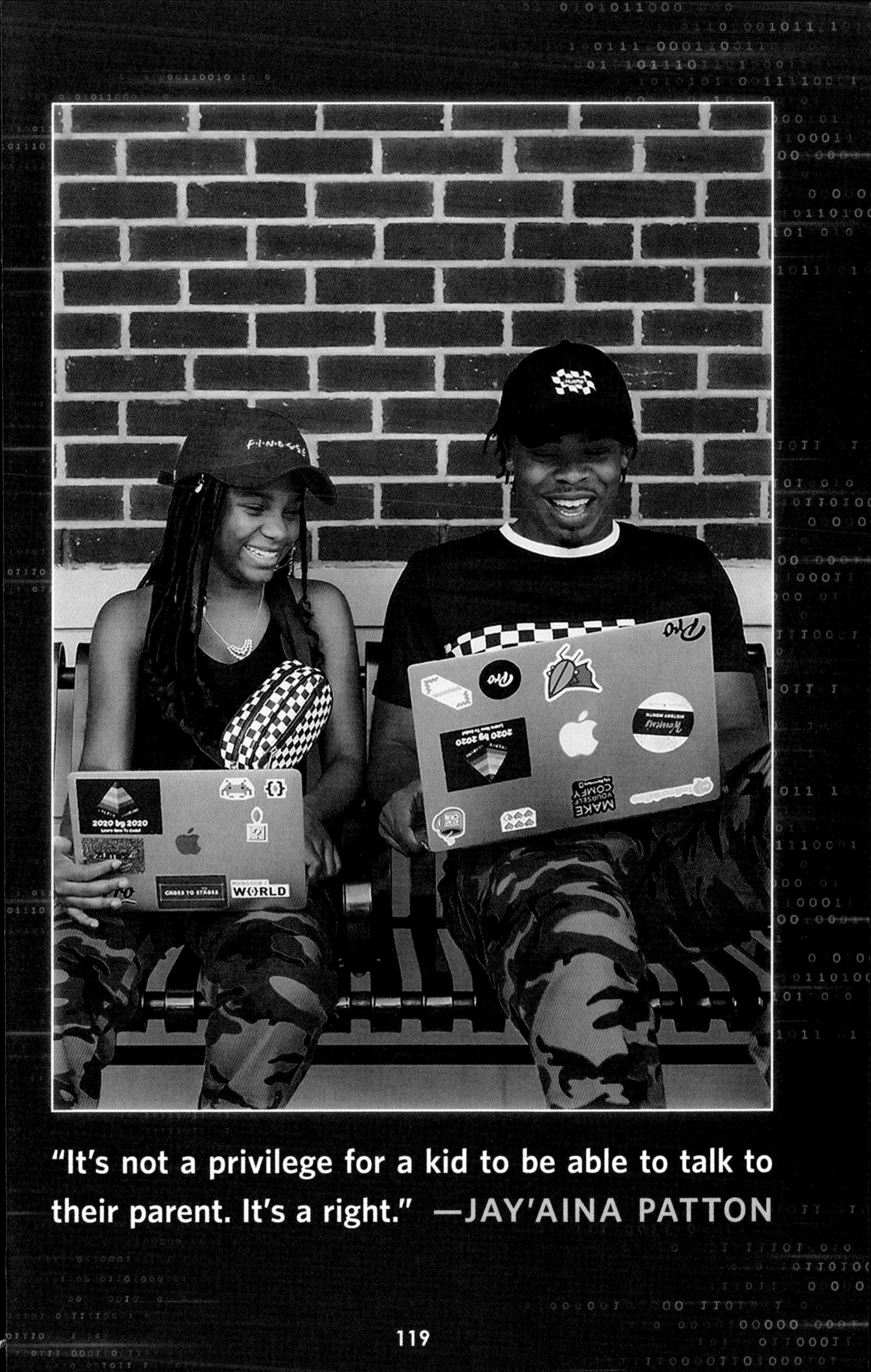
2020 by 2020
WORLD

"It's not a privilege for a kid to be able to talk to their parent. It's a right." —JAY'AINA PATTON

PHOTOPATCH
FOUNDATION

About half of people in state prisons are parents to children under 18

In fact, there are as many children with a parent in prison as there are adults in prison.

1,248,300 ADULTS IN STATE PRISONS NATIONWIDE

= about 50,000
adults in prison

= about 50,000
minor children

1,252,100 MINOR CHILDREN WITH A PARENT IN STATE PRISON

Stats from PrisonPolicy.org

The United States represents around 4 percent of the world's population but houses 20 percent of the world's prisoners (Institute for Criminal Policy Research, 2018). 58.5 percent of state parent inmates and 44.7 percent of federal parent inmates in the United States report having never been visited by their children (USDJ, 2008). An estimated 2.7 million children in the US have a parent who is incarcerated.

Since founding Photo Patch, Jay Jay and Antoine Patton have helped connect more than 75,000 youth to their incarcerated parents, and sent more than one million photos to mothers and fathers in prison. They continue to help kids keep in touch with their parents while they're in jail. Additionally, they organize family-friendly events that teach young people how to code, create games, and turn their passion for gaming into a source of income.

JAY'AINA "JAYJAY" PATTON

is an 18-year-old coder, app developer, youth leader, and entrepreneur. She's a big fan of anything tech-related and especially loves getting hands-on. Jay Jay is an advocate for diversity in the tech field and beyond and aspires to make a real impact on the world. She also enjoys a multitude of activities such as singing/rapping, dancing, piano, and volleyball. Jay Jay is a super goofy, kindhearted, and overall very happy girl who loves to keep herself and others smiling.

KIARA VALDEZ is an Afro-Dominican writer and editor from New York City. She has a love for the color lilac and spends her free time reading, writing, and enjoying a long list of other hobbies she can't keep up with.

MARKIA JENAI is an African American illustrator from Detroit, Michigan. She works in the realms of historical fiction and nonfiction. Markia has illustrated artwork for middle grade chapter books such as *Lena and the Burning of Greenwood*, the picture book *The Story of Juneteenth*, and the graphic novel *It's Her Story: Josephine Baker.*